A FIELD GUIDE TO BUTTERFLIES OF AUSTRALIA

This updated edition published in 2024 by Reed New Holland Publishers Sydney

Level 1, 178 Fox Valley Road, Wahroonga, NSW 2076, Australia

newhollandpublishers.com

Copyright © 2024 Reed New Holland Publishers
Copyright © 2024 in text: Garry Sankowsky
Copyright © 2024 in images: Garry Sankowsky, Geoff Walker and other contributors as credited on pp 4–5

First published in 2020

All rights reserved. No part of this publication may be reproduced, stored in a retrieval system or transmitted, in any form or by any means, electronic, mechanical, photocopying, recording or otherwise, without the prior written permission of the publishers and copyright holders.

A record of this book is held at the National Library of Australia.

ISBN 9781760796884

Managing Director: Fiona Schultz
Publisher and Project Editor: Simon Papps
Designer: Andrew Davies
Production Director: Arlene Gippert
Printed in China

10 9 8 7 6 5 4 3 2 1

Keep up with Reed New Holland
and New Holland Publishers

ReedNewHolland
@NewHollandPublishers and @ReedNewHolland

A FIELD GUIDE TO BUTTERFLIES OF AUSTRALIA

UPDATED EDITION

THEIR LIFE HISTORIES AND LARVAL HOST PLANTS

Garry Sankowsky

Photography by Geoff Walker & Garry Sankowsky

ACKNOWLEDGEMENTS

Thank you to my wife Nada for doing the initial editing for spelling, typos and grammar. Thank you also to Nada and Daphne Bowden (Butterfly and Invertebrates Club) for proof reading.

This book would not have been possible without the dedication, time, effort and money spent by Geoff Walker in tracking down and photographing most of Australia's butterflies.

PHOTOGRAPHIC CREDITS

All images of live butterflies by **Geoff Walker** unless otherwise stated.

Geoff's photographic equipment:
Canon EOS series with Canon 180mm lens and Canon twin-flash. All photos taken on Manual setting with flash.

All life history and host plant images by **Garry Sankowsky** unless otherwise stated.

Garry's photographic equipment:
Pentax – various models over the years, including *istDL, K5, K7, K20-D, current equipment Pentax K70 and K1, Nikon D-750. Lenses: Sigma 28-80 macro zoom, Sigma 18-200 zoom, Raynox DCR-150 and DCR-250 close up attachments, Pentax 18-135mm zoom, Nikon 18-55mm zoom, Nikkor AF-S 70-300mm zoom. Flash units: Nikon SB-700, Nikon SB-15 used both on Nikon and Pentax cameras for close ups, Ray-Flash ring flash adapter for ultra close ups and Pentax AF-360. Most photographs taken with manual settings and flash always on.

Cliff Meyer: p206, *Chaetocneme critomedia* male.

Craig Hunter: p44 bottom left image.

Densey Clyne: p282; p283 larvae on Ant Plant; p313 larvae and pupae; p317 eggs, larvae, far right; p339 larvae.

Bob Miller: p9 *Arhopala madytus* pupa; p51 *Graphium macleayanum* larvae and pupa bottom right; p140 larvae; p141 larvae and pupae; p198 four bottom larvae and two pupae; p200 larva and left pupa; p282 larvae and pupa on left; p197 pupae; p201 top right larva and two pupae; p203 larvae and pupae; p207 two right larvae and pupae; p226 larva and pupa; p258; p282 two top larvae; p293 larvae and pupae; p294 bottom larvae and pupae; p310; p311 larvae and pupae; p314 top two larvae; p317 centre larvae and pupae; p319 larvae and pupae; p320 top right larva and bottom pupae; p328 egg, larva and pupae; p329 larvae and pupa on right; p331 larvae; p332 larvae; p369 larva centre and right; p371; 373 egg, larvae and pupae.

Flickr, Creative Commons: p40 *Murraya koenigii* fruit; p271 larvae and pupae.

Frank Pierce: p282 larvae and pupa on left; p333 *Rapala varuna* female.

Garry Sankowsky: p25 *Pachlioptera polydorus* underside; p33 *Papilio aegeus ormenus*; p37 *Papilio ambrax* on flowers; p39 *Papilio capaneus* adults, bottom images; p43 all images; p56 *Graphium eurypylus* laying egg; p58 all images; p106 adult on right; p109 bottom adult image; p110 all images; p115 male on *Heliotroium* flowers; p119 pair mating; p122 three bottom adult images; p125 adult on pupal case; p133 pair mating; p134 all images; p136 all images; p137 all images; p147 bottom female images; p150 all images except bottom left; p.151 bottom male and female adult images; p152 bottom right males and bottom left female; p155 all images; p157 all images; p159 far right adult, p. bottom right adult, p. bottom left and right adults; p168 adult on pupa case; p169 adult on pupa case; p172 *Ypthima arctous* images; p173 bottom two adults.

Glenn Leiper: p17 *Ornithoptera richmondia* larva pre-pupal stage; p18 *Pararistolochia laheyana*; p31 *Citrus australis*; p32 *Citrus glauca, Citrus australasica*; p64 *Senna barclayana* flowers; p65 *Senna sophera*; p71 *Senna acclinis*; p73 *Chamaecrista maritima, C. nomame*; p73 *Neptunia gracilis*; p74 *Galactia tenuiflora*; p93 *Korthalsella*; p174 *Imperata cylindrica*; p177, p257 *Alexfloydia repens*; p179, p180 *Gahnia*; p208 *Dioscorea transversa*; p210–4 *Lomandra*; p231, p236 *Gahnia aspera*; p234 *Gahnia sieberiana*; p244 *Patersonia sericea*; p245 *Patersonia fragilis*; p278 *Oxalis chnoodes, Oxalis perennans*; p291 *Pomaderris lanigera*; p292 *Avicennia marina*; p308–9 *Amyema quandang*; p313 *Muellerina eucalyptoides*; p314 *Diplatia furcata*; p348 *Pimelea linifolia*; p350, p351 *Boronia*; p381 *Desmodium heterocarpon*; p385 *Vigna vexillata*.

Kim Starr: p150 *Portulaca* bottom left.

Lorraine Harris: p12 *Ornithoptera euphorion* male.

Mark Hopkinson: p9 *Badamia exclamationis*; p198 small larva, shelter and bottom pupa; p200 two pupae

on right; p205 larvae and pupae; p284 larvae and pupae; p285, p287 larvae and pupa; p288, p289 larvae and pupae; p290 larva and pupa; p294 two top larvae; p297 larvae and pupae; p298, p299, p300 larva and pupa; p314 bottom larvae and pupae; p320 larva with ants and larva with pupa; p329 pupa on left; p330 pupa; p331 pupa; p332 larvae; p340 larva on left.

Ross Field: p92 *Delias nysa* larvae and pupae; p172 *Heteronympha solandri*; p188 larva and pupa; p190 larva and pupae; p191 larvae and pupae; p207 left larva and pupa; p219 larva and pupa; p220 larvae and pupae; p.222 larva and pupa; p228, p229, p230 larva and pupa; p232 larva and pupa; p240, p241 larva and pupa; p246 pupae; p254 pupa; p256 larva and pupa; p259 larvae and pupae; p261 larva and pupa; p263 larvae and pupa; p264, p266 larvae and pupae; p268 larva and pupa; p278 larvae and pupae; p282 pupae in centre and bottom right; p291 larva and pupa; p292 larva; p295 pupa.

Ross Kendall: p100 larvae and pupae; p307, p308 larva and pupa; p315, p318, p325 larva and pupa; p326 larva and pupae.

Wes Jenkinson: p84 eggs; p89 *Delias haypalyce* pupae.

CONTENTS

Introduction		7
Photographing Butterflies		10
	Swallowtails	11
	Whites and Yellows	63
	Crows and Tigers	102
	Glasswings, Lacewings and Cruisers	124
	Emperors	138
	Nymphs	141
	Browns, Palmfly and Owl	170
	Skippers, Flats, Awls and Darts	192
	Blues, Coppers and Hairstreaks	273
Cultivating Mistletoes		391
Index		394
References and Further information		400

INTRODUCTION

Butterflies are probably the best-known group of insects because of their bright colours and the fact that most of them fly during the day. While the majority are tropical there are still reasonable numbers in the cooler climates of southern Australia.

Australia does not have many species compared to other countries that fall within the tropical region – only about 400 species. As a comparison, New Guinea has 1,600 and South America about 7,500.

This book should be read in conjunction with *All About Butterflies of Australia* (Reed New Holland, 2016) to get an overall view of just what butterflies are about. To save space most of the information in that book has not been repeated here. This publication has concentrated on illustrating as far as possible the adult butterflies, their early stages and the related host plants that the larvae feed on.

What makes this book different from other field guides is that all the illustrations of the butterflies are actual photos of live specimens. In most cases, this is how you will see them in the wild. It is just not possible to have every species as it would take a lifetime to gather live images of all the butterfly species as quite a few are very rare and extremely difficult to find.

The first thing you should do is make yourself familiar with the different families of butterflies as this will save a lot of time when trying to identify a particular specimen. The distribution maps are essential sources of information; while sometimes there is a remote possibility of finding a species outside of the range shown, mostly this is not the case. One possible reason for seeing a butterfly that is not usually in your area is the release of butterflies at weddings and other gatherings. Generally these butterflies will be very common species that are easy to breed, but it is just possible, if you are in the south, that the released species could be from the tropics. This does not cause any problems as every butterfly has very specific host plants on which the larvae of that species must feed. They cannot run amok and devour your garden.

In the 1973–74 season a number of butterflies moved south with the wet winter followed by a very active monsoon season over northern Australia. One species, the Blue-banded Eggfly, was seen as far south as Byron Bay in New South Wales. Events like this happen from time to time but usually a few cold winters will wipe out these populations.

Because butterflies mostly fly quickly and are often difficult to get a very good look at, the best way to identify them (apart from catching them) is to photograph them and study the image. The next section of the book gives some tips on doing this.

This book in not written for scientists, rather it is aimed at the general public, students and anyone generally interested in butterflies. Scientific terms have been kept to a minimum. Text has been sacrificed to enable the maximum number of images. You know the old saying...

Host Plant names for species that occur in Queensland are as per the Queensland Herbarium in Brisbane (BRI). Other species are according to the Australian Plant Name Index (APNI). The Queensland Herbarium does not always accept every taxonomy paper and the author usually agrees with their decision. A good example is *Aristolochia*. The Australian species were split into two genera, *Aristolochia* and *Pararistolochia*. *Aristolochia* has dry fruit that opens like a basket to disperse wind-blown seed; *Pararistolochia* has fleshy fruit with hard seed that are dispersed by birds feeding on the fruit. This split was made in a paper by Michael Parsons (Mich.J.Parsons,

1996, *Bot. J. Linn. Soc.* 120(3): 218). A paper was published in 2014 (Buchwalder and Wanke, 2014, *Australian Systematic Botany* 27: 48–55) that combined the two genera into *Aristolochia* based mainly on DNA. The Queensland Herbarium has not accepted this combination so both genera are used in this publication.

To avoid clutter on the pages, captions are seldom shown under images of eggs, larvae (caterpillars) or pupae (chrysalises). It should be obvious what these are. From left to right is an egg (if shown) or eggs if they are laid in clusters, various stages of the larvae as they develop, then the pupa, often with side and above views. The following page shows examples of various eggs, larvae and pupae. The images are not to scale; in fact none of the images in the publication are to scale. Larger species will be shown smaller than life size and the smaller species will be shown at least life size and if space permits up to twice life size. These larger images show the markings of these small butterflies much more clearly. The approximate size of each species is shown under the name. This is the size with wings at normal open, resting position. This will be slightly larger than that of set specimens shown in some other publications. Occasionally larger specimens will be seen but more commonly they will be smaller as the size of the adult butterfly depends on the quality and the amount of host plant available to the caterpillar. Distribution maps refer only to the butterflies.

Scientific terms used in this book

Alkaloids: Nitrogenous organic compounds of plant origin that are toxic to humans.

Epiphytic: Grows on branches or trunks of trees.

Exudate: Sap that oozes from wounds in a plant.

Gallery rainforest: Narrow strip of rainforest growing in the flood plain of a stream.

Haustorium: Large swollen base of Mistletoe where it attaches to a branch.

Hill-topping: Male butterflies, especially those in the Lycenidae family, spend a lot of time on hilltops. Females visit these sites from time-to-time and often mating occurs.

Larva (pl. **Larvae**): Caterpillar.

Lithophytic: Grows on rocks or boulders.

Mud-puddling: The males of most species of butterflies will gather on damp ground to take in nutrients during hot weather. This happens mainly in the tropics.

Montane: In the mountains.

Pupa (pl. **Pupae**): Chrysalis

sp. aff.: The plant has no official scientific name but resembles the species named.

Abbreviations

NSW	New South Wales	**Tas**	Tasmania		Male
NT	Northern Territory	**Vic**	Victoria		Female
SA	South Australia	**WA**	Western Australia		

Common Names of Australian Butterflies

In 2007 a paper 'A Provisional List of Common Names for Australian Butterflies' was published by M.F. Braby, A.F. Atkins, K.L. Dunn, T.A. Woodger and W.N.B. Quick. It was proposed to standardise the common names of Australia's butterflies. The names decided on were first published in *Butterflies of Australia* by M.F. Braby (2000). However, the final result was to abandon many of the standard common names as published in *Butterflies of Australia* by I.F.B Common and D.F. Waterhouse (1972/1981) and invent new ones. This present book follows the lead taken in *The Butterflies of Australia* by Albert Orr and Roger Kitching (2011) where they retained all the standard names, accepted new names for species that did not previously have a common name, and adopted some other new ones where the name grouped related species together.

Assorted Eggs.

Assorted Larvae.

Assorted Pupae.

Photographing Butterflies

Because butterflies often fly fast and it is difficult to have a good look at their markings for identification purposes, the ideal way to identify them is to take a photograph so that you then have plenty of time to carefully work out which species it might be.

Digital cameras have made great advances in the last ten years and you do not really need a top of the range DSLR (digital single lens reflex) camera and a large telephoto lens; in fact the best cameras for this purpose are a reasonably good compact camera with a 40–60x zoom lens that is stabilised. The images below were taken with a Canon Powershot SX60HS camera, which has a 60x zoom lens and another feature that is very useful, a viewfinder separate from the LCD screen. Holding a camera up to your eye enables you to hold it much more steadily than if you were holding it in front of you and looking at the large LCD screen on the back. Having an LCD screen that flips around is also useful because when it is not in use it can be turned inwards for protection.

Most major brand manufacturers make similar models. The features to look for are:

1. Zoom lens 40–60x optical zoom (digital zoom is of no use as it only crops the image).
2. Separate viewfinder.
3. LCD screen that flips around.
4. Image stabilisation in the lens.

Unless you are a skilled camera operator I suggest you use the P (program mode) setting. All cameras will have the ability to change the exposure up or down in this mode. If you are within a few metres of the butterfly, pop up the flash. Apart from getting better light on the subject this usually results in a larger aperture (f stop) and faster shutter speed. Get to know you camera and take plenty of practice shots.

The butterflies do not have to be in perfect condition, just so long as their markings are well defined. You may need to have shots from different angles to positively identify some species. The Skipper on the top right belongs to a group that is very difficult to identify, even if you have one in your hand.

SWALLOWTAILS
Family Papilionidae

The Swallowtail family contains the largest butterflies in the world; these are in the Birdwing group and are represented in Australia. Occurring in Papua New Guinea, the Queen Alexandra's Birdwing can have a wingspan of at least 25cm, which makes it the largest butterfly of all.

The majority of the Australian butterflies in this group can remain in the pupal stage for long periods, some for several years, which enables them to survive seasons that are not suitable for breeding. All the larvae of the Swallowtail butterflies prepare for their pupal stage in the upright position with a central silken girdle and attached at the base on a pad of silk.

The adults in the Papilionini (Papilios) group usually rest with wings spread, the Ulysses Swallowtail being one notable exception. Because of the brilliant blue colour on the upper surface they close their wings when resting and display dark camouflaged colours on the underside. The two Swordtail butterflies in the Leptocircini (Kites and Swordtails) usually also rest with wings spread. The pupae of this group can be either brown or green, depending on which colour offers best camouflage in their situation.

Chequered Swallowtail larva prepared for pupation.

Chequered Swallowtail pupa.

Male Swallowtail butterflies have hairs in the fold along the inside of their hindwings which contains chemicals (Pheromones) to stimulate the female prior to mating. The males hover over the female and dust the chemicals down over her.

One distinguishing feature of the larvae of swallowtails is that they have a pair of fleshy horns (osmeterium) on the top of their head that can be extended if they are in danger. These horns release an unpleasant chemical smell, and probably taste, to deter predators. The larvae may have fleshy spines but never ones that are sharp.

When taking nectar from flowers, Swallowtail butterflies continue to keep their wings moving in a hovering position. With the Triangle group this enables them to remain at each flower for a minimum amount of time and move off very fast. For larger butterflies such as Birdwings the hovering action takes the weight off their legs as well as being in a comfortable position for their long proboscis to reach into the nectar tube of the flower.

Osmeterium starting to extend on a Cairns Birdwing larva.

Fleshy spines on a Big Greasy larva.

Green-spotted Triangle hovering while feeding.

Cairns Birdwing *Ornithoptera euphorion*

Wingspan: Male 140mm, female 165mm.

Found from Mt Webb, north of Cooktown, to Mackay with an apparent gap between Townsville and Mackay. Although there are no records of this butterfly from Dryander and Conway National Parks, their host plants occur there.

Adults usually fly slowly, often gliding for short distances. Males mostly rest with wings closed but females often spread their wings. While feeding they keep their wings flapping in a semi-hovering position. The butterflies feed heavily on nectar first thing in the morning when the supply is most plentiful.

Females prefer to lay their eggs off the host plant under the leaves of trees or shrubs over which the vine is growing. The glue that fastens the egg to the *Aristolochia* leaf often triggers a reaction causing sap to be released and spread over the egg. Mould then grows and kills the egg. This is probably why most eggs are not laid directly on the host plant. Bear this in mind if growing the host vines on a fence or trellis – another species of vine should also be grown with it. The larvae usually move off the host vines to moult or to make their pupae so an alternative foliage is beneficial.

Host Plants: *Aristolochia acuminata, Pararistolochia australopithecurus, P. deltantha, P. sparusifolia, P.* sp. Gillies Crater, **A. esperanzae, *A. grandiflora, *A. macroura*.

Best Garden Host Plants: *Aristolochia acuminata* or **A. grandiflora,* the latter grows much faster than *A. acuminata* and will be big enough to feed Birdwing larvae within just 12 months.

Note: Because *A. elegans* is toxic to Birdwing larvae it was erroneously assumed that this was the case with all South American species. This is definitely not so as the three South American species mentioned above are very good host plants.

Aristolochia acuminata is the best native host plant to grow for Cairns Birdwing. This vine is large and fast growing, suitable for all gardens that are frost free.

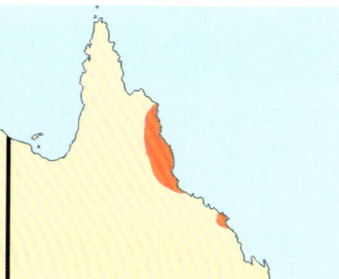

FAMILY PAPILIONIDAE – SUBFAMILY PAPILIONINAE — SWALLOWTAILS

Pararistolochia australopithecurus is a common vine of the very wet tropical rainforest. It occurs from high up on Mt Bartle Frere through to the coast north of Innisfail.

On a mature vine the leaves are quite large, being up to 30cm long by 10cm wide. Like all *Pararistolochia* species the fruit are orange or yellow, ribbed and succulent. The flowers are the largest of all the Australian species and are very showy. This is the main host plant for the Cairns Birdwing on the eastern side of the Atherton Tablelands.

Pararistolochia sparusifolia is found on the Main Coast range west of Mossman in the north Qld wet tropics, including Mt Lewis and the Mt Carbine tableland. It is the only host plant for the Cairns Birdwing in this area at altitudes above about 700m, occurring on the highest peaks of about 1,200m. The beautiful yellow flowers can be seen from about October to December. This vine requires very high humidity and is quite difficult to grow unless this requirement can be met.

Cairns Birdwing *Ornithoptera euphorion*

Pararistolochia sp. Gilles Crater is a very large vine that produces multiple stems up to 25mm diameter that reach up and spread across the canopy of the rainforest. It occurs in just a couple of localities on the eastern side of the Atherton Tableland and in the Tully River gorge. The foliage is more nutritious than *Aristolochia acuminata* and a mature vine can support a very large number of Birdwing larvae.

*Aristolochia macroura is a South American species that is an excellent host plant for all our *Aristolochia* feeding butterflies. It is very hardy and will withstand quite cold conditions. It tends to send runners along the ground and these are ideal for the Red-bodied Swallowtail as they prefer to lay low down on their host plants.

FAMILY PAPILIONIDAE – SUBFAMILY PAPILIONINAE   **SWALLOWTAILS**

**Aristolochia grandiflora* is the best of a number of South American Aristolochias that can be used as larval host plants for the Birdwings and other Aristolochia-feeding butterflies of Australia. The flowers are spectacular. The main problem with this vine is that it takes several years for the main stem to become hard and corky; large larvae can eat small vines completely to the ground.

**Aristolochia esperanzae* is a medium-sized vine from south America that can be planted so it will climb over a tree or trellis. When mature and well nourished the leaves can attain a width of 15–20cm. It is suitable for all our *Aristolochia*-feeding butterflies. Birdwing larvae reach their maximum size when using this host plant.

Richmond Birdwing *Ornithoptera richmondia*

Male with blue tint on underside.

Wingspan: Male 130mm, female 145mm.

Breeds in well-developed rainforest east of the Great Dividing Range at all altitudes, from about Gympie, Qld, to the Clarence River, NSW. Easily attracted to gardens if a plentiful supply of host plant vines is available.

Adults usually fly slowly, often gliding for short distances. Males generally rest with wings closed but females often spread their wings. On cool mornings adults sometimes rest in the sun with their wings spread in order to warm up. During the warmest part of summer they feed very early in the morning and are particularly attracted to the flowers of *Archidendron grandiflorum* (Fairy Paint Brush Tree). At times dozens of the butterflies can be seen feeding on the same tree. While feeding they keep their wings flapping in a semi-hovering position.

Males have a blue tint to the underside while the background colour of the females is variable, being black or dark grey.

Host Plants: *Pararistolochia laheyana, P. praevenosa*.

Best Garden Host Plant: *Aristolochia acuminata*. The vine should be planted so it will climb over a tree, **not on a trellis**, as this gives the females the chance to lay their eggs off the vine. This species often has only a single brood each year and the pupae can take nine months or more to hatch. Having the foliage of an evergreen tree nearby is essential for the survival of the pupae over this long period. If you want to use a local south Queensland species, then plant *Pararistolochia praevenosa*. For ten years the author grew *A. acuminata* in a garden on Mt Tamborine for the Richmond Birdwing without any egg laying problems.

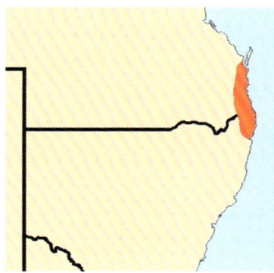

FAMILY PAPILIONIDAE – SUBFAMILY PAPILIONINAE SWALLOWTAILS

Dark form of larva.

The green colour of the Richmond Birdwing's pupa provides excellent camouflage during its long dormant period.

Larva ready to shed its skin and become a pupa.

Richmond Birdwing *Ornithoptera richmondia*

Pararistolochia laheyana is a medium-sized vine that occurs in very wet high-altitude rainforest of the southern Border Ranges of Qld, its range extending into adjacent rainforests in NSW. It is extremely common in places like Binna Burra, Qld, and Wiangaree State Forest, NSW, enabling very large numbers of this butterfly to breed each season. The vine requires constant moisture and humidity so is fairly difficult to grow in cultivation unless these conditions can be met.

Pararistolochia praevenosa is a very large vine that is found from about Gympie, Qld, to the Clarence River, NSW, in low to mid-altitude rainforest. The leaves are hard and stiff when mature but during the summer when the Birdwings are breeding flushes of soft new foliage are common.

It is very slow growing at first but after a couple of years it speeds up and eventually becomes large enough to support many larvae.

On Mt Tamborine there are huge vines that spread out over about half a hectare of rainforest.

Big Greasy *Cressida cressida*

Wingspan: Male 90mm, female 95mm.

Found in open forest and along the edge of vine thickets from about Broome, WA, across the top end of Australia and down the east coast to northern NSW.

Both sexes fly slowly – the females can often be observed flying low across the tops of grassy areas in an endless search for their small host plants. *Aristolochia indica* is naturalised in the Darwin area and used extensively there by this butterfly.

Host Plants: *Aristolochia acuminata, A. chalmersii, A. holtzei, A. meridionalis, A. nauseifolia, A. pubera, A. thozetii, *A. esperanzae, *A. grandiflora, *A. indica, *A. macroura.*

Best Garden Host Plants: *Aristolochia acuminata* when grown in full sun or the introduced *A. macroura*, which is ideal as it creeps along the ground where the females usually lay when using their tiny native host plants.

Aristolochia holtzei is a tiny upright plant that occurs in the top end of NT and in north Qld from Cape York to about Townsville. It grows in open forest where the grass cover is sparse. Unless it is in flower or fruit it is almost impossible to distinguish from grass.

Big Greasy *Cressida cressida*

Aristolochia chalmersii is a small to medium-sized vine that grows in vine thickets among boulders from Torres Strait to Lizard Island. It is deciduous and dies back to large tubers just below the surface of the ground. Occasionally Birdwings use this vine on Mt White near Coen. Mt White is a semi-deciduous dry rainforest but it is not a great distance from the much wetter rainforests of the McIlwraith Range.

Aristolochia nauseifolia is found from Torres Strait to the Rocky River on Cape York Peninsula. It is a twining vine growing to about 2m high and occurs in open forest and on the edge of vine thickets. This species has not been included in the most recent revision of Aristolochia but is definitely a valid species as named by Mike Parsons.

Aristolochia thozetii occurs in the Gove Peninsula, NT, then from Cape York to south-east Qld in amongst grass in open forest. It is a small vine that twines up grass and most years is often eaten down to the ground by the Big Greasy larvae. Underground there are numerous small tubers from which it springs back to life when the summer rains come. The above leaf variations were produced by growing seed from a wild collection that looked like the one in the basket. Other shapes also occurred in the same batch but unfortunately were not photographed. This plant appears to merge into *A. pubera* var. *pubera* with some variations.

Big Greasy *Cressida cressida*

Aristolochia pubera var. *aromatica* is the largest of the 'small' *Aristolochia* vines. It grows in open forest amongst boulders and on the edge of vine thickets, sometimes forming a clump up to 2m wide. The leaves are hairy and succulent, snapping when bent. It occurs from about Mt Carbine to Chillagoe. Perhaps this should be the real *A. pubera* as it is very pubescent (hairy) and the type locality is unknown.

Aristolochia pubera var. *pubera* appears to have a wide range but there is confusion between this and the wide leaf form of *A. thozettii* which is very widespread. This plant grows within metres of *A. pubera* var. *aromatica* so they are probably separate species. Leaf shape is very variable, as is that of *A. thozettii*.

FAMILY PAPILIONIDAE – SUBFAMILY PAPILIONINAE — SWALLOWTAILS

Aristolochia meridionalis subsp. *meridionalis* is a small vine that grows in the open forest extending from about Mirriamvale to northern NSW, east of the Great Dividing Range. It twines up stalks of grass, surviving fires and being eaten by Big Greasy caterpillars.

Aristolochia meridionalis subsp. *centralis* is an open-forest species that is found from just south of Mackay to about Gladstone near the coast, extending westward to the Carnarvon Ranges. On average it is larger than the above subspecies and supports more larvae.

Big Greasy *Cressida cressida*

*Aristolochia indica is naturalised in the Darwin area and is the main Big Greasy host in that region. It is a medium vine that can grow to about 10m long, becoming deciduous if the dry season is too harsh. It originally comes from India, Sri Lanka and Pakistan. It is thought to have been introduced to the Darwin area by Indian nuns who ran a leper colony on Channel Island. It is an excellent host for Birdwing larvae.

Red-bodied Swallowtail *Pachliopta polydorus*

Wingspan: 90–100mm.

Found in rainforest and open forest of Qld from Cape York to just south of Townsville – ranging west to Weipa in the north and the Gilbert River further south.

Adults fly slowly and in the rainforest prefer to move along streams where it is more open. Females usually lay low down on the host plant even when the vine may reach the canopy.

On Cape York Peninsula this butterfly breeds mostly on *Pararistolochia linearifolia* which occurs in the open eucalypt forest where it grows as a prostrate plant reaching a spread of 3m. It also grows on the edge of the rainforest where it becomes a small twining vine. The small size of the vine makes it an ideal host for the Red-bodied Swallowtail, whereas just a couple of Cape York Birdwing larvae virtually destroy it. In the wet tropics of north Qld the females usually lay on *P. deltantha* or seedlings of *Aristolochia acuminata*. Males and females have similar markings.

Host Plants: *Aristolochia acuminata, A. chalmersii, A. nauseifolia, Pararistolochia deltantha, P. linearifolia, P. peninsulensis, *A. esperanzae,*A. grandiflora, *A. indica, *A. macroura.*

Best Garden Host Plant: *Aristolochia acuminata* or **A. macroura.*

Red-bodied Swallowtail *Pachliopta polydorus*

Pararistolochia deltantha occurs from Iron Range on Cape York Peninsula to Mackay, in well-developed rainforest at low to mid-altitudes. It is a slow-growing medium-sized vine that develops tubers on the roots, reaching 15cm in diameter on old vines. In some areas it is extremely common and supports large numbers of Red-bodied Swallowtail and Birdwing larvae.

Pararistolochia linearifolia is a small vine that is commonly found in the open forest of Cape York Peninsula where it grows as a prostrate form covering an area 2–3m wide. This vine has enabled the Red-bodied Swallowtail to move out of the rainforest on the peninsula and become particularly abundant in the Weipa area where the vine is common.

It also grows on the edge of rainforest where it is sometimes used by the Iron Range Birdwing, although its small size means only one or two Birdwing larvae can survive on it.

The roots develop many small tubers which enable it to survive dry periods and fire.

Pararistolochia peninsulensis occurs from about the Olive River to the Rocky River on Cape York Peninsula in well-developed rainforest at low altitudes. It develops into a medium to large vine that reaches the canopy of the rainforest. The fruit are orange when mature.

Ulysses Swallowtail *Papilio ulysses*

Wingspan: Male 125mm, female 130mm.

Found in rainforest from Cape York to Sarina on the east coast, occasionally to Yeppoon, and to Weipa on the west of the Peninsula. Occurs at all altitudes but is more common below 850m. Host plants range to northern NSW but the inability of the pupae to over-winter for long periods restricts the southern range.

Adults fly in full sunshine, usually with a zigzag defensive motion, pausing for short periods while hovering on flowers. They have a preference for red or pink flowers.

Host Plants: *Melicope elleryana*, *M. rubra* and *M. bonwickii* in low- to mid-altitude areas of the wet tropics; *M. affinis*, *M. vitiflora* and *M. jonesii* in the uplands; on Cape York Peninsula *Acronychia peninsularis* in the drier rainforests, especially at Weipa, *M. peninsularis* elsewhere, and *M. elleryana* around permanent springs, of which there are many.

Best Garden Host Plants: *Melicope elleryana* for large gardens and *M. rubra* for small suburban gardens. To tempt the Ulysses Swallowtail to lay in your garden the host plants must be planted in the full sun.

The spectacular, massed flowers of *Melicope elleryana* attract numerous birds and butterflies, and many other insects, so as well as hosting the larvae of the Ulysses Swallowtail you will see a lot of activity around this tree when it is in flower. It is a medium to large tree and if grown in a suburban garden it should be heavily pruned every few years to keep it to a safe size. Its water requirements are high so it is not suitable for dry areas.

Ulysses Swallowtail *Papilio ulysses*

Male Ulysses Swallowtail feeding on flowers of *Melicope elleryana*.

Melicope peninsularis grows in well-developed rainforest from Cape York to the Rocky River. It is a small tree that grows to about 10–15m high with white flowers and large fruit, somewhat resembling *Melicope rubra*.

Melicope bonwickii is a large tree of the north Qld rainforest, ranging from about Cairns to Sarina; it is found mostly in the lowlands but it does extend to the Atherton Tablelands. Like *M. elleryana*, the pink flowers attract many birds and insects. It is more hardy than *M. elleryana* but is far too large to be planted in a suburban garden. Flowering usually occurs in April or May.

Acronychia peninsularis is a small to medium tree that occurs from Torres Strait to Cape Melville in moist to dry rainforest, common on old coastal sand dunes. It is the main host for the Ulysses Swallowtail on the Peninsula. For many years it was known as *Euodia* sp. Batavia Downs because the general appearance of the tree is that of a *Euodia* (now *Melicope*). The fruit does not completely match *Acronychia* so perhaps the butterflies know something the botanists do not.

Ulysses Swallowtail *Papilio ulysses*

Melicope affinis is a small to medium tree that occurs in the mountain rainforest on the Main Coast Range, west and south-west of Mossman, north Qld.

Melicope rubra is a very attractive medium to large shrub and definitely the best choice for those who live in a suburban garden and want to attract the Ulysses Swallowtail. An added bonus is that the flowers also attract honeyeaters. *M. rubra* is found from about the Rocky River on Cape York Peninsula south to Townsville, usually not in the very wet rainforests.

Dingy Swallowtail *Papilio anactus*

Wingspan: Male 85mm, female 90mm.

Not a rainforest species, being found in eucalypt and acacia open forest, sparse vine thickets, along the edge of well-developed rainforest where native citrus are growing and suburban gardens. Probably more widespread than shown in NT where *Citrus gracilis* grows.

Males patrol in open sunny areas watching for passing females. The females fly slowly as they search for host plants on which to lay their eggs. Both sexes can move at high speed if threatened, taking on an erratic flight path.

Host Plants: *Citrus australis, C. australasica, C. garrawayi, C. glauca, C. gracilis, Luvunga monophylla, *Citrus*.

Best Garden Host Plants: The best native citrus is *C. australis* and the best cultivated one is Bush Lemon. The plants must be growing in full sun to attract the females of this butterfly.

Citrus australis is a medium shrub, very thorny and usually found in dry rainforest. Its range in Qld extends from just north of Gympie to about Boonah. It is slow-growing but grafted plants are available from some specialist nurseries.

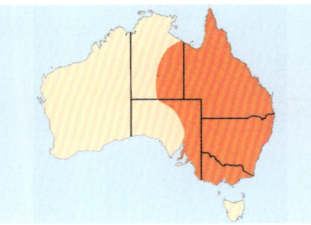

Dingy Swallowtail *Papilio anactus*

Citrus australasica is a medium to large shrub that occurs from about Gympie, Qld, to the Clarence River, NSW, usually on basalt soil in well-developed rainforest. There are a number of forms; on Mt Tamborine the ones on the top of the mountain have small fruit and yellow flesh, while near the bottom on the Southport road is a form with black fruit and red flesh. A number of these forms have been cultivated for the bushtucker trade and are available from specialist nurseries.

Citrus garrawayi is found on Cape York Peninsula, Qld. It comes in a variety of forms and inhabits a wide range of rainforest types. It is found from about the Olive River to Cape Melville National Park, extending to the west coast near Weipa. Plants in semi-deciduous rainforest near Weipa are small scraggly shrubs but in the McIlwraith Range they develop into trees up to 15m high. The fruit is not edible as the skin contains an oil that has a very strong smell and burns the lips and tongue of anyone trying to eat it. This oil contaminates the flesh when the fruit is cut or peeled.

Citrus glauca is a hardy plant that is found mostly in the inland but also near the coast in dry regions. It extends from about Bowen, Qld, to southern NSW and also into southern SA. It is slow in cultivation but grafted plants are sometimes available from specialist nurseries.

Orchard Swallowtail *Papilio aegeus*

Wingspan: Male 115mm, female 120mm.

Probably has the widest range of habitats of any of the Australian species. It ranges from very wet tropical lowland rainforest to the dry inland of central Australia, being common in gardens where cultivated citrus is grown.

Adults usually fly slowly and erratically but are capable of a very swift evasive flight when disturbed. Adults always rest with their wings spread.

Host Plants: This species has a wide variety of host plants in the Rutaceae (citrus) family which include, in order of preference, *Clausena, Citrus, Micromelum, Halfordia, Geijera, Zanthoxylum, Dinosperma, Luvunga monophylla, Flindersia, Eriostemon, Zieria, Boronia, Phebalium, *Calodendron capense, *Choisya ternata, *Citrus, *Poncirus*.

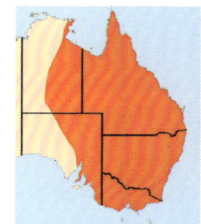

Best Garden Host Plants: Native host plant, *Micromelum minutum*, otherwise almost any cultivated *Citrus* pruned regularly to produce new growth.

Pale form female found on Cape York Peninsula.

Clausena brevistyla is distributed from Torres Strait to south-east Qld, rarely more than 100km from the coast. It is a small tree that can be grown in suburban gardens and is available from some native plant nurseries.

Orchard Swallowtail *Papilio aegeus*

Halfordia kendack occurs from about Miriam Vale, Qld, to southern NSW. This genus is used extensively by the Orchard Swallowtail. It is often found in coastal rainforest and is well worth growing to attract the butterflies.

Halfordia scleroxyla is a medium-sized tree that is common in the mountain rainforests of north Qld. All *Halfordia* species are called Kerosene Wood because the wood, which will burn when green, was used to boil the billy by early timber cutters working in the rainforest.

Zanthoxylum brachyacanthum extends from the Forty Mile Scrub in north Qld to northern NSW and is found in dry to very wet rainforest. Young plants have thorns on all parts, even the leaves.

Orchard Swallowtail *Papilio aegeus*

Halfordia sp. Temple Bay is widespread on eastern Cape York Peninsula, extending south to Cooktown. It is most common in rainforest growing on old sand dunes and is used extensively by the Orchard Swallowtail in these areas. When grown in the open it forms a dense crown.

Clausena smyrelliana is a rare small tree that is found in coastal rainforest in Qld from Bundaberg to Hervey Bay. It is a much favoured host plant for the Orchard Swallowtail. Even though it is a rare tree it is now available from some native plant nurseries.

Orchard Swallowtail *Papilio aegeus*

Luvunga monophylla only just grows within the natural range of the Orchard Swallowtail, but when planted in gardens in north and south Qld it becomes a favourite host plant for all our citrus-feeding butterflies. It is a stiff scrambling vine that ranges from Torres Strait to the Kimberley coast, just north of Broome, WA.

Geijera salicifolia var. *latifolia* is very widely distributed, ranging from about Coen on Cape York Peninsula, Qld, to near Sydney, NSW. This genus is the most used by the Orchard Swallowtail; *G. salicifolia* in eastern areas, *G. parviflora* in the inland and *G. linearifolia* in southern Australia.

Geijera salicifolia var. *salicifolia* is a tree that was once common in the Brigalow scrubs of Qld and northern NSW. It is no longer very common but used by the Orchard Swallowtail wherever it occurs.

Ambrax Swallowtail *Papilio ambrax*

Wingspan: Male 100mm, female 105mm.

Found in tropical rainforest in both lowland and upland areas from about Cooktown to Mackay. Adults fly quite quickly and the males seem to be almost always on the move. They make an ideal captive species in butterfly farms as their constant flight makes them visible. When resting they invariably sit with wings outspread. This butterfly is very reluctant to leave the rainforest so if you live much more then 5km from where they breed they may not find host plants planted in your garden.

Host Plants: In order of preference, *Zanthoxylum ovalifolium*, *Micromelum minutum*, *Clausena brevistyla*, *Zanthoxylum veneficum*, *Z. nitidum*, *Luvunga monophylla*, *Citrus inodora*, *Murraya koenigii*, *Citrus*, *Limonia acidissima*.

Best Garden Host Plant: *Zanthoxylum ovalifolium*.

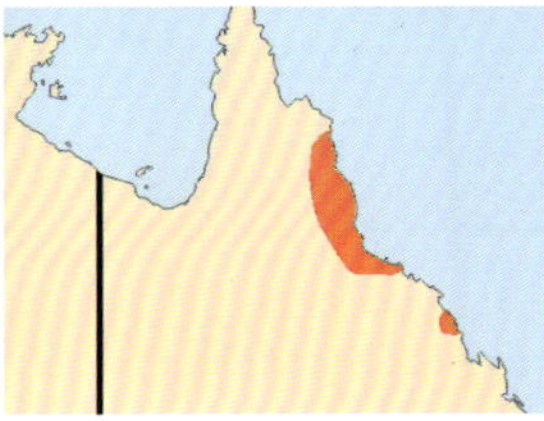

Ambrax Swallowtail *Papilio ambrax*

Zanthoxylum ovalifolium is found from about Cooktown to Ravenshoe, usually in upland moist to wet rainforest. It is a large shrub or small tree and is often available from native plant nurseries. Young plants possess thorns but mature ones have very few. When the bright red fruit opens the seed is plucked from them by honeyeaters.

Citrus inodora is found in very wet lowland rainforest from Cape Tribulation to about Babinda in north Qld. It can easily be grown in the garden but needs plenty of water and shade. The foliage is larger than most other native limes and the fruit is edible.

Capaneus Swallowtail *Papilio fuscus capaneus*

Wingspan: Male 100mm, female 105mm.

Occurs in low- to mid-altitude rainforests, vine thickets and gardens where cultivated citrus is grown. The Capaneus Swallowtail ranges from Cape York, Qld, west to at least Georgetown and south to northern NSW.

Adults usually fly slowly but are capable of extremely fast evasive flight mode if threatened. If tails cannot be observed or are broken off their slightly brown base colour distinguishes them from the Orchard Swallowtail males.

Males and females are very similar. The pupal stage of this species can last for several years. Females prefer to lay in the shade.

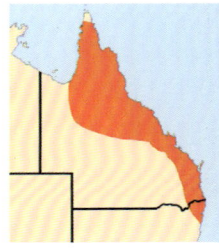

Host Plants: In order of preference, *Clausena, Glycosmis trifoliata, Micromelum, Halfordia, Citrus, Zanthoxylum, Luvunga monophylla, *Murraya koenigii, *Citrus.*

Best Garden Host Plant: *Micromelum minutum.*

Markings on both upper and the underwings vary as shown in these two images.

Capaneus Swallowtail *Papilio fuscus capaneus*

Glycosmis trifoliata (Lime Berry) is a widespread plant ranging from near Broome, WA, across the top end, with a gap in the southern Gulf of Carpentaria then from Torres Strait to about Maryborough in south Qld. As a rule it is found in the drier and coastal rainforests but not in deciduous vine thickets. It is a good garden plant as it is only a small to medium shrub and is often available from native plant nurseries in Qld. The attractive pink berries are edible but too oily to be of much use as bushtucker.

Murraya koenigii (Curry Tree) is a native of India and surrounding countries of Asia. When in flower it is a hive of activity as numerous butterflies seek nectar. One problem with this plant is that it suckers and some control is needed to limit the spread. It is an excellent host plant for Ambrax, Capaneus and Orchard Swallowtails.

FAMILY PAPILIONIDAE – SUBFAMILY PAPILIONINAE   SWALLOWTAILS

Zanthoxylum veneficum is a rainforest tree of the north Qld wet tropics region where it ranges from the Mt Windsor Tableland to about Ravenshoe, occurring in both low and high altitudes. Young plants are covered in thorns but the mature trees have very few. Citrus-feeding Swallowtails lay their eggs chiefly on juvenile plants up to about 3m high.

Micromelum minutum is a very useful butterfly-attracting shrub to have in the garden. Apart from three of the citrus-feeding swallowtails using it as a host plant, the flowers attract almost all butterflies except Birdwings and the Ulysses Swallowtail. The bright orange/red fruit are eaten by honeyeaters and figbirds.

It is advisable to plant more than one plant so you have one or more in the semi-shade and the same in full sun.

The natural distribution of *Micromelum* is from the Kimberley coast, WA, across the top end and from Torres Strait, Qld, to northern NSW. It is rarely found more than 200km from the coast, favouring coastal rainforest and semi-deciduous to deciduous vine thickets.

Apart from attracting the butterflies in your garden you will see species that are passing by, such as the White-spotted Flash in the picture on the right. This butterfly does not breed within 100km of the author's garden but twice now adults have been observed feeding on the *Micromelum* flowers.

To attract the Capaneus and Canopus Swallowtails the plant must be planted in at least part shade.

Canopus Swallowtail *Papilio fuscus canopus*

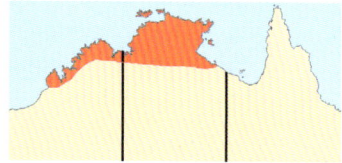

Wingspan: Male 100mm, female 105mm.

Found in rainforest, including semi-deciduous and deciduous vine thickets from about Broome, WA, across the top end and almost to the Qld border in the Gulf of Carpentaria.

Adults usually fly slowly and erratically unless threatened. Females prefer to lay their eggs on plants in the shade. Male and female are very similar.

Host Plants: *Micromelum minutum*, *Glycosmis trifoliata*, *Zanthoxylum parviflorum*, *Citrus*, and possibly *Glycosmis macrophylla*. It is interesting to note that the distribution of the Canopus Swallowtail aligns almost exactly with the distribution of both *Micromelum* and *Glycosmis* in WA and NT.

Best Garden Host Plant: *Micromelum minutum*.

The white line on the side of the pupa is different from that on the Capaneus Swallowtail.

Zanthoxylum parviflorum is a small tree that is found from the Kimberley coast, across the top end of WA and NT to the south-west Gulf of Carpentaria, then from Torres Strait to Cape Melville in Qld. It mainly occurs in coastal or island rainforest but also in rainforest in protected gorges amongst sandstone such as Kakadu National Park.

Young plants have many thorns on leaves, stems and trunk but adult plants loose most of these except on the trunk, where they resemble large rose thorns.

Chequered Swallowtail *Papilio demoleus*

Wingspan: Male 88mm, female 90mm.

Australian mainland mostly in open woodland, plains and savannah country. In south-east Qld occurs in open eucalypt forest and suburban gardens where the host plant *Cullen tenax* grows. Adults fly rapidly, usually keeping less than 2m from the ground. During large migrations, which occur regularly, huge numbers spread out across as much as half the continent.

Host Plants: Probably all native *Cullen* species but they lay less often on the very hairy species. Favourite hosts are *Cullen tenax, C. australasicum, C. cinereum, C. balsamicum, C. pustulatum, C. leucanthum, Luvunga monophylla*. They will also lay on introduced *Cullen* species such as **C. pinnata*. During migrations the females will often lay on cultivated citrus,

especially Bush Lemon. On the Mitchell Plateau, WA, *Luvunga monophylla* is used where it grows in semi-deciduous vine forests.

Best Garden Host Plant: Any of the above species of native *Cullen*.

Cullen tenax is a small herbaceous plant that grows in open forest and grassland areas, reaching a height of 1.5m if necessary to get above the grass. It is very long lived as it develops a large tuber and can survive fires and drought. It is the main host of the Chequered Swallowtail in eastern Australia, ranging from near Kirrima in north Qld to eastern SA. It often establishes in lawns in Brisbane but lawnmowers are not compatible with the butterflies' survival.

Chequered Swallowtail *Papilio demoleus*

Cullen pustulatum is confined to the northern half of Australia, from coast to coast. It grows from 1.5–2m high and makes an excellent host for the Chequered Swallowtail. Juvenile plants have leaves with three leaflets. Like all *Cullen* species it should be grown in the full sun.

Cullen balsamicum is found in inland northern Australia, usually 100km or more from the coast, in WA, NT and Qld, north of a line above about Cloncurry. It grows in open areas where there is very low vegetation and forms large colonies in areas of the Barkly Tableland. It can reach a height of 4m. The stems and leaf stalks release a sticky substance which also covers the fruit. Plant in full sun.

Cullen sp. aff. *tenax* occurs mostly west of the main coastal ranges and is sometimes referred to as 'Tall Western Grassland Form'. Originally it was named *Psoralea tenax.* var. *major* and for some unknown reason this was dropped when the name was changed to *Cullen tenax*. This plant is a small shrub to about 1.5m high with leaves much larger than *C. tenax* and is definitely the best host plant to grow for the Chequered Swallowtail as almost all the other *Cullen* species are little more than annuals. This one, like other forms in the *C. tenax* group, has a large tuber and lives for a very long time.

Cullen australasicum is very common and widespread in inland Australia, being found in all states except Tas. It forms large colonies following a good wet season. While most populations are in the dry inland it extends to the coast between Townsville and Mackay where it is relatively dry. It is an easy plant to grow, the seed being available from native seed suppliers.

Cullen cinereum covers almost the whole continent, except Tas and the very high rainfall areas. It can be found in huge colonies, spreading as far as the eye can see. It is quite easy to grow and seed is readily available.

Four-bar Swordtail *Protographium leosthenes*

P.l. leosthenes

Wingspan: Male 65mm, female 70mm.

Found in all types of rainforest, with a preference for the drier ones. Very common in Hoop Pine rainforests in south-east Qld and monsoon rainforests in northern Australia. The adults usually fly slowly, using for the most parts their forewings with the tails trailing behind, which makes them instantly recognisable as they fly past. This flight habit also makes it less likely that they will break off their tails when moving through the rainforest to lay eggs. Capable of very rapid flight when disturbed.

There are two subspecies:
- *P.l. geimbia* in NT, mostly in Kakadu National Park.
- *P.l. leosthenes* in Qld from Cape York to south of Coffs Harbour.

This species can remain in the pupal stage for several years and the butterflies almost always emerge when ideal breeding conditions prevail.

Host Plants: In order of preference, *Melodorum leichhardtii, Desmos polycarpus, D. wardianus, M. rupestre* (NT), *Uvaria rufa, M. unguiculatum, M. crassipetalum, M. scabridulum, M. uhrii, Miliusa horsfieldii*.

P.l. geimbia

Best Garden Host Plant: *Melodorum leichhardtii*. Most of the host plants of this butterfly are large scrambling vines which can be kept pruned to a weeping shrub. However, this does present a problem. The pupa of the Swordtail is almost impossible to see on the plant, where it might remain for more than a year. Hence there is a high probability that pupae will be cut off and discarded with the prunings.

SWALLOWTAILS

Uvaria (Melodorum) leichhardtii is an extremely widespread plant, ranging from Torres Strait, Qld, to about Coffs Harbour, NSW. It is found in most types of rainforests, from very wet lowland regions to high altitudes of 1,000m on the Mt Windsor Tableland, north Qld. It is most common in coastal and lower rainfall rainforests but not usually in deciduous vine thickets. This is an extremely easy plant to grow in the garden and available from many native plant nurseries.

Uvaria (Melodorum) rupestre is found only in NT, mainly in Kakadu National Park and the surrounding area, in vine thickets on sandstone. It is very common where it occurs and is the most used host plant for the NT race of Four-bar Swordtail. *Desmos wardianus* is a more favoured plant in this area due to the abundance of soft new foliage, but is not as common.

Uvaria rufa is found in Qld from Torres Strait to a little south of Coen on Cape York Peninsula. In this area it is a major host plant for the Four-bar Swordtail. At the start of the storm season in November-December it produces a flush of large soft foliage that can support many larvae. The edible fruit is closely related to a species in Asia which is called Custard Finger. It is a large vine but with a very open habit.

Five-bar Swordtail *Graphium aristeus*

Wingspan: Male 60mm, female 65mm.

The **Five-barred Swordtail** occurs in a wide range of rainforest types at low altitudes, from wet lowland rainforest near Cairns to deciduous vine thickets on Cape York Peninsula. Permanent colonies occur mostly where their host plants grow amongst large boulders. The larvae pupate in the leaf litter and often under these boulders (first observed by Graham Wood) where they can remain dormant for several years. When there is a population explosion they spread out, laying their eggs on their host plants in completely different habitats. However, they never establish colonies in these areas unless there are large numbers of host plants present.

The limiting factor on their population in their breeding areas near Cairns is that the host plants mostly grow on the slopes along fast flowing streams and in the wet season large numbers of pupae in the leaf litter would be washed away. This is not such a problem near Cooktown where their breeding area is mostly flat.

They range from Cape York to Rockhampton, but I do not believe they breed in the Rockhampton area. The nearest Miliusa plants are about 150/200 km to the north and they are probably only visitors to this area. The adults fly very fast and are difficult to identify on the wing. Males are often seen mud puddling after rain. In good seasons when their population density becomes very high they spread out and can be seen up to 200 km from where they bred. Every so often they breed in very large numbers.

Male patrolling the leaf litter

Like most butterflies the females usually mate while their wings are drying. Unlike all other swallowtails they lay their eggs in large batches of from 50 to 80 on a single leaf. The eggs are carefully placed an equal distance from each other. This is because the larvae of swallowtails eat their own eggshell after hatching so they need space to do this when they all hatch together. The larvae stay clustered together for the first two instars after which they then spread out into smaller groups. Each morning males patrol backwards and forwards over the leaf litter under the host plants looking for freshly emerged females. By not searching for females on the host plant it enables the females to carefully lay their batches of eggs without being molested. The egg laying process often takes half an hour or more as she carefully places each one a certain distance from the other.

FAMILY PAPILIONIDAE – SUBFAMILY PAPILIONINAE — SWALLOWTAILS

Batch of eggs showing their placement on the leaf. The larvae usually make this leaf their first plant meal. One egg was infertile and three sucked out by a spider or ant.

First instar larvae

Second instar larvae

Small cluster of third or fourth instar larvae

Mature larva

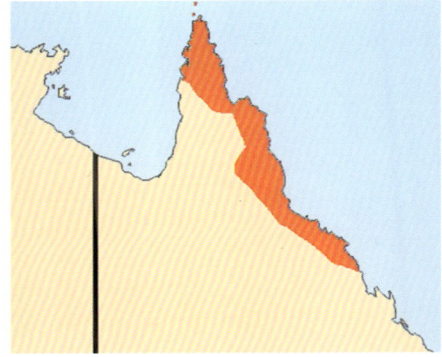

Pupae in leaf litter

Five-bar Swordtail *Graphium aristeus*

Host Plants: *Miliusa traceyi, M. brahei, M. horsfieldii. Huberantha nitidissima (Polyalthia)* is listed as a host plant but may be very much a secondary host, used only when most of the *Miliusa* plants in the area have been eaten. The butterfly never breeds where only *P. nitidissima* grows on its own, even if it is amongst large boulders.

Best Garden Host Plant: *Miliusa brahei*.

Miliusa traceyi is a typical monsoon rainforest tree inasmuch as it is deciduous. Usually in September or October the leaves turn yellow and fall. Just as the first storms of summer commence it bursts into new growth and flowers at the same time. The new growth is soft and juicy and this is the time that the Five-bar Swordtails emerge from their dormant pupae and target this tender growth with large numbers of eggs. The small black fruit are eaten by birds.

Miliusa brahei is a small to medium tree that is found across the top end of Australia from just north of Broome, WA, through the Kimberley and NT to about Nhulumbuy, then in Qld from Torres Strait to south of Sarina in monsoon or well-developed rainforest. This is the main host plant used where the butterfly breeds south of Cooktown. Crush the leaves of this plant and have a sniff, you should be rewarded with the smell of Raspberry Jelly – or not – depending on your own individual olfactory sense.

Miliusa horsfieldii is a small to medium tree that is found in lowland rainforest from Cape York to Cairns. Just before flowering it throws all its leaves and produces a massive flush of soft green foliage along with the flowers. This plant rarely grows where there are permanent colonies of the Five-bar Swordtail but is utilised for a single brood when there is a population explosion causing the butterflies to spread out and find new host plants in a different area. It is not known what happens to these temporary breeding colonies – they just seem to disappear.

Macleay's Swallowtail *Graphium macleayanum*

Wingspan: Male 70mm, female 72mm.

Found in mountain rainforests in Qld, occurring at lower altitudes further south. The only Swallowtail found in Tas.

There are two subspecies:
- *G.m. macleayanum* from McIlwraith Range on Cape York Peninsula, Qld, to far eastern Vic.
- *G.m. moggana* in the highlands of southern NSW, Vic and Tas.

G.m. moggana.   G.m. macleayanum.

Adults spend a lot of time feeding on flowers and most of the day flying rather than resting. Because of this they are an ideal butterfly to have in your garden, being visible most of the time. Males patrol open sunny areas on the lookout for passing females.

Host Plants: In north Qld the most commonly used plant is *Doryphora aromatica*. They also use *Daphnandra repandula* and a wide range of plants in the Lauraceae (Laurels) family, especially *Cryptocarya* and *Endiandra*. In south-east Qld *Cryptocarya*, *Cinnamomum* and *Daphnandra apatela* are utilised while further south the following are used; *Doryphora sassafras*, *Tasmannia* and *Atherosperma*.

Best Garden Host Plants: Depending where you live, *Doryphora aromatica* in north Qld, *Daphnandra apatela* in south-east Qld, *Tasmannia* in southern areas.

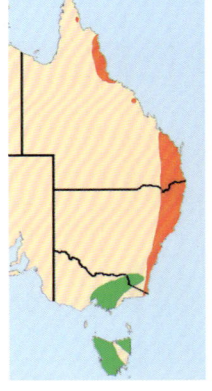

Macleay's Swallowtail *Graphium macleayanum*

Daphnandra repandula is a small to medium tree that is found in the high-rainfall rainforests of the wet tropics of north Qld as well as Eungella, near Mackay. It has finely serrated leaves and fruit that open up to expose seed clothed in soft, long brown hairs.

Doryphora aromatica (Northern Sassafras) is a small to medium tree found in the high-rainfall rainforests of the wet tropics of north Qld. The leaves are serrated and have a strong aromatic smell when crushed.

The butterflies quite often lay their eggs high up on mature trees, so finding larvae in undisturbed rainforest is very difficult.

Blue Triangle *Graphium choredon*

Male Blue Triangle spreading his hair pencils during courtship flight to dust pheromones down onto the female.

Wingspan: Male 80mm, female 85mm.

All the host plants are in the Lauraceae (Laurels) family and are rainforest plants, but because of the introduced Camphor Laurel (*Cinnamomum camphora*) being widespread and native host plants being planted in gardens and as street trees the habitat of this butterfly can be anywhere east of the Great Dividing Range from Cape York, Qld, to Vic.

Adults fly fast and usually erratically, stopping momentarily to feed on flowers. When they land the wings are generally closed but sometimes on a cool morning they will sit in the sun with wings spread to gather warmth, as the individual in the top left image is doing.

Host Plants: Almost all native plants in the Laurel family with the one definite exception, *Cryptocarya laevigata*. The females have a definite preference for species with few hairs and red new growth. Their wide range of host plants includes most species of the following genera; *Beilschmiedia*, *Cinnamomum* (these are very high on the most favoured list), *Cryptocarya*, *Endiandra*, *Litsea* (all species are used), *Neolitsea*, with *N. brassii* being the most favoured native host plant. *N. dealbata* is rarely used, probably because it is often quite hairy.

Best Garden Host Plant: *Neolitsea brassii*. Camphor Laurel cannot be recommended as it is a declared weed in both NSW and Qld. The Qld legislation states: 'It must not be given away, sold, or released into the environment without a permit.'

Blue Triangle *Graphium choredon*

Cryptocarya vulgaris occurs in well-developed rainforest from low to mid-altitudes and ranges in Qld from about the Pascoe River on Cape York Peninsula to Bundaberg. It is a very hardy plant and even though the new growth is not red many females are tempted to lay on it.

Cinnamomum baileyanum is a typical laurel that Blue Triangles favour for egg-laying. It has soft, red and glossy new growth, being found in rainforests from Cape York to Cooktown, then in south-east Qld.

Pale Blue Triangle *Graphium eurypylus*

Wingspan: Male 80mm, female 82mm.

Natural habitat is rainforest of most types, but rarely occurs above 700m. The host plants are in the Annonaceae (Custard Apple) family and this and other related plants are readily accepted by the larvae. Cultivated Custard Apple is common in gardens and this has enabled the Pale Blue Triangle to spread well beyond its natural habitat. The common name comes from freshly hatched butterflies which are pale green.

There are two subspecies in mainland Australia:
- *G.e. lycaon* from Cape York, Qld, to central NSW, occasionally to Vic.
- *G.e. nyctimus* across the top end of WA and NT.

Adults fly rapidly and visit flowers regularly. Like all Triangles they do not stay long on each flower and keep their wings flapping continuously while feeding. When resting they usually sit with their wings closed.

Host Plants: In order of preference, *Polyalthia, Uvaria, Desmos, Cyathostemma, Miliusa, Goniothalamus australis, Artabotrys carnosipetalus, *Annona, *Rollinia, *Michelia*.

Best Garden Host Plants: *Uvaria leichhardtii* or *Huberantha nitidissima (Polyalthia)*.

G.e. lycaon.

G.e nyctimus.

 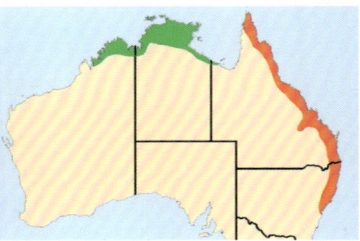

Pale Blue Triangle *Graphium eurypylus*

The colour of some females fades to yellow quite quickly. The cause of this is not known.

Huberantha nitidissima (Polyalthia) is widespread across the top end of NT and in eastern Qld, extending into northern NSW. It occurs most often in coastal or dry to moist rainforest. It is a very hardy plant and available from native plant nurseries. The fruit is eaten by birds.

Cyathostemma micranthum occurs from the Kimberley region of WA, around the top end and down to about Cooktown, Qld. It is usually found in coastal rainforest, monsoon rainforest or vine thickets. It is common in the Kimberley region and the author found the Pale Blue Triangle breeding on this plant on Bigge Island.

It is a small woody vine that scrambles over trees. The flowers are very small but the glossy black fruit is more noticeable and is eaten by birds.

Meiogyne (Fitzalania) heteropetala is a large shrub that is found in Qld in coastal and dry rainforest from Orpheus Island (north-east of Townsville) to about Rockhampton.

Meiogyne (Fitzalania) bidwillii occurs in Qld from Eurimbulah Creek (Seventeen Seventy) north of Bundaberg to Hervey Bay in coastal, gallery and Hoop Pine rainforest. It is a large understorey shrub that has flowers of an unusual colour; they are dark purple to black when mature. The bright orange fruit is edible.

Meiogyne (Fitzalania) sp. Groote Island is a very rare understorey shrub that is restricted to Groote Island, growing in monsoon and coastal rainforest. There is not much rainforest on Groote Island and this plant should be classified as critically endangered and a determined effort made to propagate it so that its survival is assured.

Green Triangle *Graphium macfarlanei*

Wingspan: Male 90mm, female 92mm.

Found in coastal and monsoon rainforest from Cape York to about Townsville. Rarely occurs above 300m. Usually breeds at Kuranda each year but very rarely visits the Atherton Tableland.

Adults fly swiftly and are fairly difficult to distinguish from the Pale Blue Triangle. To a trained eye the red on the underside of the wings stands out. When they land the underside is distinctly green rather than pale blue.

Host Plants: Strangely enough the females seem to be more attracted to introduced plants, namely Soursop and Custard Apple. In order of preference native host plants are *Miliusa brahei, Uvaria (Melodorum) leichhardtii, Huberantha nitidissima (Polyalthia), Miliusa traceyi, Desmos polycarpus.*

Best Garden Host Plants: **Annona muricata* (Soursop) or the native plant *Miliusa brahei.*

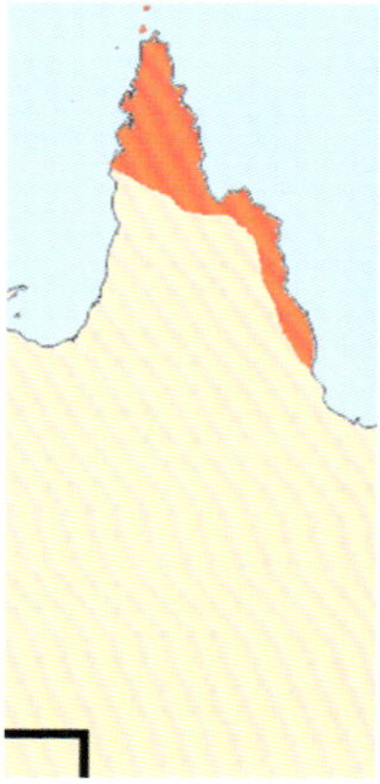

FAMILY PAPILIONIDAE – SUBFAMILY PAPILIONINAE — SWALLOWTAILS

Annona muricata (Soursop).

Green-spotted Triangle *Graphium agamemnon*

Wingspan: Male 85mm, female 90mm.

Occurs from Cape York to Rockhampton in moist to very wet rainforest, occasionally in semi-deciduous vine thickets and usually at low to mid-altitudes.

Adults are very fast flying, stopping for short periods on flowers. Eggs are usually laid in shade. Adults move slowly through the rainforest and the wing markings make them very difficult to keep track of.

Host Plants: *Artabotrys, Cyathostemma, Desmos, Goniothalamus, Haplostichanthus, Meiogyne, Miliusa, Mitrephora, Monoon, Polyalthia, Pseuduvaria, Uvaria, Xylopia,* *Annona (Custard Apple and Soursop), **Michellia champaca.*

Best Garden Host Plants: *Uvaria leichhardtii,* *Annona (Custard Apple and Soursop).

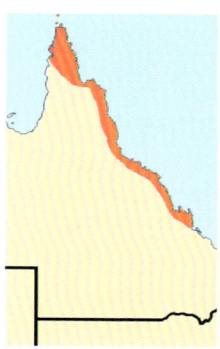

Pseuduvaria froggattii is a large understorey shrub that is confined to the lowland rainforest of the north Qld wet tropics. It is found from about Bloomfield, south of Cooktown, to Julatten. The large soft leaves of the new growth are ideal for the rapid development of the larvae.

There are five different *Pseuduvaria* species and all are restricted to the rainforest of the north Qld wet tropics. All grow in the shade and this is ideal for the Green-spotted Triangle.

FAMILY PAPILIONIDAE – SUBFAMILY PAPILIONINAE
SWALLOWTAILS

Monoon patinatum (patinata) is a medium to large tree found in the wet tropical lowland rainforest of north Qld from about Gordonvale to Innisfail. Its large soft new growth is ideal for the butterfly larvae to feed on. It eventually produces a mass of yellow flowers which are very prolific and hang under the branches.

Though this plant may look like *Cananga* it certainly does not smell like it. The flowers have a strange smell that possibly attracts beetles.

Monoon australe (Polyalthia australis) is a medium to large tree that is found in lowland monsoon rainforest from the Kimberley area in WA, across the top end of NT, then in Qld from Cape York south to about Townsville. It is a major host plant for the Green-spotted Triangle wherever it occurs within the range of the butterfly.

Polyalthia xanthocarpa (Haplostichanthus ramiflorus) is a medium-sized understorey shrub of the north Qld wet tropics. It is found in lowland rainforest from just north of Cape Tribulation to the Mossman River. Every time this plant flushes the female Green-spotted Triangle butterflies are quick to lay on it. It is an ideal host plant as this butterfly lays its eggs in the shade and that is where *Polyalthia xanthocarpa* grows.

Green-spotted Triangle *Graphium agamemnon*

Meiogyne cylindrocarpa is a small to medium shrub with a very narrow and neat growth habit. It is an understorey plant that grows in monsoon rainforest from the Kimberley region, WA, across the top end of NT and then in Qld from Cape York to Iron Range. The bright red-orange fruit is very attractive to the eye and also to birds.

Xylopia maccreae is a slow-growing small tree that can be grown in coastal gardens of Qld and northern NSW. It will flower when in part shade, and though the white flowers are quite attractive it rarely produces many of them at any one time. The fruit are unusual as they turn inside-out when ripe, exposing the bright orange to red inside. It is found from Cape Flattery to Mackay, in lowland rainforest, especially coastal and gallery types.

WHITES and YELLOWS
Family Pieridae

This family is represented in all states of Australia, but as with most groups the greatest number of species are found in the northern half of the continent. Overall these butterflies are quite active and very noticeable when on the wing. At times some of the species occur in huge numbers and participate in migrations that consist of millions of individuals. These migrations can cover hundreds of kilometres and can go on for many days. The species that most often move in large numbers are the Common Migrant, Lemon Migrant and Caper White. These migrations happen when a local population has exploded and most of the host plants have been eaten. The majority of these butterflies die without establishing new colonies and their direction of travel is usually into the wind as they are spurred on by the scent of a few molecules of their host plants being carried along. Often the migration goes round in a circle as the wind changes. Before the Brigalow Scrub was almost completely destroyed, vast numbers of Lemon Migrants could be seen each summer in Qld between Rockhampton and Sarina on the inland road. The numbers were at times so high they could completely clog the radiator grill of a vehicle. Their host plant in this area is *Cassia brewsteri* and this plant used to be very common, but the clearing of the scrub has reduced the numbers to just a scattered few and the butterfly numbers will never be the same as they used to be.

The larvae of the Whites and Yellows usually have very few markings; they usually have some hairs, although never dense like some moth larvae, while larvae of the Jezebel group have quite long hairs. The pupae are attached by a central girdle and pad of silk at the base like the Swallowtails but not necessarily in a vertical position. Some are on top of a leaf where they are somewhat camouflaged. The eggs are quite small for the size of the butterflies and usually pointed at both ends.

Adult males often gather in large numbers on damp ground to suck up nutrients; this behaviour is called 'mud-puddling' and is also practiced by most other butterfly families, especially in the warmer climates. This is more common in the drier rainforests (Hoop Pine rainforests and vine thickets) of central and north Qld. In some seasons huge numbers can be seen extracting nutrients from damp ground.

The adults of this group survive the winter/dry season as butterflies, spending a lot of time resting; moving about occasionally on warm days to feed.

The Lemon, Orange and Yellow Migrants continue to breed in the north if fresh foliage of their host plants is available. Jezebels breed mostly during the winter months except in the far south.

Male Caper Whites and Australian Gulls on damp ground.

Northern Jezebel larvae showing the long white hairs.

Grey Albatross pupa on top of a leaf.

Common Migrant egg.

Common Migrant *Catopsilia pyranthe*

Size: Male 65mm, female 70mm.

Found in northern and eastern Australia in open forest and vine thickets. Adults mill about slowly in their breeding colonies, but when migrating they fly swiftly, often in very large numbers.

Host Plants: Annual/semi-annual *Senna* plants, including *S. barclayana, S. planitiicola, S. sophera (S. clavigera)*. The seed pods are eaten by cattle and spread far and wide by cattle trucks. The Common Migrant generally uses *Senna* species that have more or less cylindrical seed pods, rather than those with flat pods. The combined distribution of these three host plants matches perfectly with that of the Common Migrant butterfly but no doubt there are many more *Senna* species that are host plants. *Cassia* plants are not used. There are a number of records listing *Cassia* species as host plants, but this could be because *Senna* species were previously included in the *Cassia* genus. These records are considered one-offs or dubious, so have not been included.

Best Garden Larval Food Plant: *Senna sophera* or *S. planitiicola*.

Senna barclayana is a shrub from 1–1.5m high. It is often confused with *S. sophera*, and it is very difficult to tell the difference, but the one illustrated was identified by the Queensland Herbarium. This species is found over most of eastern Australia, although less commonly in the far north.

Senna sophera (clavigera) is a semi-annual shrub that can grow 2m high in favourable conditions but is usually smaller. It is found in eastern Australia from west of Cairns, Qld, to southern NSW, extending west of the Great Dividing Range but is more common closer to the coast. Usually in its second year of growth a mass of seed pods will be produced, then the plant dies in the following dry season.

Senna planitiicola is found mostly in the northern half of Australia, being more common in the inland. It is the tallest of the three host plants and can reach 3m in garden situations; normally it is between 1–2m. The foliage often has a blue tinge. Most *Senna* species produce nectar from glands near the base of their leaves; the nectar attracts ants. These ants do not attack the larvae of the Common Migrant.

Lemon Migrant *Catopsilia pomona*

Size: Male 66mm, female 70mm.

Found in northern and eastern Australia; at times their extensive migration flights reach all areas of the mainland. There are two distinct forms:
– Wet-season form (top two images) is more lemon or even lime in colour.
– Dry-season form (bottom three images) is white with lemon centre and pink antennae. In this form some females appear with very dark red/brown markings on the underside. Adults fly very fast with an erratic flight pattern.

Host Plants: *Cassia brewsteri, C. marksiana, C. queenslandica, C. tomentella, C.* sp. Kalpowar, *C.* sp. Paluma Range, *Senna coronilloides, S. magnifolia, S. venusta, *S. alata, *C. didymobotrya, *C. fistula, *C. javanica, *C. siamea.* Apparently able to use any *Cassia* species from South-East Asia as host plants, but very few from South America. This is usual for all our butterflies.

Best Garden Host Plant: Native host plant, *Cassia* sp. Paluma Range; introduced, **C. fistula.*

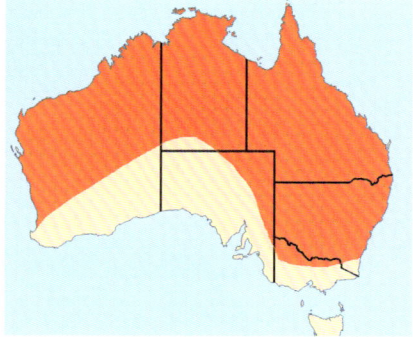

Senna notabilis is a shrub that is found throughout most of inland Australia, being more common in the tropics. The unusual colour of the foliage and pods make it easy to identify.

FAMILY PIERIDAE – SUBFAMILY COLIADINAE — WHITES AND YELLOWS

Cassia brewsteri in a multi-stemmed shrub or small tree that is usually found in the Brigalow belt in Qld from just south of Greenvale to about Springsure.

A similar looking but very much larger rainforest plant is found from about Biggenden to Cooroy in south-east Qld. It grows as an emergent tree in the rainforest or as a large spreading one when growing in the open. Listed as *C. brewsteri* in herbaria.

Cassia queenslandica is a large spreading tree found in rainforest from Cooktown to the Clohesy River in north Qld. It is much too large to be planted in a suburban garden. Old flowers turn orange

Cassia sp. Paluma Range is probably the most spectacular of all the Australian Cassia species. It is found in and along the edge of rainforest from Mt Fox to Shoalwater Bay in north Qld. It forms a column shape and is ideal for most gardens. The mass of bright yellow flowers follows a flush of new growth with purple underside. It is readily available from native plant nurseries in Qld.

Lemon Migrant *Catopsilia pomona*

Cassia sp. Kalpowar is a medium to large shrub – an ideal size for a suburban garden. It was discovered on Kalpowar Station, north of Cooktown, about 20 years ago. It is available from some native plant nurseries.

Cassia tomentella is a large shrub to small tree that grows in vine thickets from just south of Sarina to south-east Qld. It is readily available from native plant nurseries and suitable for suburban gardens.

Senna magnifolia is a multi-stemmed shrub with large glossy leaves and showy heads of flowers. It occurs in the dry savannah forest in a relatively narrow band from just west of Mareeba to Bowen then across to the Kimberley region of WA. It is an ideal garden plant for the dry tropics of Australia.

Orange Migrant *Catopsilia scylla*

Size: Male 66mm, female 70mm.

Most common in tropical Australia from the Kimberley region, WA, across to Townsville, Qld, then extending down the east coast to southern NSW. Usually found in vine thickets where the host plant generally grows. It readily visits gardens if a suitable host plant is available.

Host Plants: *Senna leptoclada, S. oligoclada, S. gaudichaudii, S. surattensis, *S. auriculata.*

Best Garden Host Plant: **Senna auriculata* – this is the species most readily available.

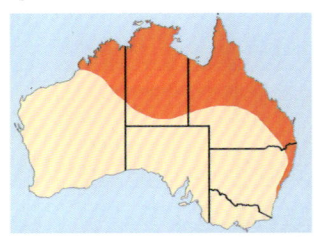

Senna gaudichaudii is a weeping shrub that can develop into a climber if planted close to other plants. In cultivation, flowering occurs all year round. It is very hardy and will grow in a wide range of areas. Pruning once a year will keep it bushy and attractive.

Yellow Migrant *Catopsilia gorgophone*

Size: Male 66mm, female 70mm.

Found in eastern Australia from about Cooktown, Qld, to southern NSW and up to about 300km inland. It breeds during summer in inland areas, moving towards the coast at the end of the wet season. On the Atherton Tableland it is most common from May to October. Both this and the previous species have a white form. These white forms are indistinguishable from each other and also resemble the Common Migrant.

Host Plants: *Senna acclinis, S. sulfurea, S. gaudichaudii, S. surattensis, *S. auriculata*.

Best Garden Host Plant: **Senna auriculata*.

Senna surattensis is a small to medium shrub that forms colonies by suckering. It is very hardy and an ideal host plant for Yellow and Orange Migrants. The species name means it was first found in Surat in India, and some taxonomists consider it to be introduced into Australia. It is now pantropical.

FAMILY PIERIDAE – SUBFAMILY COLIADINAE — WHITES AND YELLOWS

Senna acclinis is a shrub that grows from about 2–3m high with rather thin branches and narrow seed pods. It occurs from about Townsville, Qld, to northern NSW in dry and coastal rainforest. Cultivation is easy from seed and it is often available from native plant nurseries.

*Senna auriculata is a native of India, Myanmar and Sri Lanka. It has been introduced to many tropical and subtropical countries of the world and used extensively as an ornamental plant in gardens. It is a medium-sized shrub that grows to about 4m high with bright yellow flowers. The large soft leaves are ideal for the larvae of the Orange and Yellow Migrants.

No-brand Grass Yellow *Eurema brigitta*

Size: Male 38mm, female 40mm.

Adults fly slowly and often fairly close to the ground. This species is somewhat nomadic and populations move around depending on the abundance of host plants. Found from Cape York, Qld, to southern NSW and in the Darwin area, NT.

The Grass Yellows are very difficult to identify on the wing as they rarely sit with wings spread and most have rather indistinct markings on the underside of the wings.

Host Plants: *Chamaecrista concinna, C. maritima, C. nomame, Neptunia dimorphantha.*

Best Garden Host Plant: Any of the above. These plants are never available from nurseries but *N. dimorphantha* can be obtained from native seed suppliers.

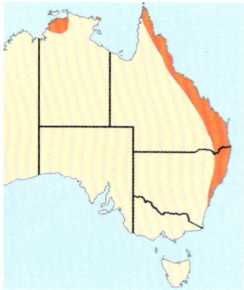

Lined Grass Yellow *Eurema laeta*

Size: Male 36mm, female 38mm.

Occurs across the top end of Australia from just north of Broome, WA, to about Rockhampton, Qld. Usually common and quite widespread. Like all the species in this group, populations multiply quickly when good rains occur which boost the supply of their small host plants.

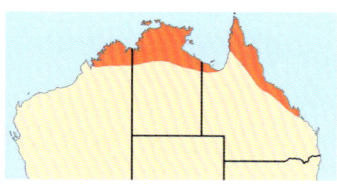

Host Plant: *Chamaecrista mimosoides.* This tiny plant is never available from nurseries but if seed is collected and scattered in a garden bed it will germinate readily and reseed each season.

Macleay's Grass Yellow *Eurema herla*

Size: Male 36mm, female 38mm.

Found across northern and eastern Australia from Broome, WA, to southern NSW.

Host Plants: *Chamaecrista concinna, C. maritima, C. mimosoides, C. nomame, C. nigricans.*

Best Garden Host Plant: *Chamaecrista mimosoides.*

Chamaecrista nomame.

Chamaecrista maritima.

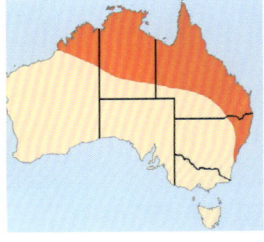

Small Grass Yellow *Eurema smilax*

Size: Male 32mm, female 34mm.

Found over the whole of mainland Australia. A very common butterfly with a wide selection of host plants. Does not occur in rainforest but will breed nearby when suitable host plants are available.

Host Plants: *Senna acclinis, S. coronilloides, S. gaudichaudii, S. artemisioides, S. odorata, S. petiolaris, S. surattensis, Neptunia gracilis, N. monosperma, *S. alata, *S. auriculata, *Cassia fistula.*

Best Garden Host Plant: *Senna gaudichaudii.*

Neptunia gracilis is a perennial herb or shrub that has a prostrate habit and can spread for about 2m. It has very fine leaflets and yellow flowers.

Scalloped Grass Yellow *Eurema alitha*

Size: Male 36mm, female 38mm.

Unusual because it has a completely different range of host plants from any of the other Grass Yellows. Found in the top end of NT and then from Cape York to south-east Qld in vine thickets and savannah woodland where the scrambling host plants grow.

Host Plants: *Galactia tenuiflora, G. muelleri, Glycine tabacina*.

Best Garden Host Plant: *Galactia tenuiflora*.

Galactia tenuiflora is a small climbing herb that can be found over most of northern Australia, extending down the east coast to about Sydney. The small pink flowers are sparsely arranged on the plant and often absent. It is not the sort of plant that would be available from nurseries but is easily recognised in the wild.

FAMILY PIERIDAE – SUBFAMILY COLIADINAE   WHITES AND YELLOWS

Common Grass Yellow *Eurema hecabe*

Size: Male 40mm, female 44mm.

Like the Small Grass Yellow this species is very widespread and common because of the diverse range of host plants. Some are rainforest plants so this butterfly can even be found in the wet tropical rainforest as well as open forest, parks and suburban gardens. Males gather in large numbers on damp ground during summer.

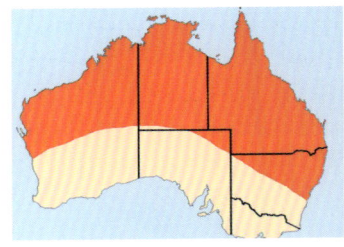

Host Plants: *Albizia* seedlings and small suckers, *Cassia*, *Chamaecrista*, *Cleistanthus apodus*, *Senna*, *Acacia* (species with true leaves consisting of many small leaflets), *Indigofera*, *Paraserianthes*, *Sesbania*, *Swainsona*, *Breynia*, *Phyllanthus*, *Aeschynomene*, **Aeschynomene*, **Albizia*, **Breynia*, **Leucaena*, **Medicago*, **Senna*, **Trifolium*.

Best Garden Host Plant: *Breynia*, even the variegated cultivated species.

Male Common Grass Yellows mud-puddling.

Breynia stipitata is a small to medium shrub that grows in rainforest where there is sufficient light, such as in clearings or along streams and around edges. The bright red fruit is a characteristic of *Breynia* species but is toxic and should not be eaten. A hardy plant, it will grow in most gardens. Occurs over a very wide area, from the Kimberley region, WA, to Vic.

Common Grass Yellow *Eurema hecabe*

Breynia cernua is a small shrub that is found in coastal and monsoon rainforest, vine thickets and moist open forest from the Kimberley area in WA round to tropical north Qld south to about Townsville.

Breynia sp. Iron Range is a shrub that grows to about 4m high and is found from about the Pascoe River to the Rocky River on Cape York Peninsula. Foliage turns red when in full sun. Readily available from native plant nurseries.

Narrow-winged Pearl White *Elodina padusa*

Size: 46mm.

Found in northern and eastern Australia in a wide range of habitats from vine thickets to open forest in arid areas.

The Pearl Whites are a difficult group to identify on the wing so check the distribution maps to narrow the list of possibilities.

Host Plants: *Capparis canescens, C. lasiantha, C. mitchellii.*

Best Garden Host Plant: *Capparis mitchellii*, suitable only for low rainfall areas. *C. canescens* is extremely slow growing and *C. lasiantha* is a mass of tangled spines.

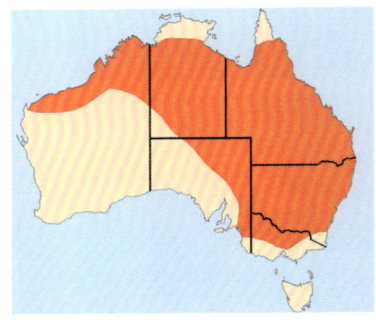

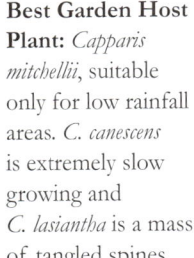

Capparis lasiantha is a very thorny vine, and while it is easy to grow, it should be planted where you will not come into contact with it. The foliage is a very unusual colour, and the plant can become massed with blossoms in the summer.

It is found in the northern half of Australia, in open forest; usually occurring inland but sometimes near the coast in dry areas.

Southern Pearl White *Elodina angulipennis*

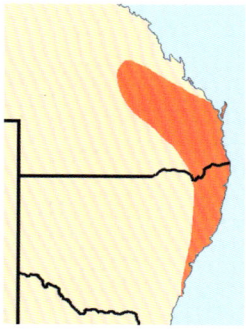

Size: 46mm.

Found from the Blackdown Tableland, west of Rockhampton, to central NSW. Occurs in coastal and subtropical rainforests as well as in various types of dry rainforest.

Host Plants: *Capparis arborea, C. canescens, C. velutina.*

Best Garden Host Plant: *Capparis arborea.* This plant is very slow growing but will eventually become a small tree.

Capparis canescens is a very widespread plant that unfortunately is very difficult to grow in cultivation. As is the case with quite a few *Capparis*, this species grows very slowly and takes a long time to establish. It is an extremely hardy plant and survives fire very well and even cultivation. The root system is so deep that even years after land is cultivated and crops grown on it, this plant can pop up from roots deep in the ground.

Glistening Pearl White *Elodina queenslandica*

Size: 46mm.

Two subspecies:
- *E.q. kuranda* from just north of Cooktown to south-east Qld.
- *E.q. queenslandica* from Cape York to Cape Melville.

This is a rainforest butterfly which does not usually lay on *Capparis* plants in the open forest. However, it is quite happy to breed in a garden with suitable host plants and a selection of other rainforest plants.

Host Plants: *Capparis arborea, C. lucida, C. ornans, C. sepiaria.*

Best Garden Host Plant: *Capparis lucida*. This is the only *Capparis* species that grows quite quickly, has thorns only when young and produces continuous flushes of new growth suitable for all *Capparis*-feeding butterfly larvae.

Notes: Females usually lay their eggs on the old leaves of the host plant and this is one of the few butterflies whose larvae are able to start feeding from the hardest foliage on the plant. Pearl White larvae are almost impossible to see on the plant as they chew from the side of the leaf in a wavy pattern then when not feeding rest along the chewed edge. The larva even has a stripe on its back that looks like the leaf edge when viewed side on. Several examples are shown below.

Glistening Pearl White *Elodina queenslandica*

Capparis arborea is a small tree that occurs in a wide range of rainforest habitats in eastern Australia from Cape York, Qld, to central NSW. Its habitat ranges from semi-deciduous vine thickets 200km west of Cairns to upland rainforest in the southern Border Ranges of Qld. It is slow growing but will develop into a large shrub within 10 years. Juvenile plants contain many thorns but fully mature plants have smooth stems.

Capparis sp. aff. *ornans* is a very large vine that grows in low- to mid-altitude rainforest from about Cape York to Ingham, Qld. It has many thorns in all stages of growth. The flowers are very large, being 10cm or more across. In the author's garden Pearl Whites breed on it all year round.

Northern Pearl White *Elodina walkeri*

Size: 46mm.

A very small butterfly but the problem with using size as one of the criteria for identification is that other Pearl Whites can also be very small if the larvae have to feed on a stressed caper plant with low moisture content, which they often do. Found from the Kimberley area in WA, across the top end, on Gulf islands and from Cape York to about Cairns, usually in coastal or dry rainforest/vine thickets.

Host Plants: The only host plant recorded is *Capparis sepiaria* but it is highly likely other species are utilised, especially *C. quiniflora* and *C. lucida*.

Best Garden Host Plant: *Capparis sepiaria*. This is an extremely spiny vine and not the type of plant that most people would plant in their garden.

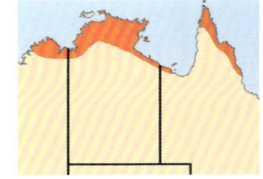

Capparis sepiaria is an easy vine to grow, but it is extremely thorny and should be planted where it can climb over a tree and be well out of the way. When it is completely mature (which takes many years) it has no thorns. It grows at a reasonable speed and will become large enough to support larvae in three or four years. The flowers are small, but are produced en masse and have a beautiful perfume.

Delicate Pearl White *Elodina perdita*

Size: 40mm.

A rainforest species that is found in coastal and dry rainforest from about Townsville to Mackay.

Host Plant: *Capparis sepiaria*.

Chalky Pearl White *Elodina parthia*

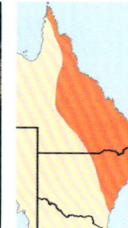

Size: 44mm.

Found in open eucalypt forest and woodland, and occasionally in deciduous vine thickets where various species of *Capparis* host plants grow. Occurs in eastern Australia from Cape York to southern NSW and well inland.

Host Plants: *Capparis arborea, C. canescens, Capparis nummularia (C. spinosa* var. *nummularia), C. sarmentosa, C. velutina,* *C. *spinosa* (edible caper, grown in plantations in Australia).

Best Garden Host Plant: *Capparis arborea*.

Capparis nummularia (previously *C. spinosa* var. *nummularia*) is a very thorny scrambling shrub or vine that is found over the northern half of Australia, usually inland, but also in dry coastal areas and islands. It is closely related to the commercial caper and looks very similar.

Australian Gull *Cepora perimale*

Size: Male 54mm, female 56mm.

Found in a wide range of habitats including monsoon rainforest, deciduous and semi-deciduous vine thickets, open forest and woodland in northern and eastern Australia. Ranges from the Kimberley region, WA, across the top and down eastern Qld to southern NSW, occasionally reaching Vic.

Host Plants: *Capparis arborea, C. canescens, C. jacobsii, C. lucida, C. mitchellii, C. sepiaria, C. umbonata, C. velutina.*

Best Garden Host Plant: *Capparis lucida.*

Capparis lucida is the best *Capparis* to grow as it is easy to germinate and grows very quickly. A special bonus is that is has very few thorns. The seedlings have some thorns, but by the time it is 1m high the thorns have disappeared. Pearl Whites and Gulls will lay on it when in part shade but for the Caper Whites it must be in full sun.

Caper White *Belenois java*

Size: Male 66mm, female 68mm.

Found over most of Australia except the south-west, even reaching Tas on occasion. No *Capparis* plants are recorded this far south so the butterfly could not breed there. Large migrations are seen over eastern and northern Australia in most years.

Host Plants: *Apophyllum anomalum, Capparis arborea, C. canescens, C. jacobsii, C. lasiantha, C. lucida, C. mitchellii, C. nummularia, C. sarmentosa, C. umbonata, C. velutina.*

Best Garden Host Plant: *Capparis lucida.*

Female – dark form.

Apophyllum anomalum, sometimes called Native Broom because it is leafless with weeping branches; it looks like the European Broom, except it does not have yellow flowers. It is a small tree that is found in the dry inland of eastern Australia, extending to the coast in low rainfall areas. Caper White butterflies lay on this plant wherever it occurs.

Common Albatross *Appias paulina*

Size: Male 66mm, female 68mm.

A rainforest butterfly that is found in northern and eastern Australia from the Kimberley region, WA, to central NSW. Occasionally migrations reach Vic. Breeds in all types of rainforest and at times occurs in huge numbers, especially in drier rainforests where their host plants grow in great profusion. The larvae can only eat the very soft new growth of host plants and the females lay on new shoots before the leaves have expanded.

Vast numbers of males can sometimes be seen mud-puddling during summer in softwood rainforests of central Qld.

Host Plants: *Drypetes deplanchei, D. acuminata, D.* sp aff. *deplanchei.*

Best Garden Host Plant: *Drypetes deplanchei.*

Drypetes deplanchei is a very widespread and extremely hardy plant which forms a dense habit. When young the leaves are holly-like, but become smoother on the edges when mature. It is usually found in coastal/softwood rainforests and vine thickets. Birds eat the bright red fruit.

Grey Albatross *Appias melania*

Size: Male 72mm, female 72mm.

Restricted to the wet tropical region of north Qld and is usually found in mid- to high-altitude high-rainfall rainforest. Most seasons see large migrations of these butterflies moving from one area of rainforest to another. In exceptional seasons females have been seen 200km inland laying on *Drypetes deplanchei* growing in vine thickets. It is not known if they survive but they are not sighted in these areas the following season. Females lay eggs on the new shoots and the larvae feed on the ensuing soft new growth.

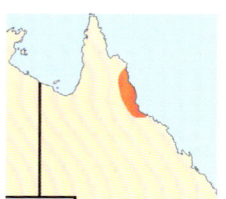

Host Plants: *Drypetes acuminata*, *D*. sp. aff *deplanchei*.

Best Garden Host Plant: *Drypetes* sp. aff *deplanchei*.

Males mud-puddling.

Drypetes acuminata is a small to medium tree that is found in high-altitude rainforest in the wet tropics of north Queensland. The **Common Albatross** also uses this plant and the following species so larvae of both species can occur together. They are almost impossible to tell apart – the only way is to hatch out the pupae.

Drypetes sp. aff. *deplanchei* is a small tree that grows in low- to mid-altitude rainforest in the wet tropics of north Qld and in well-developed rainforest on Cape York Peninsula. It has serrated leaves when juvenile but these are lost on a mature plant. It is quite hardy and much easier to grow than *D. acuminata*.

Cabbage White *Pieris rapae*

Size: Male 50mm, female 52mm.

One of only four butterflies that have been introduced into Australia from other countries. Like the Wanderer butterfly this species rarely uses any Australian native plants as a host. The one exception is *Crateva religiosa* when grown in gardens. This plant is only found on Cape York Peninsula so it is mostly out of the range of the butterfly. Anyone who has a vegetable garden will probably know this species. Quite often gardeners mistake some of our white butterflies for this one.

Host Plants: *Brassica, *Cakile edentula, *C. maritima,* Canola (a cultivar of *Brassica napus*), *Hirschfeldia incana, *Lepidium africanum, *Sisymbrium officinale, *Cleome, *Reseda, *Tropaeolum.* Host plants are mostly in the Brassicaceae (cabbage) family except for *Cleome* and *Crateva*. Clouds of these butterflies can be seen in areas where Canola is cultivated.

Golden Canola is now widely cultivated for the canola oil industry. Many plants go wild and can be seen along roadsides in areas where it is grown commercially. The wild plants often end up with white flowers after a couple of generations, as shown in the

image on the left. In both the cultivated crops and the wild growing plants the Cabbage White breeds up in huge numbers.

FAMILY PIERIDAE – SUBFAMILY PIERINAE WHITES and YELLOWS

Imperial Jezebel *Delias harpalyce*

Size: Male 78mm, female 84mm.

Occurs in the eastern half of NSW and most of Vic. Inhabits open forest up to about 800m where the various mistletoe host plants grow on eucalypts and acacias. A common butterfly throughout most of its range. Mature larvae often gather together and form a mass of web on which they make their pupae.

Host Plants: Mostly *Amyema miquelii*, *A. pendula*, *Muellerina eucalyptoides*; less commonly *A. congener*, *A. preissii*, *A. quandang*.

Best Garden Host Plant: Any of the first three mistletoes listed above.

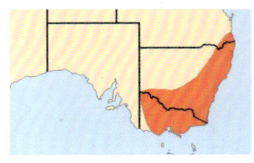

Amyema preissii is commonly found growing on Acacias and other small trees or shrubs in dry regions. It is uncommon in the tropics but common in southern New South Wales and Victoria. It is often called **Wire-leaf Mistletoe** which is a very apt name, as the leaves are stiff, round and pointed. It is very attractive when in flower and it becomes very obvious on its host. The small cream fruit are spread by birds.

Spotted Jezebel *Delias aganippe*

Size: Male 74mm, female 78mm.

Widespread in the south-east and south-west of Australia, inhabiting open forest where its parasitic host plants grow. Large migrations reach Melbourne in September/October and for some unknown reason considerable numbers of eggs are laid on olive trees in plantations. The larvae cannot eat this plant so all die unless rescued by butterfly enthusiasts. From time to time they are seen in north Qld on the dry side of the Atherton Tableland where they lay on *Santalum lanceolatum*.

Host Plants: *Amyema cambagei*, *A. conspicua*, *A. linophylla*, *A. melaleucae*, *A. miquelii*, *A. preissii*, *A. quandang*, *Exocarpus aphyllus*, *E. cupressiformis*, *E. strictus*, *Santalum acuminatum*, *S. lanceolatum*, *S. spicatum*.

Best Garden Host Plant: Any *Santalum* species.

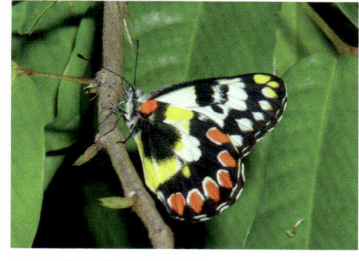

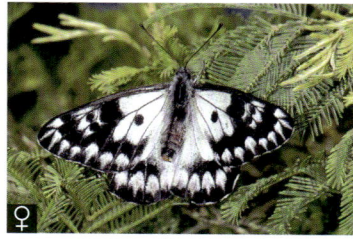

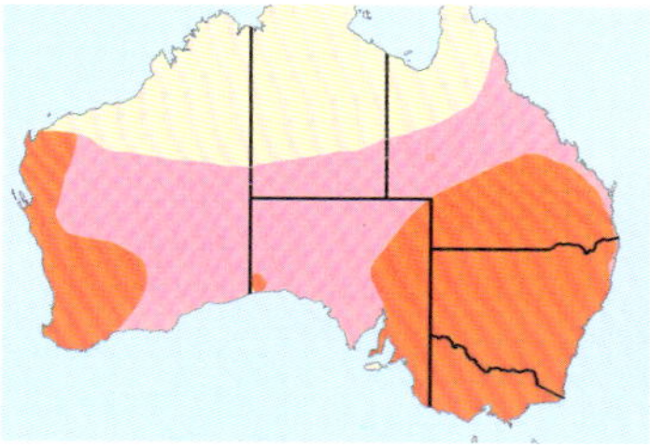

Possible distribution due to habitat and host plant distribution.

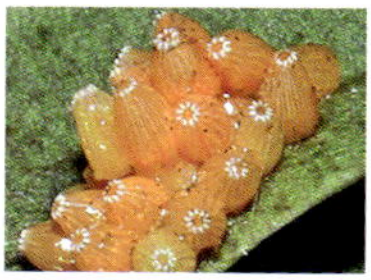

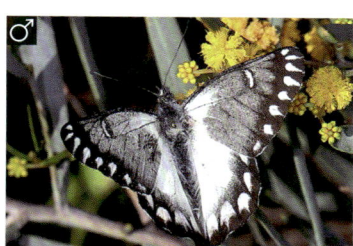

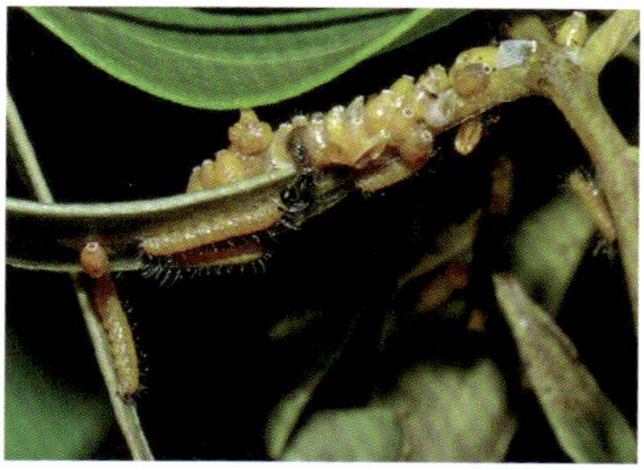

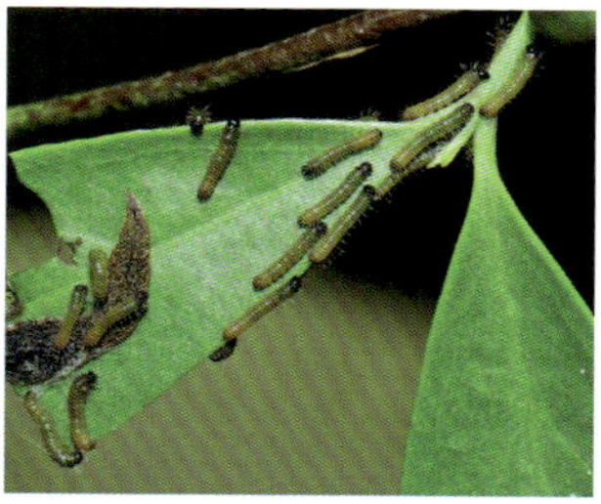

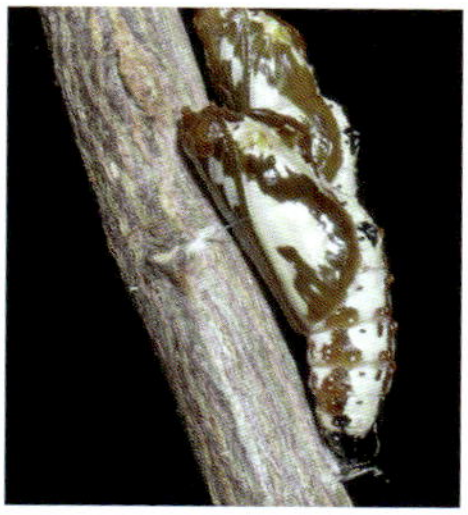

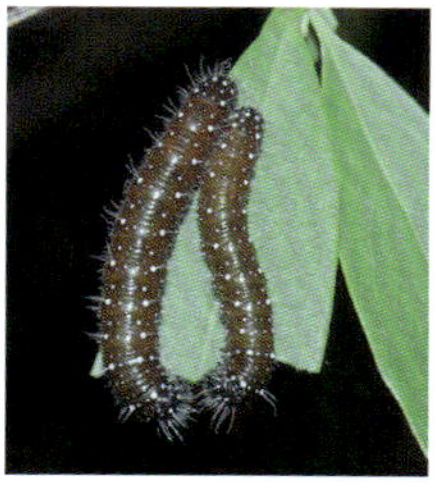

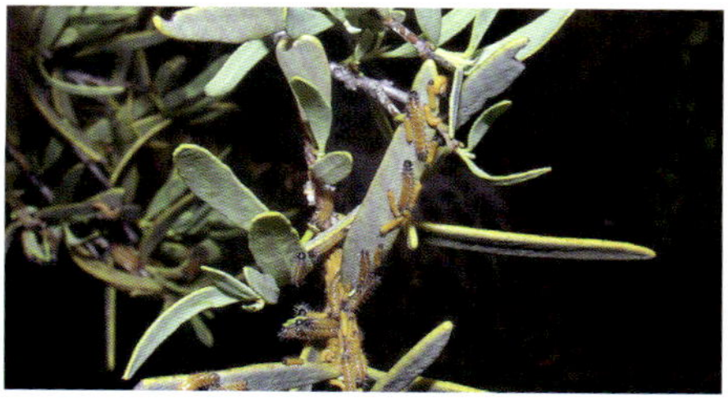

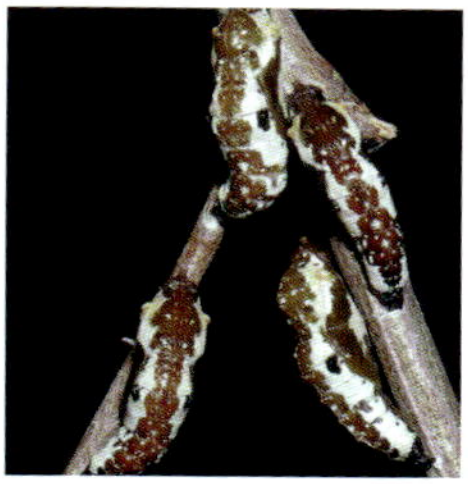

WHITES AND YELLOWS

Santalum lanceolatum is a parasitic tree that is found throughout mainland Australia, ranging from coastal sand dunes to the dry inland and up to 1,000m altitude. It does not occur in rainforest but can be found along the edge of vine thickets. It suckers readily and usually forms colonies of suckering stems. It is also a host plant for the Northern Jezebel butterfly.

Exocarpos cupressiformis is a parasitic shrub or tree that is found mostly in south eastern Australia but does extend into the tropics reaching the dry side of the Atherton Tableland. It has very tiny leaves and appears to be leafless with a weeping habit that somewhat resembles a Cypress Pine. Like *Santalum* it suckers and is often seen in colonies, possibly consisting of only one plant.

Nysa Jezebel *Delias nysa*

Size: Male 58mm, female 60mm.

Quite widespread and has two subspecies:
- *D.n. nysa* ranges from about Cooktown, Qld, to eastern Vic.
- *D.n. nivira* occurs in Qld from the Pascoe River to the southern end of the McIlwraith Range on Cape York Peninsula.

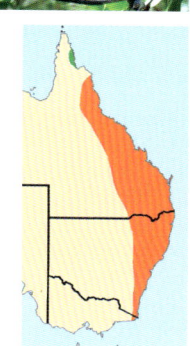

The host plants are very small leafless mistletoe plants that resemble the commonly cultivated Zygocactus because they consist of flattened and segmented stems. One of these plants is rarely large enough to support a batch of larvae. Like all Jezebels this species lays eggs in clusters. These mistletoes, in the *Korthalsella* genus, have runners that are under the bark of the host plant, breaking through at intervals to form a small colony. The only situations where the mistletoe, and thus the butterfly, is common, is in dry rainforest where there are stands of *Geijera* trees. In some areas almost every *Geijera* plant is infested with *Korthalsella taenioides*. Most of these dry rainforests/vine thickets have been destroyed with the clearing of the Brigalow scrub belt in Qld.

Host Plants: *Korthalsella japonica*, *Korthalsella taenioides*.

Korthalsella japonica form *rubra* is widespread, being found from Iron Range on Cape York Peninsula, Qld, to Vic in a very wide range of habitats. *Korthalsella* plants are quite small and mostly go unnoticed. They are probably the least collected of any mistletoe genus. It is almost certain that the Nysa Jezebel uses all the species in this genus. Coincidentally, the range of the Nysa Jezebel matches that of this species of *Korthalsella*. The Nysa Jezebel is common only where there are numerous *Korthalsella* plants in a relatively small area. This is usually in dry rainforest.

Korthalsella taenioides forma *taenioides* (*Korthalsella rubra* subsp. *geijericola*) is common on *Geijera* plants in the drier parts of Qld. Various species of *Korthalsella* are often referred to as 'zygocactus mistletoes' because they lack leaves, and the leaf function is performed by flattened stems in joints. Wherever you see the Nysa Jezebel these strange little mistletoes will be somewhere nearby. The rhizome of this group of mistletoes runs under the bark of the host plant and suckers pop out through the bark all along a branch. This helps them to survive when the Jezebel larvae chew all available green material from a plant.

Yellow-banded Jezebel *Delias ennia*

Size: Male 62mm, female 64mm.

Two subspecies:
- *D.e. tindalii* on Cape York Peninsula from the Rocky River to the Pascoe River.
- *D.e. nigidius* in the wet tropics region of north Qld.

While the host plant is very common the butterfly is quite localised. Adults fly very fast with an evasive flight pattern and are extremely difficult to identify on the wing. The eggs of this species are much smaller than those of any of the other Jezebels.

Host Plant: *Notothixos leiophyllus*.

Yellow-banded Jezebel *Delias ennia*

Notothixos leiophyllus (Golden Mistletoe) is found from about Townsville, Qld, northwards, its range extending into Papua New Guinea. It is usually found growing on another species of mistletoe. At times this is not obvious as the *Notothixos* foliage overwhelms that of the host species. While this mistletoe is often found outside rainforest, the Yellow-banded Jezebel will lay its eggs only on plants in rainforest or a rainforest-type garden. The rhizome of this plant runs under the bark and bursts out at regular intervals if not growing on another mistletoe species. Leaves are sometimes silver on the underside.

Mangrove Jezebel *Delias aestiva*

Size: Male 70mm, female 72mm.

The only species in this group that does not live on a mistletoe-related plant. There are two subspecies:
- *D.a. aestiva* in the top end of NT
- *D.a. smithersi* on the west coast of Cape York Peninsula, Qld.

Host Plants: *Excoecaria ovalis*, *E. agallocha*. These are known as 'blind-your-eye mangroves' and their sap is toxic.

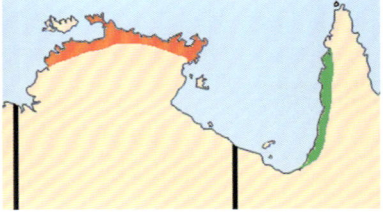

Delias aestiva aestiva.

Orange Jezebel *Delias aruna*

Size: Male 80mm, female 82mm.

Found on Cape York Peninsula and ranges from Torres Strait to Massy Creek, east of Coen. Usually occurs in rainforest but also inhabits paperbark and palm forests. Females are much paler above, have a smaller area of orange and have yellow spots around the edges of the wings.

Host Plants: *Dendrophthoe glabrescens* is the only recorded host plant but it is almost certain that they use other species of mistletoe as well.

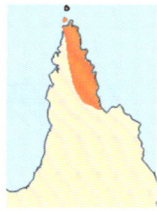

Dendrophtnoe glabrescens is an extremely widespread mistletoe, which occurs from the Kimberley, WA, across the top and down eastern Australia (extending well inland) to southern NSW. This mistletoe is most commonly found on *Eucalyptus* trees but can establish on many other unrelated plants, including common garden plants; often on oleander shrubs along with other mistletoes. The base (haustorium) forms a large swelling where it joins the branch of the host plant (see bottom right image).

Northern Jezebel *Delias argenthona*

Delias argenthona argenthona.

Delias argenthona fragalactea.

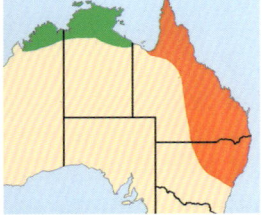

Size: Male 72mm, female 74mm.

Two subspecies:
- *D.a argenthona* from Cape York, Qld, to southern NSW.
- *D.a fragalactea* from just north of Broome, WA, to the central Gulf of Carpentaria

Not a rainforest butterfly, rather it prefers open forest areas, parks and suburban gardens. Uses a wide range of mistletoe species as host plants. It is common to find Northern Jezebel larvae on mistletoes growing on *Callistemon* and *Melaleuca* (all are now technically *Melaleuca*) planted as street trees.

Host Plants: *Amyema bifurcata, A. cambagei, A. miquelii, A. miraculosa, A. pendula, A. quandang, A. sanguinea, Decaisnina signata, Dendrophthoe curvata, D. glabrescens, D. odontocalyx, D. vitellina, Diplatia furcata, Lysiana maritima, L. spathulata, Muellerina celastroides, Santalum lanceolatum.*

Best Garden Host Plant: *Santalum lanceolatum.*

Northern Jezebel *Delias argenthona*

Amyema sanguinea is the most spectacular of all mistletoes and rivals many trees with its brilliant red display of flowers. It is the one mistletoe that most people notice as they drive around. It develops into large clumps and the blue-grey foliage contrasts well with the bright red flowers.

Like all mistletoes it can be grown by collecting ripe fruit and carefully squashing out the seed and glueing them onto the underside of a branch. Unless you are lucky you will need to attach a large number of seeds as it is only about one in a hundred that actually takes. The plant is most commonly seen on smooth-bark eucalypts so this would be the best host. Oleander also makes a good host for this and many other mistletoes.

Decaisnina brittenii subsp. *brittenii* is a tropical mistletoe found in NT and Qld south to about Bowen. It is most commonly found on *Eucalyptus*, *Acacia* or *Lophostemon*.

Decaisnina angustata is another tropical species occurring right across the top end of Australia north of a line from about Broome, WA. *Eucalyptus* and *Acacia* are the most favoured hosts.

FAMILY PIERIDAE – SUBFAMILY PIERINAE WHITES AND YELLOWS

Union Jack *Delias mysis*

Size: Male 70mm, female 72mm.

Two subspecies:
- *D.m. mysis* from about Cooktown to Yeppoon, rare south of Mackay.
- *D.m. waterhousei* from Cape York to the Rocky River on Cape York Peninsula.

Usually a rainforest butterfly, spreading out to melaleuca wetlands near the coast.

Host Plants: *Amylotheca dictyophleba, Dendrophthoe curvata, D. glabrescens, D. vitellina.*

Best Garden Host Plant: Any of the above mistletoes.

Amylotheca dictyophleba occurs in eastern Australia from Torres Strait, Qld, to southern NSW, generally east of the Great Dividing Range. It will accept a wide range of hosts including the Sandpaper Fig and oleander.

Dendrophthoe curvata is found from Torres Strait to about Rockhampton, also in Papua New Guinea. It attaches to a wide range of hosts including vines, shrubs and trees. It is also used by *Delias argenthona* and *D. nigrina*.

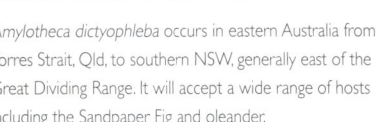

Common Jezebel *Delias nigrina*

Size: Male 68mm, female 70mm.

Occurs in eastern Australia from Cape York, Qld, to Vic, most commonly east of the Great Dividing Range. Usually in upland rainforest in the north while further south it inhabits lowland rainforest, eucalypt forest, parks and gardens.

Host Plants: *Amyema, Amylotheca, Benthamina, Dendrophthoe, Lysiana, Muellerina.*

Best Garden Host Plant: Mistletoes are very difficult to get established but the Common Jezebel breeds on most of the species that grow on callistemons, melaleucas and oleanders in suburban gardens and streets, so if mistletoe establishes on a tree in your garden keep a close eye on it. It will probably be a host plant for a *Delias* butterfly.

Dendrophthoe curvata is a tropical rainforest mistletoe that grows in Qld from Torres Strait to about Rockhampton, extending to Papua New Guinea and Indonesia.

FAMILY PIERIDAE – SUBFAMILY PIERINAE — WHITES AND YELLOWS

Amyema bifurcata is very widespread north of a line about level with Sydney, NSW. It is usually on *Eucalyptus* or *Corymbia* but also at times on *Acacia* and *Grevillea*.

Amyema queenslandica is a tropical rainforest mistletoe that is found north of Townsville, Qld, with its range extending to Papua New Guinea. It parasitises a wide range of plants, usually high up in trees or on smaller trees in disturbed areas where high levels of light are available.

CROWS and TIGERS
Family Nymphalidae – Subfamily Danainae

The Crow and Tiger butterflies are very long lived (up to 12 months) and many of them spend the winter/dry season in large colonies in sheltered gorges or in dense foliage along streams. In Australia they do not go into complete hibernation but rather spend a lot of time resting while grouped closely together. On warm days they take to the wing and feed on nearby nectar. These colonies are always sheltered, have fairly high humidity and a supply of nectar for the winter/dry season. Sandstone gorges and inland streams with *Pandanus*, *Calamus* (Lawyer Cane) and other dense foliage are the main areas that they select.

The larvae of this group feed mostly on toxic plants in the Apocynaceae (both Asclepiadaceae and Apocynaceae subfamilies). Only the Common Crow and the Hamadryad use Apocynaceae – all the other species use the subfamily Asclepiadaceae. The larvae all have fleshy spines, sometimes quite long for the size of the caterpillar, and are usually marked with a striped pattern with colours of black, white, orange or yellow. This colour pattern is a usual warning in nature to signal to predators that these larvae are dangerous and in this case toxic.

The pupae of the Crow butterflies are most unusual insomuch as they are shimmering silver or gold, looking like they are made of metal. The Tigers mostly have green pupae with gold and silver markings.

Wintering colony of Common Crow butterflies.

Golden pupa of the Two-brand Crow.

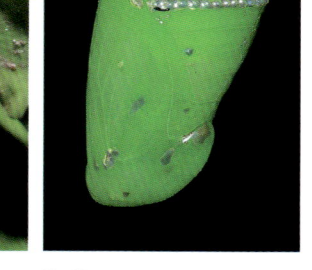

Larva of Common Crow showing long fleshy spines and striped markings.

Blue Tiger pupa.

Cairns Hamadryad *Tellervo zoilus zoilus*

Size: Male 45mm, female 50mm.

Found in well-developed rainforest at low to mid-altitudes, ranging from Cape Melville to south of Townsville. Adults fly slowly and feed for long periods on small flowers. At night they often gather in small groups, sleeping close to each other on small twigs in the rainforest understorey.

Host Plants: All *Parsonsia* species that grow within their range, except for the densely hairy ones.

Best Garden Host Plant: *Parsonsia velutina* or *P. straminea*.

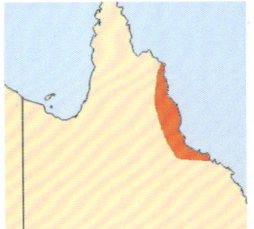

Parsonsia velutina is a very widespread vine occurring from the Kimberley, WA, across to Cape York, Qld, then south to about Sydney, NSW, in most types of rainforest. The tiny yellow flowers attract huge numbers of small butterflies. It is the main host plant for the Cairns Hamadryad butterfly.

As it grows quite large it should be planted where it can be cut back from time to time to bring it under control.

Cairns Hamadryad *Tellervo zoilus zoilus*

Parsonsia latifolia is a medium to large vine that is found from about Cooktown to Rockhampton in well-developed rainforest at low- to mid-altitudes. Unlike most *Parsonsia* species this vine has a milky sap. In the author's garden it is a favourite host plant for the Cairns Hamadryad.

Parsonsia lenticellata is a small twining vine with very narrow leaves. It is found from just north of Cairns, Qld, to northern NSW, usually in dry rainforest or on steep well-drained hillsides where the more hardy species of rainforest plants grow. Where it grows near Cairns the Hamadryad butterflies use it regularly.

Cape York Hamadryad *Tellervo zoilus gelo*

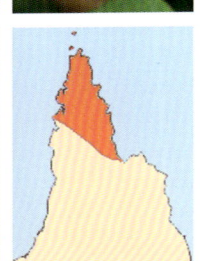

Size: 53mm.

Occurs in north Qld from Cape York to about the Rocky River, east of Coen, in well-developed rainforest. It is found on both sides of the peninsula down to about Weipa.

Host Plants: *Parsonsia ferruginea, P. velutina* (and probably many other species as well).

Best Garden Host Plant: *Parsonsia velutina*.

Parsonsia ferruginea (Rusty Parsonsia) is a medium to large vine that occurs from Cape York to Cape Melville in well-developed rainforest. All parts of the new growth are densely covered in rusty brown hairs. As well as being a host plant for the Cape York Hamadryad it is used by the males of all species of Crow and Tiger butterflies, which obtain alkaloids from the stems and leaves by scratching and licking them. It is a very hardy vine but not available from native plant nurseries to date.

Two-brand Crow *Euploea sylvester*

E.s. pelor.

E.s. sylvester.

Size: Male 78mm, female 80mm.

Two subspecies:
- ■ *E.s. sylvester* in Qld on Cape York Peninsula and down the east coast to about Rockhampton.
- ■ *E.s. pelor* in the top end of NT.

Inhabits mostly monsoon, coastal or dry rainforest and vine thickets where the host plants are most common. Adults usually fly slowly unless disturbed. Males congregate on various plants to extract alkaloids (see bottom butterfly image), especially from dry fruits of *Crotalaria* and *Parsonsia*.

Host Plants: *Marsdenia geminata, M. pleiadenia, M. straminea, M. tricholepis.* The host plants for this species were previously in the genus Gymnema. Plants in this genus have now been placed in Marsdenia so they are no longer easily identifiable by name.

Best Garden Host Plant: *Marsdenia geminata* or *M. pleiadenia*.

Marsdenia pleiadenia is a medium-sized vine that has a very wide distribution, being found in dry rainforest and vine thickets in the north-west of WA, and from about Mt Garnett, Qld, to central NSW.

CROWS AND TIGERS

Marsdenia tricholepis is a medium to large twining vine that is found in monsoon and coastal rainforest in Qld from Torres Strait to about Mackay. It is an ideal host plant for the Two-brand Crow as even the older leaves are quite soft. It is a favourite host plant in the author's garden.

Marsdenia geminata is a widespread tropical vine that is found from the Kimberley, WA, across the top and down the east coast to about Townsville, Qld. It usually occurs in monsoon or dry rainforests and vine thickets. A typical habitat in north Qld is the vine thickets on the limestone bluffs at Chillagoe.

Marsdenia straminea is an uncommon vine that is restricted to the wet rainforests of the Atherton Tableland in north Qld. It is a small to medium-sized vine and tends to scramble over the ground, layering itself as it goes and eventually climbing trees.

Eichhorn's Crow *Euploea eichhorni*

Size: Male 78mm, female 80mm.

Only occurs from Torres Strait to just south of Townsville, even though its host plant is much more widespread. Adults fly slowly and usually within a few metres of the ground and are almost always found only a relatively short distance from where the host plant is growing.

Adults mix in with other species of Crows in wintering colonies along streams and in gorges from about June to September.

Host Plant: *Gymnanthera oblonga*. Other host plants are listed in publications but the author has never seen the butterfly where *Gymnanthera* does not grow. Because the larvae are very similar to those of the Common Crow there is some doubt as to the validity of these listings.

Best Garden Host Plant: *Gymnanthera oblonga*.

Gymnanthera oblonga is a medium sized twining vine with thick milky sap that is commonly found along the edge of mangroves but also along inland rivers. It extends from just north of Broome in Western Australia to about Bundaberg in Queensland. North of a line through about Townsville it is found along most streams, especially those that have a reduced flow for most of the year allowing vegetation to grow in the stream bed. In cultivation it is very easy to grow, requiring full sun or a very well lit situation. It can be grown from either seed or cuttings.

Common Crow *Euploea corinna*

Size: Male 82mm, female 84mm.

Found in low- to mid-altitude rainforest, monsoon and coastal rainforest, semi-deciduous and deciduous vine thickets, and suburban gardens.

Adults usually fly slowly except when moving to their wintering colonies. They take nectar from many flowers and the males extract toxic alkaloids from a number of plants such as *Crotalaria*, *Heliotropium* and *Parsonsia*. During the winter/dry season huge numbers of these butterflies gather in sheltered gorges, along the edges of mangroves or along permanent streams with *Pandanus* and *Melaleuca*. They shelter in the *Pandanus* but use the nectar of the *Melaleuca* to sustain them.

Host Plants: They have a huge range of host plants – almost all the native plants in the Apocynaceae and subfamily Asclepiadaceae as well as quite a number of *Ficus* (figs). These host plants include the following genera; *Carissa*, *Ichnocarpus*, *Parsonsia*, *Brachystelma*, *Ceropegia*, *Cynanchum*, *Gunnessia*, *Gymnanthera*, *Hoya*, *Marsdenia*, *Secamone*, *Tylophora*, and many species of *Ficus*. The introduced Oleander (*Nerium oleander*) is often used in gardens. In the dry tropics the introduced Rubber Vine (*Cryptostegia grandiflora*) is extensively used and enables large numbers of butterflies to breed.

Best Garden Host Plant: Oleander (*Nerium oleander*).

Male Common Crow extracting alkaloids from *Crotalaria grandiflora*.

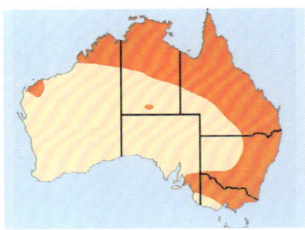

Common Crow *Euploea corinna*

Common Crow butterflies massed in wintering colonies. This is only a tiny fraction of the butterflies that had gathered at this site and there are many hundreds of such sites scattered across northern Australia each year. A few *Euploea sylvester* are also in this colony.

Parsonsia straminea (Common Silkpod) is a very widespread vine which will grow in most gardens in eastern and northern Australia. It is found from Cooktown, Qld, to central NSW in rainforest, open forest and in swampy *Melaleuca* habitats. The flowers have a perfume that is noticeable up close, but not usually from more than a few metres away.

The vine looks best grown up a large tree where it will cascade back down and form quite a thick mass of foliage. When in flower it attracts many butterfly species.

Juvenile foliage.

Marsdenia hemiptera is a vine that is well worthy of cultivation. The flowers are not as large as in some *Hoya* species (to which they are related), but are, nevertheless, very attractive. It is found in Qld from Cape York to about Tully, in wet to dry rainforest, usually at low altitudes.

Common Crow *Euploea corinna*

Carissa laxiflora is the most attractive member of the genus, and can be kept as a small shrub to about 2m high. When in semi-shade the flowers are pink, but in the sun they are usually white. It is very hardy and the least thorny of the group. It is found in Qld from Torres Strait to about Coen in vine thickets and monsoon rainforest.

Butterflies are attracted to the flowers which have a pleasant perfume.

Carissa spinarum (*Carissa ovata*) is a very hardy vine, but as it has thorns it should not be planted where you will come into contact with it in the garden. It can be pruned and kept as a shrub, but be careful when you are pruning as the sap can burn your skin.

The bright white flowers have a beautiful perfume, and the small, black fruit are eaten by birds.

Eastern Brown Crow *Euploea tulliolus*

Size: Male 70mm, female 75mm.

Distributed from Cape York, Qld, to northern NSW in moist to dry rainforests, most commonly in coastal regions.

The adults fly slowly and settle regularly, usually with their wings closed. In the dry season/winter large colonies can be found in sheltered areas of coastal rainforest and along streams where a nectar supply is available. This species is much more common in south-east Qld than in the north. This is difficult to understand as the host plant is equally abundant in all areas.

Host Plant: *Trophis scandens*.

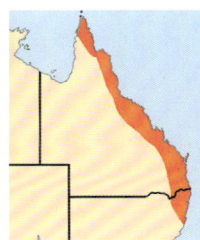

Trophis scandens is a large vine that can reach the canopy of the rainforest. It is found in all types of low- to mid-altitude rainforest, but is perhaps most common in the drier types. It has a wide distribution, ranging from the Kimberley area, WA, around the top end and down the east coast almost to Vic, rarely occurring more than 250km inland.

The spectacular red fruit are eaten and spread by birds.

The bark has an unusual sandpaper texture giving rise to the common name of Burny Vine; it burns your leg if you trip over it.

White-margined Crow *Euploea darchia*

Size: 70mm.

Two subspecies:
- ■ *E.d. darchia* in the top end of WA and NT.
- ■ *E.d. niveata* in Qld from Torres Strait to about Townsville.

E.d. darchia is sometimes common around Darwin but the Qld subspecies is usually not so common, occurring sporadically and in small numbers.

Host Plant: *Trophis scandens*

E.d. niveata.

E.d. darchia.

Trophis scandens – see previous page for information.

Lesser Wanderer *Danaus petilia*

Size: 60mm.

Very widespread, covering all the mainland and part of Tas. Often occurs in large numbers, mostly relying on introduced host plants rather than native ones. Various species of *Asclepias* from America and *Gomphocarpus* from Africa have provided this butterfly with opportunities to breed well beyond its natural range. In the north of Australia the widespread weed *Calotropis procera* from Africa enables it to breed throughout the dry tropics at any time of the year.

Adults usually fly slowly, and seek out sheltered gullies and areas along streams to rest in during the hot part of the day. Males extract toxic alkaloids from *Heliotropium* and *Crotalaria*. The pupae can be pink or green.

Host Plants: *Brachystelma, Cynanchum carnosum, Rhyncharrhena, Oxystelma esculentum, Tylophora erecta, T. floribunda, T.* spp. aff. *flexuosa,* *Asclepias, *Gomphocarpus, *Calotropis.

Best Garden Host Plant: *Asclepias or *Gomphocarpus.

Male on *Heliotropium muelleri*.

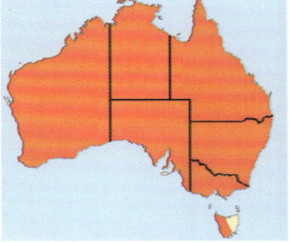

*Asclepias curassavica is an attractive plant from North America that is often sold in nurseries in southern Australia but is considered a weed in the north. It is easy to grow and as it is a perennial will last for many years.

Lesser Wanderer *Danaus petilia*

Tylophora erecta is a small, mostly erect, multi-stemmed vine that is found in open forest from the top end of NT and in Qld from Cape York Peninsula south to about Rockhampton. It is not readily available from nurseries but grows easily from seed.

Tylophora sp. aff. *flexuosa* is a small twining vine that occurs from Cape York, Qld, to about the Rocky River, NSW. It usually grows in permanently damp ground along streams or mangroves. *T. flexuosa* from WA and NT is not a host plant.

Cynanchum floribundum is a very widespread vine which is found in most of the dry regions of Australia, being more common in the centre and west of the continent. It often forms a tangled mass on the ground but climbs over small trees and shrubs when they are available. The small flowers are usually white but can be pale pink or mauve. Milky sap exudes from any broken parts of the plant.

**Calotropis procera* is a small to medium shrub that grows to about 3m high, with large soft leaves and attractive heads of flowers. It originates in Africa but is now naturalised across the top end of Australia in open areas, especially along the flood plains of streams. It is used extensively as a host plant by both the Lesser Wanderer and the Wanderer. A similar cultivated species is **Calotropis gigantea*.

Orange Tiger *Danaus genutia*

Size: Male 75mm, female 80mm.

Confined to the top end of WA and NT and usually found along streams or in swampy areas where the main host plant, *Oxystelma (Sarcostemma) esculentum*, grows. Adults usually fly slowly, settling often, usually low down and with wings spread. Breeding occurs all year round.

Host Plants: *Oxystelma esculentum, Cynanchum ovalifolium, C. pedunculatum.*

Best Garden Host Plant: *Oxystelma esculentum, C. ovalifolium*

Oxystelma (Sarcostemma) esculentum is a twining vine that occurs from the top end of NT to the southern Kimberley region, WA. It grows along streams and billabongs in mud or moist sand and scrambles over the vegetation along the banks. The large pink flowers are quite spectacular and this plant has potential as an ornamental.

Lesser Wanderer larvae are almost always present on the vine along with those of the Orange Tiger. They can be distinguished easily; the Orange Tiger larva has only two pairs of feelers and the Lesser Wanderer has three.

Cynanchum pedunculatum is very widespread in tropical Australia, mostly occurring in vine thickets. It produces large amounts of seed and often forms colonies of many vines at all stages. Large numbers of many types of butterflies are attracted to the tiny flowers.

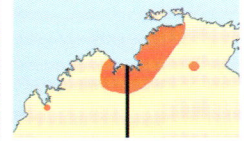

Black-and-white Tiger *Danaus affinis*

Size: Male 75mm, female 75mm.

Found in mangroves, fan palm rainforests and vine thickets where various species of host plants grow.

The adults usually fly slowly, rarely more than 2m above the ground, often settling on twigs. They may rest either with wings spread or closed.

Host Plants: *Ceropegia cumingiana, Cynanchum carnosum, Cynanchum leptolepis, Cynanchum ovalifolium, Cynanchum pedunculatum, Sarcolobus hullsii*. Occasionally they lay on various *Marsdenia* vines but these are not major host plants.

Best Garden Host Plant: *Cynanchum ovalifolium*.

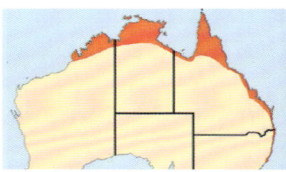

Cynanchum carnosum is a mangrove vine that grows in the mud just below the high-tide level. It scrambles all over the mangrove trees and is usually very common where it occurs. Even though it only occurs naturally in a mangrove community it is easy to grow in cultivation so long as the roots are kept permanently wet.

Black-and-white Tiger *Danaus affinis*

Cynanchum leptolepis is a large deciduous vine that is found in semi-deciduous and deciduous vine thickets. It is widespread, occurring from the Gulf of Carpentaria to Torres Strait and south to central Qld. It is unusual because not only does it lose its leaves but also many of the stems die back. It survives by having a large network of roots, up to 25mm thick, about 15–30cm underground. When the first storms arrive at the end of the year the new growth bursts out of the ground and the vine puts on up to 10m of growth in a few weeks. Wherever it occurs there is usually a breeding colony of Black-and-white Tigers during the wet season.

Cynanchum ovalifolium is a small vine that is found mostly on Cape York Peninsula, north of about Cape Melville but also in west Arnhem Land. It usually grows in well-developed rainforest or fan palm rainforest. If grown in a garden anywhere within the range of the Black-and-white Tiger it will attract the females to lay. Eggs are usually laid on the soft pink/red growth.

Ceropegia cumingiana ranges from Torres Strait to Mt Stuart (near Townsville) but populations south of Cape Melville are isolated and restricted to just a small number of vine thickets. North of Coen it is very common and occurs in large numbers in some vine thickets and is the main host plant for the Black-and-white Tiger in these areas. It is deciduous and dies back to a mass of tuberous roots that can survive long dry periods.

In cultivation it is best grown in a hanging basket and care should be taken not to water it when it dies back or the very soft tubers will rot. All the foliage is very soft so it makes an excellent host plant.

Wanderer *Danaus plexippus*

Size: Male 105mm, female 110mm.

Found in open forest, farms and gardens over eastern Australia and in the Perth area of WA.

Adults fly slowly, often gliding for short distances usually within a few metres of the ground. When resting they sit with wings spread or closed. In the tropics they breed all year round but in southern areas they form wintering colonies like our native species of *Danaus* and *Euploea*.

Host Plants: Introduced Milkweeds from North America and Africa, mainly *Asclepias, *Calotropis and *Gomphocarpus and including *Asclepias curassavica, *Gomphocarpus fruticosus, *G. physocarpus, *G. cancellatus; *Calotropis procera in the dry tropics where it has become naturalised from just west of the Atherton Tablelands, Qld, to the Kimberley region, WA, and *C. gigantea in gardens. Larvae can survive on the native plant *Marsdenia rostrata* although the females do not lay on it. They do lay however on another native plant, *Tylophora williamsii*, but the larvae die.

Best Garden Host Plant: *Asclepias or *Gomphocarpus species that are suited to your climate.

*Gomphocarpus physocarpus originates in south-east Africa and has been naturalised in many countries. In Australia it is very common and widespread in the eastern half but also occurs in south-west WA. It generally grows as an annual plant and due to the prolific seed production it often forms large colonies.

Blue Tiger *Tirumala hamata*

Male on *Heliotropium muelleri*.

Male on *Crotalaria* flowers.

Group of males on dead *Strychnos psilosperma* leaf.

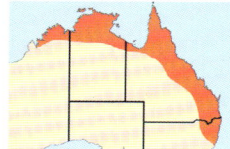

Size: Male 90mm, female 95mm.

Occurs in coastal, Hoop Pine, and monsoon rainforest, also semi-deciduous and deciduous vine thickets. Used to be extremely common in the Brigalow vine forests of central Qld but this habitat is all but extinct now. Adults fly slowly through the forest where they breed but move more quickly when migrating to their wintering sites. In April they begin heading towards the coast where they will spend the dry season/winter in coastal rainforest or on islands. Massive numbers congregate on many of the islands on the Great Barrier Reef by June, where they remain until about October, after which they move back to the mainland and spread out in readiness for the breeding season. Male butterflies extract alkaloids from the flowers and leaves of various toxic plants, especially *Heliotropium*, *Crotalaria* and *Parsonsia*.

The Blue Tiger is found from the Kimberley region of WA, around the top end and down to northern NSW. Migrations sometimes reach Vic but no host plants grow south of about Coffs Harbour, NSW.

Host Plants: *Secamone elliptica* is the most widespread one and is found over the entire range of the butterfly; *Heterostemma*, of which there are three species in Qld and one in NT; *Marsdenia velutina*, *M. glandulifera*. *Cynanchum carnosum* is often used as a host plant in south-east Qld but does not seem to be utilised at all in the north.

Best Garden Host Plant: *Heterostemma* sp. Bellenden Ker.

Mature larvae change colour a few days before they make their chrysalis.

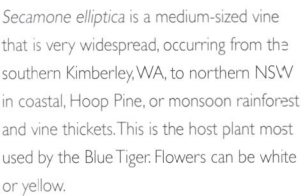

Secamone elliptica is a medium-sized vine that is very widespread, occurring from the southern Kimberley, WA, to northern NSW in coastal, Hoop Pine, or monsoon rainforest and vine thickets. This is the host plant most used by the Blue Tiger. Flowers can be white or yellow.

Heterostemma magnifica occurs in swampy rainforest in NT.

Heterostemma acuminatum occurs from Cape York, Qld, to northern NSW. It is the only species that exudes a milky sap when leaves or stems are cut.

Heterostemma sp. Bellenden Ker is restricted to the wet tropical lowland rainforest of north Qld. It is very fast growing and has spectacular flowers. Now available from nurseries and grown by many butterfly enthusiasts.

Marsdenia velutina is found in the top end of Australia north of about a line through Ingham, Qld. It is usually found in monsoon or coastal rainforest and vine thickets, forming a large, multi-stemmed vine that can die back in very dry times and spring to life again after good rains. The flowers vary in colour and the leaf shape varies from almost round to oblong.

Heterostemma sp. Mt Edith is confined to the high-altitude rainforest of north Qld.

GLASSWINGS, LACEWINGS and CRUISERS
Family Nymphalidae – subfamily Heliconiinae

The majority of the butterflies in this group are restricted to the tropics, with only three of them being found in southern states. The host plants of this group belong to plants in the order Violales, which includes the families Flacourtiaceae, Passifloraceae and Violaceae. Larvae in this group are covered in sharp spines which form a defence against being eaten by most birds. The species that lay on plants in the Passifloraceae family (*Passiflora* and *Adenia*) usually lay their eggs in groups; each one has its special place on the plant where it lays and is unique in the way in which the eggs are arranged.

All the butterflies in the Nymphalidae family appear to have only four legs – the front two are very short and used only to identify food and their host plant. All butterflies have sensors on their front feet to identify their host plant and they do this by scratching on the leaves to release the scent.

None of these species can remain in the pupal stage for long periods so they either live in the tropics where they can breed all year or go into semi-hibernation to survive the winter/dry season.

Australia now has one introduced butterfly in this group – the Tawny Coster. It originates from South Asia and was first recorded in NT in 2012. It is now present throughout most of tropical Australia.

The Glasswing is one of Australia's least colourful butterflies but has the widest distribution of any species in the Heliconiinae group, covering most of the mainland except the central southern region.

Eggs of Red Lacewing, usually laid on the stem of a vine about 10–30cm from the end.

The larva of the Cruiser butterfly has the longest and most formidable spines of any species in the Nymphalidae family.

Female Cruiser showing how Nymphalidae butterflies use only four of their six legs most of the time.

Red Lacewing *Cethosia cydippe*

Size: Male 90mm, female 92mm.

Found in lowland and gallery rainforest from Torres Strait to Townsville. Seldom found above about 200m, the Red Lacewing is a rare visitor to the Atherton Tableland.

Adults fly slowly along the edge of rainforest, resting from time to time, usually with wings open but sometimes closed. As a rule females lay their eggs near the ends of the host plant stems that hang from trees. The larvae stay together until they are ready to pupate, then they scatter and often end up ten or more metres away from the vine. The bright black and yellow markings of the larger larvae are typical warning signs in nature. In this case they carry toxins obtained from the host plant.

Host Plants: *Adenia heterophylla* subsp. *heterophylla*, *Passiflora* (*Hollrungia*) *kuranda*, *P. aurantioides* (not to be confused with *Passiflora aurantia*, which is a true *Passiflora*). It is unfortunate that the genus *Hollrungia* has been lumped in with *Passiflora*; the Red Lacewings do not naturally lay on *Passiflora*.

Best Garden Host Plant: *Adenia heterophylla* subsp. *heterophylla*.

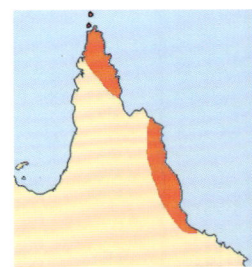

Red Lacewing *Cethosia cydippe*

Adenia heterophylla subsp. *heterophylla* develops into a large vine, and like all vines in the family Passifloraceae it climbs by means of tendrils. If you buy it from a nursery, check where the stock comes from. If it originates from the Bamaga area or somewhere near Cape York it will be quite hardy and will be able to withstand the south-east Qld climate; plants from the wet tropical lowlands need much more water and cannot tolerate temperatures much below 15°C. The spectacular red fruit split when ripe and expose the seed for birds to eat and spread.

Passiflora (Hollrungia) kuranda is a very large, hardy vine that naturally grows from sea-level to about 900m altitude. It has a limited distribution, ranging from about Cape Tribulation to the Clohesy River, south of Kuranda. This vine is used extensively by the Red Lacewing larvae when it occurs at low altitudes; when growing higher up the Cruiser butterfly breeds on it. The plant is more nutritious than *Adenia* and larvae develop to full size by eating much less than they do on *Adenia*.

Passiflora (Hollrungia) aurantioides is quite a rare vine that is restricted to very wet lowland rainforest in Qld between the base of Mt Bellenden Ker and Mission Beach. It is a large vine that scrambles over the canopy of the rainforest. Even though it occurs naturally in the hot wet lowlands it has no problem growing on the Atherton Tablelands at 750m. Unlike *P. kuranda* the old leaves are quite soft and so it makes an excellent host plant for both the Red Lacewing and the Cruiser.

Orange Lacewing *Cethosia penthesilea*

Size: Male 80mm, female 82mm.

Inhabits monsoon rainforest and vine thickets in the top end of NT. Even though the *Adenia* host plant is very common in the Kimberley region of WA this butterfly does not occur there.

Adults fly slowly through and along the edge of the rainforest, often settling very low to or even on the ground. The butterflies may rest either with wings open or closed.

Host Plants: *Adenia heterophylla* subsp. *australis*. In captivity the females lay readily on a non-hairy form of *Passiflora foetida* that grows in the lowlands of the north Qld wet tropics as well as *P. aurantia* and *P. herbertiana*. They do not lay on the hairy form of *P. foetida* that is found growing wild in NT.

Best Garden Host Plant: *Adenia heterophylla* subsp. *australis*. This vine is largely deciduous in its natural habitat but can retain leaves all year with regular watering. Should it loose its leaves it should no longer be watered until new growth appears after the dry season, or the roots may rot. Old vines have a large above-ground tuber and stems that can spread out over an extensive area of the forest.

Orange Lacewing *Cethosia penthesilea*

Adenia heterophylla subsp. *australis* is a widespread vine occurring from just north of Broome, across the top end of WA and NT to Groote Island. It is found in semi-deciduous, deciduous and evergreen vine thickets and monsoon rainforest. It is also found on islands along the Kimberley coast. To attract the Orange Lacewing it is best grown so that it climbs over and through trees. If it is in the full sun it will attract the Glasswing and the introduced Tawny Coster butterflies, at times being completely demolished by their larvae.

A huge *Adenia* vine growing in a deciduous vine thicket near Kununurra, WA. At the start of the storm season this vine will burst into new growth with stems stretching out 20–30m in all directions. The giant tuber is wedged in amongst the rocks and protected from fire. In the author's opinion this should be a separate species as the only thing it has in common with *Adenia heterophylla* is that it is an *Adenia*.

Cruiser *Vindula arsinoe*

Size: Male 95mm, female 100mm.

Found in well-developed rainforest in Qld from Torres Strait to Rockhampton, from sea-level to about 900m altitude.

Adults have a powerful erratic flight, landing frequently and often slowly opening and closing their wings. As well as using nectar they often feed from fallen fruit on the ground.

Host Plants: *Adenia heterophylla* subsp. *heterophylla*, *Passiflora (Hollrungia) kuranda*, *Passiflora (Hollrungia) aurantioides*, *P. aurantia*, *P. herbertiana*, non-hairy *P. foetida*, **Passiflora caerulea*. The introduced **P. subpeltata* and **P. suberosa* will attract the females to lay but the plants are toxic to the larvae and they all die. If you live within the range of the Cruiser butterfly you should eradicate these vines from your property.

Best Garden Host Plant: *Passiflora aurantia*.

Passiflora aurantia is a medium-sized vine that is very widespread, being found from Torres Strait, Qld, to south of Sydney, NSW, usually in coastal rainforest or semi-deciduous and deciduous vine thickets. After a number of years the main vine may die, but the following year suckers will appear from the roots that remain viable underground. It is a very ornamental vine with large flowers which are white or pale pink when they open and gradually change colour to red as they age.

As well as being a much favoured host plant for the Cruiser butterfly it is also used extensively by the Glasswing. In captivity the Orange Lacewing and the Tawny Coster lay readily on this plant and the larvae develop normally.

Cruiser *Vindula arsinoe*

Passiflora herbertiana is a large vine that grows very rapidly but has quite a short life. Lifespan is usually from two to four years but in that time it generally reaches the canopy of the upland rainforest where it grows and produces a large amount of fruit. The seeds remain dormant for several years. In north Qld its range extends from Mt Lewis to about Ingham. The southern range is from about Gympie, Qld, to southern NSW. Ants suck nectar from special glands just below the leaf.

**Passiflora caerulea* is a medium-sized vine that is sometimes used as root stock for grafted commercial passionfruit. It originates from South America and in some areas is considered a weed as it suckers from the roots. However, unlike some other South American species it is used by the Cruiser and Glasswing butterflies as a host plant. It is also used by the Orange Lacewing in captive-bred situations. It is a very hardy vine but needs some control to restrict its spread.

This non-hairy *Passiflora foetida* is found in the lowlands of the north Qld wet tropics where it usually grows in disturbed areas and gardens. It is used extensively by the Cruiser and Glasswing butterflies as a host plant and by the Orange Lacewing in butterfly farms. It is a small to medium vine, quite cold sensitive and requires plenty of moisture. The origin of the plant is not known as it does not match any of the known varieties of *P. foetida*. A search of the Internet shows that it also occurs in South-East Asia and is used by Lacewing butterflies there.

Glasswing *Acraea andromacha*

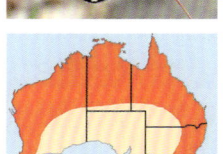

Size: Male 58mm, female 60mm.

Occurs in open forest, disturbed rainforest, vine thickets and grassland, depending on which host plant is used. Because one host plant is widespread and not associated with rainforest the Glasswing is found over most of northern Australia.

Adults fly slowly, usually fairly close to the ground, settling regularly. Eggs are usually laid in neat batches on leaves of the host plant.

Host Plants: *Adenia heterophylla* subsp. *heterophylla*, *A. heterophylla* subsp. *australis*, *Hybanthus aurantiacus*, *H. enneaspermus*, *H. monopetalus*, *H. stellarioides*, *Passiflora aurantia*, *P. cinnabarina*, *P. herbertiana*, **P. caerulea*, **P. mollissima*, **P. foetida* (non-hairy variety only). Females lay eggs on the introduced **P. suberosa* and **P. subpeltata* but the larvae die.

Best Garden Host Plant: *Passiflora aurantia* or *P. cinnabarina*.

Hybanthus monopetalus is widespread in eastern Australia and more common in southern areas.

Hybanthus stellarioides is found throughout eastern Australia.

Tawny Coster *Acraea terpsicore*

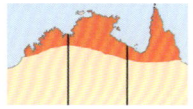

Size: Male 58mm, female 63mm.

Found in grassland and savannah woodland, often in disturbed areas, ranging from near Broome, WA, across the top of NT and Qld at least as far south as Townsville.

Notes: The Tawny Coster originates in South Asia and was first detected near Darwin, NT, in 2012. Adults fly slowly, usually within a couple of metres of the ground, settling low down on grass or even on the ground, with wings spread. The larvae are extremely difficult to distinguish from those of the Glasswing.

Host Plants: *Hybanthus spp*, *Passiflora aurantia*, **P. caerulea*, **P. foetida* (variety growing near Darwin, NT), occasionally *Adenia heterophylla* subsp. *australis* and *A. h. heterophylla* when growing outside or on the edge of the rainforest.

Best Garden Host Plants: *Adenia heterophylla* subsp. *australis*, *A.h.* subsp. *heterophylla* or *Passiflora aurantia* when grown in the open.

Tawny Coster *Acraea terpsicore*

Hybanthus enneaspermus is a small herb that is found in most of Australia, being more common in the northern half. It grows amongst the grass or in disturbed areas.

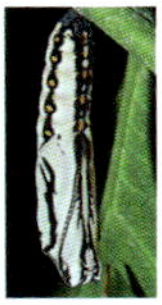

The Tawny Coster has adapted to this particular strain of *Passiflora foetida* near Darwin, NT. It has densely hairy leaves and the fruit have green vertical stripes. The form growing in north Qld does not have fruit marked this way. The Tawny Coster may have adapted to this particular strain over some time as the individuals that appeared in north Qld in 2017 will not feed on it. The author obtained plants from Darwin and placed two batches of eggs on them. The resulting larvae all starved to death rather than eat the vine. They do, however, thrive on the non-hairy form of *P. foetida* that grows in the wet lowlands of north Qld.

Glasswing larvae also refuse to eat this plant and the similar hairy one that occurs in both wet and dry areas of north Qld.

Australian Vagrant *Vagrans egista*

Size: Male 58mm, female 64mm.

Occurs in low- to mid-altitude rainforest in Qld from Cape York to Townsville. Adults fly rapidly but settle frequently, often on the trunk of trees, or sides of buildings, mostly with head facing down. Eggs are mostly laid on spider web, dead twigs on the host plant or on the ground. Larvae often hang on a silken thread for the night.

Host Plants: *Flacourtia* sp. Shipton's Flat, *Homalium circumpinnatum*, *Xylosma* sp. Bolt Head, *X.* sp. Hunter Creek, sometimes on *Scolopia braunii*.

Best Garden Host Plant: *Homalium circumpinnatum*.

Homalium circumpinnatum is a small tree that is found in well-developed rainforest in Qld from the Pascoe River to Bowen, at low to mid-altitudes. The flowers have an extremely unpleasant smell. It is a hardy fast-growing plant and will quickly attract the Vagrant butterfly to your garden if you live within the range of the butterfly.

Xylosma sp. Temple Bay is a medium to large shrub found in coastal rainforest in Qld from Cape York to the Pascoe River.

Xylosma sp. Hunter Creek is an extremely rare plant, being found only on the lower reaches of Hunter Creek near the base of Mt Lewis, north-west of Cairns, Qld. This area is on Brooklyn holding which is now owned by the Australian Wildlife Conservancy.

In the author's garden both the Vagrant and the Rustic butterflies lay their eggs on this plant every time it flushes with new growth. At the moment it is not available from native plant nurseries but it should be in the future.

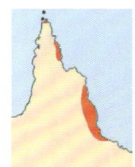

Australian Rustic *Cupha prosope*

Size: Male 60mm, female 64mm.

This species is found in low- to mid-altitude rainforest from Cape York, Qld, to northern NSW, being very common in coastal rainforest.

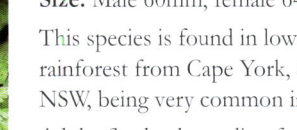

Adults fly slowly, settling frequently with wings spread. They are very localised and usually do not fly far from their host plants. The adults are long lived and several generations are often on the wing at the same time. Breeding only occurs when the host plants flush with soft new growth.

Host Plants: *Flacourtia* sp. Shipton's Flat, *Scolopia braunii*, *Xylosma ovatum*, *X.* sp. Hunter Creek, *X.* sp. Temple Bay, *X. terrae-reginae*, **Flacourtia inermis*, **F. indica*, **F. jangomas*, **Oncoba spinosa*.

Best Garden Host Plant: *Flacourtia* sp. Shipton's Flat.

Flacourtia sp. Shipton's Flat is a large shrub or small tree that is found from Torres Strait to Shipton's Flat, south of Cooktown in well-developed lowland and monsoon rainforest. It is a very hardy plant and an excellent host plant for the Rustic as it flushes with new growth several times each year. If you live within the natural range of the Rustic and have this plant in your garden the butterflies will always be around. When ripe the fruit is quite tasty and can be used for making jam. Usually there are separate male and female plants but there are a few bisexual plants making it into the nursery trade.

Scolopia braunii is a very widespread small tree that is found from Torres Strait, Qld, to about the Hunter River, NSW. It is most common in coastal rainforest but its range also extends into the mountain rainforests up to 1,200m. The Rustic butterfly does not usually occur at these altitudes. *Scolopia* has bright red new growth but does not flush as often as *Flacourtia* so is not quite as useful as a host plant. It is readily available from native plant nurseries.

Xylosma sp. Mt Lewis is confined to the high-altitude rainforest on the main coast range west of Mossman in north Qld. It is a small to medium tree that produces a mass of small red fruit that is eaten by birds. It has a high water requirement and survives better in gardens in southern Qld than it does in those areas of the Atherton Tableland where rainfall is below 1,200mm.

Xylosma terrae-reginae is a small to medium shrub that is found from about Rockhampton to Brunswick Heads in moist to dry rainforest, especially coastal. One problem with this host plant is that most of the leaves are soft at times and the Rustic larvae can completely defoliate it. If this happens several times in a row the plant may die. Plant in semi-shade for best results.

*Oncoba spinosa is a small to medium shrub that originates from Africa and is often grown in gardens in the north Qld tropics because of the large and attractive flowers. When given sufficient moisture the leaves become large and soft, supporting many Rustic larvae.

Leopard *Phalanta phalantha*

Size: Male 52mm, female 54mm.

Inhabits monsoon rainforest, deciduous and semi-deciduous vine thickets, and is confined to the north-west corner of NT. The host plant is recorded from the Gove Peninsula but the Leopard does not appear to occur there.

Adults fly slowly through and around the forest where they breed, settling frequently, usually with wings spread.

Host Plants: *Flacourtia territorialis*, **F. inermis*, **F. rukum*. In captivity they readily accept *Scolopia braunii* as well as other *Flacourtia* species.

Best Garden Host Plant: **Flacourtia inermis,* mainly because it is much larger, and commonly grown in gardens and as a street tree in Darwin.

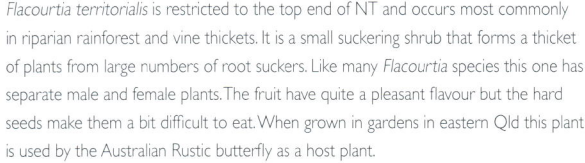

Flacourtia territorialis is restricted to the top end of NT and occurs most commonly in riparian rainforest and vine thickets. It is a small suckering shrub that forms a thicket of plants from large numbers of root suckers. Like many *Flacourtia* species this one has separate male and female plants. The fruit have quite a pleasant flavour but the hard seeds make them a bit difficult to eat. When grown in gardens in eastern Qld this plant is used by the Australian Rustic butterfly as a host plant.

Australian Fritillary *Argynnis hyperbius*

Size: Male 65mm, female 68mm.

Favours moist gullies, coastal wetlands and swamps where an abundance of the Violet host plant grows. This very rare butterfly has been found from Gympie, Qld, to northern NSW but seldom in any abundance.

The adults are extremely localised, not flying far from where they are breeding. They fly slowly, close to the ground and spend a lot of time resting with wings closed. Twenty or more years may pass between sightings of this species so if it has not been seen for ten or more years it should not be assumed that it has become extinct. Where the author saw this butterfly the females were laying on violets growing in a fairly open situation in short grass. The caterpillar is quite striking and cannot be confused with that of any other butterfly.

Host Plant: *Viola betonicifolia*.

Best Garden Host Plant: *Viola betonicifolia*. Anyone living within about 50km of the coast and in the above mentioned area should grow this plant just in case the butterfly makes another appearance. All the violet needs is permanently moist soil and not too much competition from creeping prostrate plants.

Viola betonicifolia is a small herb that lives in moist gullies and coastal wetlands. In ideal conditions leaves can grow to 25cm long. Seeds are spread by exploding capsules, which enables the plant to spread rapidly if there is not too much competition. The mass of purple flowers is quite showy.

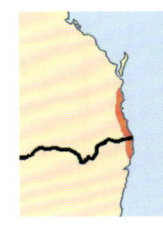

Tailed Emperor *Charaxes sempronius*

Size: Male 95mm, female 105mm.

Occurs in northern and eastern Australia in open forest, vine thickets, suburban gardens and most types of rainforest at low to mid-altitudes.

Charaxes have a very strong thick thorax which gives them powerful flight. When moving about within their breeding areas they usually fly quite slowly but can move extremely fast when required. Only two species occur on mainland Australia but there are about 180 in Africa.

Charaxes butterflies do not feed on nectar, instead they eat sap oozing from tree trunks, rotten fruit, dung and even dead animals. In Africa, where there are many species, butterfly collectors use traps baited with fruit, rather similar to the method for catching crabs.

Host Plants: This butterfly has so many host plants that it is difficult to make a definitive list. Most are in the broad Leguminosae group and specifically the two subgroups – Caesalpiniaceae (Cassias) and Mimosaceae (Acacias and Albizias). They utilise all five species of native Cassias as well as those from Asia that are commonly grown in gardens in Australia. They have been found to lay on a very large number of Acacias but have a definite preference for those with true leaves. All native Albizias are used as host plants. Host plants outside of this group include *Celtis*, *Adenanthera* and *Brachychiton acerifolius*.

Best Garden Host Plant: *Acacia baileyana* (Cootamundra Wattle) or any species of *Albizia*.

Albizia lebbeck is found naturally in Australia across the top end, from the Kimberley, WA, to Cape York Peninsula, Qld. Most of the trees planted in parks, school grounds and in homestead gardens are not of Australian origin but come from India. Because it is eaten by cattle the seeds get spread far and wide by cattle trucks moving stock. The one illustrated here is from Cape York Peninsula. The Tailed Emperor does not mind where the plant comes from and utilises it extensively. It is a large spreading tree and not at all suitable for suburban gardens.

Albizia retusa is found in Australia from about the Olive River to Musgrave on Cape York Peninsula. It grows to a very large tree in well-developed rainforest but only a large shrub in vine thickets. All *Albizia* species have separate male and female flowers but this species is very showy because the male flowers are pink and the female ones white. It is available from some native plant nurseries.

Albizia procera is a small to medium tree that is found across tropical Australia from the Kimberley, WA, to just north of Rockhampton, Qld, in low- to mid-altitude rainforest in the wet tropics and in rainforest along streams and near springs in the dry regions. All *Albizia* species are excellent host plants for the Tailed Emperor.

Orange Emperor *Charaxes latona*

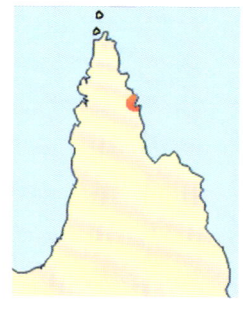

Size: Male 90mm, female 95mm.

Restricted to high-rainfall well-developed rainforest in the Iron Range/Claudie River region of Cape York Peninsula, Qld.

Adults usually fly rapidly, settling on foliage and tree trunks with wings closed.

Like all *Charaxes* species the adults do not feed on nectar but utilise sap, rotten fruit, dung or dead animals.

It is hard to understand why this butterfly is restricted to the Iron Range area as the host plant is common from Torres Strait to about Townsville. The plant illustrated below was actually photographed at Iron Range. The species name is a little confusing as you can see by the photograph that this variety (*riparia*) is not tri-nerved.

Host Plant: *Cryptocarya triplinervis* var. *riparia*.

Best Garden Host Plant: Only a handful of people live within the range of this butterfly so attracting it to gardens is not really an option.

Cryptocarya triplinervis is a medium to large tree that is common in rainforest from Torres Strait, Qld, to northern NSW. The variety *riparia* that is found at Iron Range extends down to about Townsville.

NYMPHS
Family Nymphalidae – Subfamily Nymphalinae

Members of this group are usually just referred to as Nymphs. The majority of them are confined to the tropics with some species extending along the east coast down to northern NSW; only four species are more widespread in the southern states.

The host plants of these butterflies are quite varied, though the family Acanthaceae is used by seven species, all of which have adapted to introduced garden plants or weeds in the same family, which gives them a chance to extend their range if climatic conditions are suitable.

The pupae of the Nymphs are not able to remain dormant for long periods and they all must either keep breeding all year round or go into hibernation or semi-hibernation for the winter/dry season. It is usually the freshly hatched butterflies that hibernate, thus giving them the best chance to mate and breed when conditions are suitable. Hibernating butterflies can often be found in hanging baskets or potted plants under the eaves of a house where it is sheltered.

The larvae of all species in the Nymphalinae subfamily have sharp spines which are usually black; the one exception is the Common Eggfly which has brown spines. This is an easy way to distinguish the larvae of the Common Eggfly and those of the other two Eggflies, whose spines are black.

Blue-banded Eggfly larva.

Common Eggfly larva.

When feeding on flowers the Nymphs often have their wings partly open, or they continuously open and close them. This gives you a chance to have a good look at both sides and to photograph them. Left: Australian Leafwing. Right: Common Eggfly.

White Nymph *Mynes geoffroyi*

Size: Male 62mm, female 64mm.

Found in low- to mid-altitude rainforest including gallery rainforest from Cape York, Qld, to northern NSW. Adults fly fairly rapidly and are difficult to identify on the wing. They usually settle on leaves with head facing out from the tree or down. Larvae remain together in a compact group, sometimes even pupating together along a branch or under a large leaf of their host plant. The butterfly image on the bottom right shows the rare pale form.

Host Plants: *Dendrocnide cordifolia*, *D. excelsa*, *D. moroides*, *D. photinophylla* (all stinging trees), *Nothocnide repanda*, *Pipturus argenteus*.

Best Garden Host Plant: *Pipturus argenteus*.

Nothocnide repanda is a large vine that occurs from Torres Strait to the Rocky River on Cape York Peninsula in well-developed rainforest. It has large soft leaves with no stings so is an ideal host for the White Nymph. Unfortunately it is not currently available from nurseries.

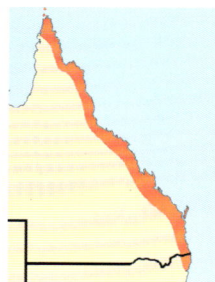

Dendrocnide cordifolia is a shrub confined to the wet tropics of north Qld. It is extremely dangerous and should never be touched. The fruit are purple when mature.

Dendrocnide moroides is a large shrub that occurs from the Pascoe River, Qld, to northern NSW in moist to wet rainforest at low to mid-altitudes. Touching almost any part of the plant can cause an extremely painful sting. Extreme care should be taken when near this plant.

Dendrocnide photinophylla is found in moist to very wet rainforest from the McIvor River, north of Cooktown, Qld, to just north of Sydney, NSW, usually at low to mid-altitudes. While it has stings on the leaves and soft stems they are rather sparse and if stung the pain only lasts for half an hour or so. With care the plant can actually be handled without getting stung. It is a major host plant for the White Nymph as all the leaves are soft and edible by the caterpillars.

White Nymph *Mynes geoffroyi*

Male plant

Pipturus argenteus is a large shrub or small tree that is found in the top end of NT then from Torres Strait, Qld, to northern NSW, usually in moist to wet rainforest or along streams and near springs in lower-rainfall rainforest.

Female plant

Pipturus sp. Archer Creek is found in deciduous and semi-deciduous vine thickets in north Qld in areas such as Chillagoe. The leaves are furry to touch, quite thick and fleshy. It is an excellent host for the White Nymph but is not widely grown. *Pipturus* have separate male and female plants.

Common Eggfly *Hypolimnas bolina*

Extreme aberration of female.

This not quite so colourful form of the female is quite common.

Size: Male 92mm, female 98mm.

Found along the edge of rainforest, shaded gullies, stream banks, parks and suburban gardens over most of northern and eastern Australia. Males establish territories in open sunny areas, usually resting upside-down on leaves, ready to dash out and chase passers-by, even birds. Females fly close to the ground searching endlessly for host plants to lay eggs on. Larvae hide on the ground when not feeding, move around quite a lot and will feed temporarily on non-host plants (such as Clover) when searching for more host plants.

Host Plants (in order of preference): *Sida rhombifolia, Alternanthera angustifolia, A. denticulata, A. nodiflora, *Synedrella nodiflora, Pipturus argenteus, *Galinsoga parviflora, Persicaria*. The author has never seen females laying on the following but the larvae certainly will eat them: *Asystasia, Dipteracanthus, Hygrophila, Pseuderanthemum*. In captivity the females will lay readily on *Asystasia gangetica* and *Pipturus argenteus*.

Best Garden Host Plants: Any *Alternanthera, *Sida rhombifolia* or *Synedrella nodiflora*.

Common Eggfly *Hypolimnas bolina*

Alternanthera angustifolia occurs in the top end of WA and NT, and most of Qld, usually in the lower rainfall areas, in open forest. This very widespread plant is common along footpaths in towns, growing up against power poles. Like other species of this genus, it is a small plant. In the wild, it is often found in areas that remain very moist for most of the summer.

It should not be exterminated as a weed. Most people look at *Alternanthera* species and think they are weeds. While they may look this way they are valuable host plants for the beautiful Common Eggfly butterfly.

Alternanthera nodiflora (Common Joyweed) is found over most of Australia, usually in areas where the soil remains damp for long periods following rain, such as near lagoons and along streams. It is a small, mostly prostrate herb that may spread out for half a metre or so and is often very common where it occurs.

Alternanthera nana occurs in the top end of NT, and from Torres Strait to south-east Qld, in open forest. It is a small prostrate plant that rarely spreads more than 50cm. If you have it occurring naturally you should leave it where it is, as it is a much favoured host plant for the Common Eggfly.

Synedrella nodiflora (Cinderella Weed) is an introduced herb from tropical America that is naturalised in the northern half of Qld. It has small yellow flowers and sharp-tipped seed pods (when dry). In ideal conditions it can grow to 1m high and often forms large colonies. It is a much favoured host plant for the Common Eggfly. Freshly mowed plants attract the females and entice them to lay many eggs.

Sida rhombifolia (Paddy's Lucerne or Sida Retusa) is now naturalised over most of the warmer regions of the world and is common in most parts of Australia. It is a woody herb that can grow to a little over 1m high. The Common Eggfly utilises this host plant more than any other. Sometimes where there are large numbers of seedlings many dozens of larvae can be found resting on the ground among these plants, feeding mostly at night, staying concealed beneath the foliage during the day.

Danaid Eggfly *Hypolimnas misippus*

Size: Male 68mm, female 75mm.

Usually found in flat open country where there are patches of bare ground which allow their host plant to flourish. Particularly common in farming areas where cultivated ground is left long enough for the host plant to establish. Occurs in northern and eastern Australia south to northern NSW.

Adults fly fairly rapidly and usually close to the ground, resting with wings spread. Females can be seen searching over open fields for the host plant.

Host Plants: *Portulaca oleracea* (Pig Weed), *P. australis*.

Best Garden Host Plant: *Portulaca oleracea*.

Portulaca australis

Portulaca oleracea is a small prostrate herb that spreads to about 30–40cm, with fleshy leaves and small yellow flowers. It occurs over the whole of Australia, including Tas. It is an edible plant, and when cooked the taste closely resembles that of beans.

Blue-banded Eggfly *Hypolimnas alimena*

H.a. darwinensis.

H.a. lamina.

Size: Male 80mm, female 85mm.

Found along the edges of rainforest, up to about 800m altitude, in evergreen and semi-deciduous vine forest, also in suburban gardens and parks. Males stake out territories in open sunny areas and chase everything that passes. Females fly slowly close to the ground and often settle there, with wings spread. Two subspecies are named:
- ■ *H.a. lamina* in Qld.
- ■ *H.a. darwinensis* in NT.

Host Plants: *Pseuderanthemum variabile* when growing in the open, *P.* sp. Mt White, *Brunoniella spiciflora*, *Asystasia australasica*, **A. gangetica*.

Best Garden Host Plant: **Asystasia gangetica*.

As the name suggests, *Pseuderanthemum variabile* is just that. Above are some of the leaf shapes and colours. The height varies from about 2–60cm. It is quite possible that there are a number of species involved as the ones above with white or silver in the leaves are in the author's garden and they do not cross with each other or the more typical forms.

They are very easy to grow – just collect ripe seed or a few seedlings and you are in business. The plant has exploding capsules that spread the seeds very efficiently.

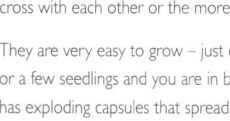

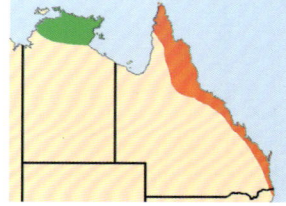

Leafwing *Doleschallia bisaltide*

Size: Male 75mm, female 80mm.

Found from Torres Strait to northern NSW in low- to mid-altitude rainforest, especially in coastal areas and along streams with a narrow band of rainforest along the banks.

Adults have a rapid flight except when the female is laying, she then flies slowly, very close to the ground while searching for plants of *Pseuderanthemum*. Females lay only on host plants in the shade at the time she finds them and usually on the flower heads. The colour on the underside of the wings of males is quite variable. Larvae usually rest on the ground during the day when not feeding. Because *Pseuderanthemum* plants are quite small, larvae have to utilise several plants to reach maturity. It is possible that they can detect nearby plants rather than roam randomly for their next feed.

Host Plants: *Asystasia australasica*, *Pseuderanthemum variabile*, *P.* sp. Mt White, *Isoglossa eranthemoides*, **Asystasia gangetica* – occasionally on *Brunoniella* when close to the rainforest and **Strobilanthes anisophyllus* and **S. dyerianus* in gardens. Larvae will eat *Graptophyllum pictum*, *Dipteracanthus*, *Hemigraphis* and **Pseuderanthemum bicolor* but females rarely if ever lay on these.

Best Garden Host Plant: **Asystasia gangetica* because this is very easy to grow and females readily lay on it. If you want to stick to native plants then take the trouble to cultivate large numbers of *Pseuderanthemum variabile* and spread them around your garden.

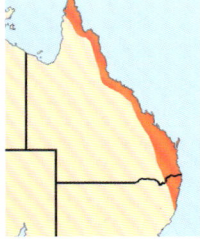

NYMPHS

Asystasia australasica occurs in Torres Strait and possibly on the mainland in the top end. It is an understorey plant in vine thickets and evergreen rainforests that grows to about 1m high and has small pale mauve flowers. It is an excellent host plant for all the butterflies that use the introduced *Asystasia gangetica* and could be used as an alternative, for those who prefer native plants, when it becomes more widely cultivated.

Isoglossa eranthemoides is an uncommon plant that occurs on the Atherton Tablelands, Granite Creek in central Qld and Mt Warning in northern NSW in wet rainforest. It is very easy to grow and spreads quite rapidly requiring a shaded and permanently moist situation.

Leafwing *Doleschallia bisaltide*

*Strobilanthes anisophyllus (Persian Shield) is a fairly commonly grown garden plant in the tropics. It is an excellent host plant for the Leafwing butterfly, especially for captive breeding. Grow it in the shade to ensure that the foliage is soft.

*Asystasia gangetica is a very common garden plant in north Qld and grown extensively by butterfly enthusiasts because it is a host plant for five species of butterflies. It grows easily from cuttings or divisions. The flowers may be white, yellow, pink, mauve or blue.

Australian Lurcher *Yoma sabina*

Size: Male 76mm, female 80mm.

Found in Arnhem Land, NT, and then in Qld from Torres Strait to about Townsville in low- to mid-altitude rainforest. The butterflies shelter in the rainforest but lay eggs in nearby eucalypt forest where most of their host plants grow. Adults are powerful fliers but usually do not fly fast. Females fly low down near the ground in search of their small host plants. Males stake out territories by resting upside-down on a leaf in the full sun and try to chase away everything that moves past.

Host Plants: *Dipteracanthus bracteatus* (Qld from Torres Strait to just south of Cooktown and then in the Nhulunbuy area of NT); *D.* sp. Kalpowar in semi-deciduous and deciduous rainforest in Qld on the western side of the McIlwraith Range and in Cape Melville National Park; *D. australasicus* in the Chillagoe area, Qld; *D. prostratus* wherever it occurs within the range of the butterfly.

Best Garden Host Plant: *Dipteracanthus australasicus*. *D. prostratus* attracts the females the best of all but as this is an aggressive weed from India it cannot be recommended as a garden plant. It already occurs from Torres Strait to the Atherton Tableland and then in the Darwin and Ord River areas.

Adult Lurcher butterflies hibernate for the winter/dry season in dense foliage; sometimes in old buildings but mostly in gorges and along streams where they shelter in *Calamus* (Lawyer Cane vine) and *Pandanus* plants. At times there are huge numbers in these wintering colonies.

Australian Lurcher *Yoma sabina*

Dipteracanthus bracteatus is the main host for the Lurcher butterfly. It is a small herbaceous plant that grows in the grass and reaches a height of up to 60cm. Underground it has tuberous roots and can die back to these if the dry season is too harsh. This also enables it to survive fire.

The Lurcher only utilises the plant when it is growing within a few hundred metres of rainforest or between patches of rainforest where the butterflies pass to and from.

The large white flowers are quite conspicuous but only last for a few hours in the sunlight. They open during the night and are most likely pollinated by hawk moths.

Dipteracanthus sp. Kalpowar is found in Qld from about Peach Creek, north of Coen, to Cape Flattery in semi-deciduous rainforest and vine thickets. It is a small plant that rarely grows more then 30cm high with deep blue flowers. So far it is not available from native plant nurseries.

Like any good weed **Dipteracanthus prostratus* (below) can grow from 2cm to 2m high, depending on the requirements to obtain light. In this instance it has completely taken over a lawn.

Dipteracanthus australasicus is very widespread and is found in scattered populations over about two-thirds of the north of Australia. It usually grows in vine thickets or sheltered gullies amongst rocks where it is protected from fire. The Lurcher butterfly only uses it when it is in vine thickets within its range. This plant is sometimes available from native plant nurseries. There are at least four subspecies named.

*Dipteracanthus prostratus is an introduced weed from South-East Asia which has colonised many areas across tropical Australia from Torres Strait to the Ord River and south to the Atherton Tablelands. It is a much favoured host plant for the Lurcher, Brown Soldier and Tiny Grass Blue, but has enormous weed potential and cannot be recommended for planting.

Iron Range Lurcher *Yoma algina*

Size: Male 76mm, female 80mm.

Occurs in lowland tropical rainforest, in Australia from the Pascoe River to the Rocky River – also in Papua New Guinea.

Adults fly slowly and carefully through the understorey of the rainforest, settling with their wings open, often in sunny patches. Females fly close to the ground searching for their host plant which grows in very damp shady locations.

Host Plants: *Hemigraphis ciliata*, **H. colorata*, **H. alternata*, **H. repanda* cultivars. It is extremely difficult to get a correct identification on cultivated varieties of this genus. The author searched more than 100 herbarium specimens on the web and decided to follow the commonly accepted names used by nurseries in Australia. Use the images on the following page when selecting plants from a nursery.

Best Garden Host Plant: **Hemigraphis colorata* (Purple Waffle Plant).

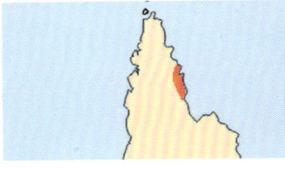

Iron Range Lurcher *Yoma algina*

Hemigraphis ciliata is a small herb that grows to about 40cm high and occurs naturally in Qld from about the Olive River to the Rocky River on Cape York Peninsula and again near Cape Tribulation, north of Cairns.

*Hemigraphis alternata (Metal Plant) is widely planted in council gardens as a ground cover on footpaths and in parks.

*Hemigraphis colorata (Purple Waffle Plant) is much softer than the Metal Plant and more suitable as a host plant. It is widely planted in gardens in the tropics.

This *Hemigraphis repanda* cultivar is often sold in nurseries in north Qld just as 'Hemigraphis'. The leaves are small and soft and it makes an excellent host plant.

*Hemigraphis reptans is a small prostrate plant that infests many tropical gardens. It is so small it often goes unnoticed. It is also used by the Brown Soldier butterfly.

Brown Soldier *Junonia hedonia*

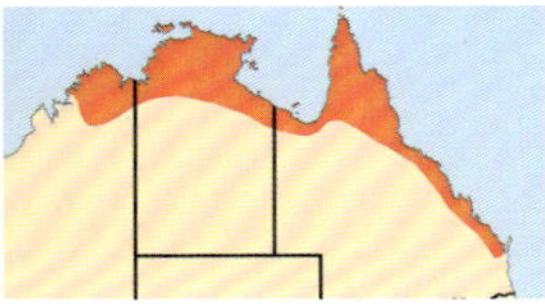

Size: Male 56mm, female 60mm.

Found in swampy areas and inland waterways where the host plant *Hygrophila* grows, and in suburban gardens and parklands where the introduced weed *Dipteracanthus prostratus* has infested.

Adults fly slowly, unless disturbed, and usually close to the ground, settling regularly with wings spread. They often rest in shaded areas on tree trunks or walls of buildings with wings closed in an upside-down position.

Host Plants: *Hygrophila angustifolia*, *H.* sp. Rocky River, **H. costata*, **Dipteracanthus prostratus*, **Hemigraphis*.

Best Garden Host Plant: *Hygrophila angustifolia*.

Hygrophila angustifolia is very widespread, occurring from about Broome in WA, across the top and down the east coast to northern NSW. There are probably two species, as one is a perennial plant that grows in swamps, especially along the coast, while the other is found in riverbeds of inland waterways and is only an annual. It germinates as the floodwaters go down, produces masses of flowers and seed, then dies.

Both are excellent host plants for the Brown Soldier, but the longer-living coastal one is the best one to grow in a garden.

Brown Soldier *Junonia hedonia*

Hygrophila sp. Rocky River is a small plant that grows to about 60cm tall and is found between Iron Range and the Rocky River on Cape York Peninsula. It grows in boggy areas and often colonises four-wheel-drive wheel tracks that are left in melaleuca habitat. Even though it is very hairy the Brown Soldier larvae breed well on it.

**Hygrophila costata* is a host plant but it is also a declared weed from central America and should not be grown. It grows much taller than the native species, up to 2m. This can prevent waterbirds from using the area as they need water that is much more shallow. This plant pales into insignificance in terms of destroying wetland habitat compared to Pond Grass (*Hymenachne amplexicaulis*), which has taken over numerous streams and wetlands in tropical north Qld.

Meadow Argus *Junonia villida*

Size: Male 52mm, female 56mm.

Inhabits open woodland and grassy areas, including coastal; quite common in gardens over most of Australia.

Adults fly rather quickly with a flapping and gliding motion close to the ground. Usually rests with wings spread unless disturbed.

Host Plants: This butterfly has a huge range of host plants that includes many common garden plants. The following are listed in order of preference for south Qld – this will vary depending where you live because of availability of the range of their host plants. *Plantago*, *Verbena rigida, **V. bonariensis*, *Evolvulus*; other hosts in alphabetical order, natives first; *Epaltes*, *Goodenia*, *Hygrophila angustifolia* (when growing in dry stream beds or gardens), *Hyptis*, *Phyla nodiflora* (grows in exposed damp areas and is extensively used), *Portulaca*, *Scaevola*, *Stemodia*, **Angelonia salicariifolia*, *Centaurium, *Hygrophila, *Plantago (most species of *Plantago* that you will see are introduced species), *Scabiosa*, *Antirrhinum*, *Russelia*, *Stachytarpheta*, *Phyla, *Veronica*.

Best Garden Host Plant: *Plantago* – whichever species is in your area.

**Verbena bonariensis* is widespread in eastern Australia and around Perth. It grows in open woodland and disturbed areas amongst grass, reaching a height of about 1.5m. There are other *Verbena* species that could be confused with this one but they have softer leaves. The foliage of this species has a sandpapery texture to the touch. Flowers can range from dark pink and mauve to purple.

Meadow Argus *Junonia villida*

*Verbena rigida is a herb from South America that is widely cultivated around the world as a garden plant. It has become naturalised in south-eastern Australia and near Perth. Wherever it occurs it is utilised by the Meadow Argus. The foliage is very stiff and sandpapery to the feel. A creeping rhizome enables it to spread and form large colonies.

Plantago debilis is found over most of Australia, being more common south of a line through about Mackay, Qld. Leaves can grow to 30cm long and it often forms colonies in grassy areas.

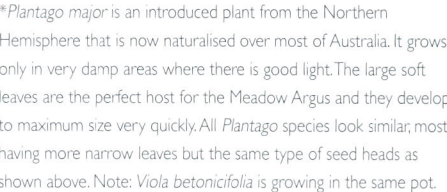

*Plantago major is an introduced plant from the Northern Hemisphere that is now naturalised over most of Australia. It grows only in very damp areas where there is good light. The large soft leaves are the perfect host for the Meadow Argus and they develop to maximum size very quickly. All *Plantago* species look similar, most having more narrow leaves but the same type of seed heads as shown above. Note: *Viola betonicifolia* is growing in the same pot.

Blue Argus *Junonia orithya*

Male dry-season form.

Size: Male 46mm, female 50mm.

Inhabits open woodland with short grass and many bare patches of soil; parks and gardens over northern and eastern Australia down to northern NSW. Adults flap and glide, usually keeping low to the ground. When they land they generally spread their wings, if disturbed they snap them shut.

Host Plants: *Rostellularia*, *Brunoniella*, *Pseuderanthemum variabile* (when growing in the full sun), *Hygrophila* (when growing in a dry stream bed or in a garden), *Buchnera*, *Veronica*, *Striga*, **Angelonia salicariifolia*, **Asystasia gangetica*, **Striga* (some introduced species are declared pests), **Thunbergia alata*.

Best Garden Host Plant: **Asystasia gangetica* when growing in the full sun.

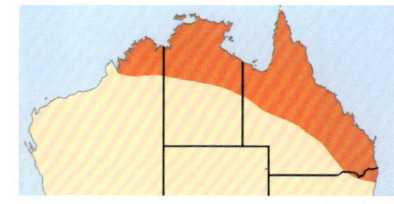

Rostellularia adscendens var *latifolia* is a prostrate plant that forms a mat on the ground and may spread for 2m or more. It is found over most of northern and eastern Australia and often goes unnoticed unless it is flowering. The small pink flowers stand out against the dark green foliage.

Blue Argus *Junonia orithya*

Rostellularia adscendens is a very widespread plant covering most of Australia, becoming less common in Vic, southern WA and SA. It has numerous subspecies, but once you have seen one you will recognise them all by the flowers.

This is definitely the main host for the Blue Argus and if you are in the range of the butterfly this is the most likely plant on which you will find the larvae. Most varieties of this plant are no more than 30cm high and are usually amongst grass.

Brunoniella acaulis is a tiny plant with just a rosette of leaves and fairly large blue flowers. It is found amongst grass in open eucalyptus and acacia forest and in lawns in the drier tropical regions of Australia.

Rostellularia adscendens subsp. *glaucoviolacea* is the tallest of all the subspecies and can grow to 60cm high. The flowers are sometimes white but often the usual pink colour. This species is restricted to north Qld, north of about Bowen and usually found in open eucalyptus forest.

Brunoniella australis is larger than *B. acaulis* as it produces stems up to 30cm long and can support several larvae. It is also used by the Lurcher butterfly when growing near vine thickets. It usually grows in the open in sparse woodland. It is found in northern and eastern Australia south to at least Sydney, NSW.

Australian Painted Lady *Vanessa kershawi*

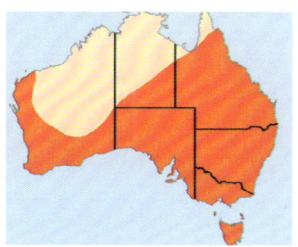

Size: Male 58mm, female 62mm.

Very common and found over most of eastern and southern Australia, including Tas, but scarce in the northern tropics. Found in areas without dense vegetation but also common in gardens, parks and the dry inland.

Adults fly rapidly but settle frequently on the ground or low vegetation. Very large migrations occur regularly and huge numbers of adults can be seen at these times flying fast and usually not much more than 2m above the ground.

Host Plants: This butterfly has a large number of host plants that belong to the Asteraceae (Daisy) family. Most of these are instantly recognisable as Daisies. The group commonly called Paper Daisies are most often used. The following genera are all daisies: *Ammobium* (Paper Daisy), *Chrysocephalum* (Paper Daisy), *Helichrysum* (daisy), *Rhodanthe* (daisy), *Xerochrysum* (Sticky Paper Daisy), *Gamochaeta* (includes the weed **Gamochaeta calviceps* Cudweed), **Arctotheca* (Cape Weed), **Artemisia* (Wormwood Weed), **Onopordum* (Scotch Thistle), **Carduus* (Scotch Thistle), **Galinsoga* (Potato Weed).

Best Garden Host Plant: Any Paper Daisy, especially the larger *Xerochrysum* species.

Xerochrysum bracteatum is a very widespread Paper Daisy that is found all over Australia, including Tas. It is probably the main host plant of the Australian Painted Lady and is typical of other species in this group. They have soft furry leaves and dry paper-like petals. Often mixed seed of paper daisies can be purchased and these produce plants with flowers of many different colours.

A number of moths use these plants as hosts and the caterpillar on the flower bud belongs to a moth.

Australian Admiral *Vanessa itea*

Size: Male 60mm, female 64mm.

Found along the edge of rainforest, in damp gullies, along streams, and in gardens, wherever the host plant Stinging Nettle grows.

Adults fly rapidly, often settling on the sides of buildings or tree trunks with head downwards. Males are seen regularly on hilltops, especially where microwave towers are. In these locations the males sit on the sides of buildings.

Host Plants: *Australina pusilla*, *Laportea interrupta*, *Parietaria debilis*, *Pipturus argenteus* seedlings, *Urtica incisa*, *U. urens*, *Parietaria judaica*, *Soleirolia soleirolii*.

Best Garden Host Plant: *Urtica incisa* or *U. urens* (Stinging Nettle).

Larval shelter.

Laportea interrupta looks very much like Stinging Nettle but is an annual plant and rarely grows more than 30cm high. Being an annual it can grow in areas that are mostly dry but remain moist for some time following the wet season. It is confined to the tropical regions of northern Australia so is only a minor host for the Admiral butterfly.

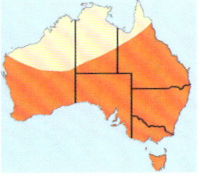

The Stinging Nettle *Urtica incisa* is very widespread in Australia and its distribution closely mirrors that of the Admiral butterfly. It is found in permanently moist areas on the edge of rainforest, damp gullies, sheltered gorges and along streams. Gloves are needed when handling it as it has quite a nasty sting, although it does not last for long. When growing it in the garden it is best to ring it off with some bird wire to avoid accidental contact by the unwary.

Common Aeroplane *Phaedyma shepherdi*

Size: Male 65mm, female 68mm.

Inhabits low- to mid-altitude rainforest, suburban gardens and parklands in eastern Australia from Cape York, Qld, to central NSW.

Adults fly with a flap-and-glide motion, settling with wings either open or closed. Larvae are difficult to find as they web chewed off pieces of leaf to the end of leaves, where they hide.

Host Plants: *Aphananthe philippinensis, Brachychiton* (all species), *Bombax ceiba, Celtis, Cordia dichotoma, Ehretia acuminata, Firmiana papuana, Grewia australis, Mucuna gigantea, Petraeovitex multiflora, Pongamia.*

Best Garden Host Plant: *Brachychiton acerifolius* or *B. populneus* – both are regularly stocked by native plant nurseries.

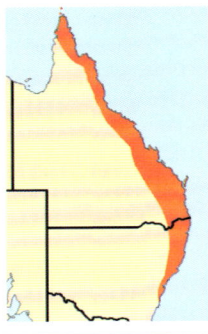

Pongamia pinnata var. *minor* is a deciduous tree that is widespread from Cape York to central Qld in monsoon forest, and more commonly in forest along streams. Old leaves turn yellow before dropping and the new growth is a spectacular copper colour.

Orange Aeroplane *Pantoporia consimilis*

Size: Male 40mm, female 42mm.

Found in low- to mid-altitude rainforest in Qld from Torres Strait to just north of Rockhampton. Like all the Aeroplanes the adults fly with a flap-and-glide motion, usually resting with wings spread.

Host Plants: *Dalbergia candenatensis* (a mangrove), *D. densa*, *Austrosteenisia stipularis*, *Senna gaudichaudii*, **S. auriculata*.

Best Garden Host Plant: **Senna auriculata*.

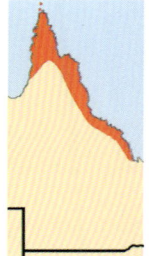

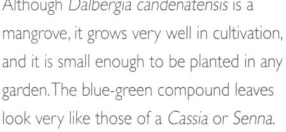

Although *Dalbergia candenatensis* is a mangrove, it grows very well in cultivation, and it is small enough to be planted in any garden. The blue-green compound leaves look very like those of a *Cassia* or *Senna*.

It occurs along the north coast of NT, and in Qld from Torres Strait to Mackay.

It is on the top of the list for host plants of the Orange Aeroplane butterfly. However, only foliage in the shade will be used by the butterfly.

Dalbergia densa is a large vine that can be kept as a weeping shrub with regular pruning. It has long, straight stems that lean on plants rather than twine around them as many vines do. To keep it as a shrub you will need to grow it in the open where it cannot reach other plants. Under a large tree is ideal as the butterfly lays eggs only in the shade.

Orange Aeroplane *Pantoporia consimilis*

The master of camouflage

The caterpillars of all Aeroplane butterflies use dead leaves and twigs to hide when not feeding but the larvae of the **Orange Aeroplane** go to extremes, especially in relation to their size. The top left image shows a new shelter that has been created where the leaves are not yet dead. The bottom left image shows another one where the leaves are dead and dried. The larvae cut the stems and tie them back on with silk. When they rest somewhere amongst the dead leaves and twigs they are virtually invisible.

Black-and-white Aeroplane *Neptis praslini*

Size: 50mm.

Found in lowland rainforest in Qld from Cape York to about Townsville. Adults mimic the toxic Cairns Hamadryad by flying fairly low with a slow gliding flight. They also have the matching eye colour of the Hamadryad. Males often sit on the upperside of leaves with wings outspread.

Host Plants: *Phylacium bracteosum* (restricted to Cape York Peninsula), *Bridelia insulana*, *Erycibe coccinea*.

Best Garden Host Plant: *Bridelia insulana*.

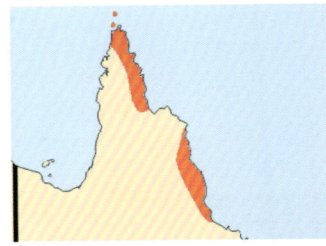

Erycibe coccinea is a very hardy vine that can be pruned and kept as a large, weeping shrub. The branches are very stiff, and the plants look like a shrub when young. The lovely flowers put on a showy display. The vine is quite widespread, occurring in the top end of NT as well as in eastern tropical Qld.

BROWNS, PALMFLY AND OWL
Family Nymphalidae – Subfamily Satyrinae

The majority of this group of butterflies are not rainforest species. Because most of them use grass as a host plant they are more common in open country, including parks and gardens with extensive lawns. One small group, the Swordgrass Browns, use a non-grass host plant. There are two species of Swordgrass Browns with the southern one having a number of subspecies. These butterflies use *Gahnia* (Swordgrass) as a host. This plant is not really a grass but a sedge.

Butterfly breeders have shown that of the grass-feeders most, if not all, are not confined to particular species of grass but more to a specific habitat. Bill Graham, a butterfly enthusiast who used to live in Canberra, advised me that he bred all the species of Browns in the Canberra region on grass purchased as lawn seed from a local hardware store. Not only did they lay on this grass but they developed normally through all stages.

In colder southern regions they have only one brood per year, spending the autumn, winter and part of the spring as larvae then changing into pupae and emerging as butterflies in December. Even in the tropics the author observed that several of the Ringlets remained in the larval stage from May until late September. This very long period as larvae and pupae amongst the grass makes them extremely vulnerable to fire. This is not such a problem in the high-rainfall areas but in drier parts, burning their habitat before the adults have hatched can wipe out an entire population. Because the larvae feed mostly on grasses or sedges they do not contain any toxic properties to protect them from birds. Instead, they make extensive use of eye-spots in their wing-patterns. This has been proven to be an effective defence strategy. As well as having eye-spots for protection, this group, as the name Browns suggests, is basically brown, so this gives them a good degree of camouflage when settled on the ground or on leaf litter.

The larvae of the Browns are usually slender, with two spikes at the rear end and in the final

This Dingy Ring rests quietly with wings closed, but if disturbed the forewing pops up revealing a large eye-spot.

stage some sort of a crown on the head. They are usually covered with hairs in the first couple of stages and smooth when mature. Utilising their colour to blend in amongst the grass, they can be either green or brown.

This small larva of the Dingy Ring is typical of the Browns.

The butterflies in this group have large wings in relation to their bodies, enabling them to move through the air with ease, and they tend to 'bob' along in an up-and-down motion. This makes it difficult for predators to catch them, even when they are not taking evasive action.

This Solander's Brown larva hides low down in a clump of grass during the day.

The adults of the Browns often feed on fallen fruit and many can be attracted to a tray of squashed bananas with a little beer added.

To help identify grass species, the online resource AusGrass2 (ausgrass2.myspecies.info) is extremely useful.

Palmfly *Elymnias agondas*

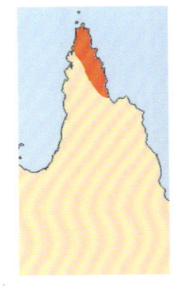

Size: Male 70mm, female 72mm.

Found in well-developed rainforest from Cape York to the Rocky River, east of Coen.

Adults fly slowly, not straying far from the areas where their host plants grow in great profusion.

Host Plants: *Calamus caryotoides* (Fish-tail Lawyer Cane).

Best Garden Host Plant: Very few people live within the range of this butterfly and because the host vine forms an almost impenetrable mass of thorns it is unlikely that anyone would plant it on purpose.

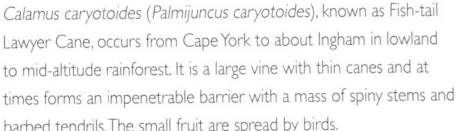

Calamus caryotoides (*Palmijuncus caryotoides*), known as Fish-tail Lawyer Cane, occurs from Cape York to about Ingham in lowland to mid-altitude rainforest. It is a large vine with thin canes and at times forms an impenetrable barrier with a mass of spiny stems and barbed tendrils. The small fruit are spread by birds.

Artemis Owl *Taenaris artemis*

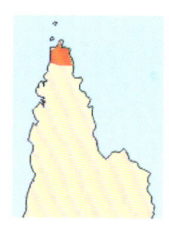

Size: Male 70mm, female 72mm.

Occurs in lowland swampy rainforest where the *Pandanus* host plant grows. In Australia this butterfly is mostly restricted to islands in Torres Strait, being a rare visitor to Cape York.

The butterflies flap their wings slowly as they pick their way through openings in the rainforest. Adults regularly feed on rotten fruit.

Host Plants: *Musa* sp. (Bananas), *Pandanus* sp., *Cocos nucifera* (Coconut Palm). In Papua New Guinea this species also uses cultivated Bananas.

Best Garden Host Plant: *Musa* (Bananas).

Pandanus conicus is a small branching tree that grows in lowland rainforest from Torres Strait to the Rocky River, usually along streams or near springs. The bright orange fruit is typical of *Pandanus* – the only exception is *Pandanus zea* fruit which looks like a cob of corn and the leaves have no spines along the edge. It is found in the same area as *P. conicus*.

Musa banksii is a small to medium suckering banana that grows in low- to mid-altitude rainforest from Papua New Guinea to about Bowen, north Qld. Suckers do not appear until the first bunch of fruit has matured.

Dingy Ring *Ypthima arctous*

Size: Male 34mm, female 38mm.

A very common butterfly that occurs in open eucalypt and acacia forests with a sparse grass cover, or along streams in the drier parts of its range. It occurs from the top end of NT to Vic, rarely more than 200km from the coast. If conditions are cool they will spread their wings to absorb heat from the sun.

Recorded Host Plants: Many grasses including *Imperata cylindrica* (Blady Grass) and most lawn grasses.

Evening Brown *Melanitis leda*

Size: Male 80mm, female 84mm.

An extremely variable butterfly. It has distinct wet (summer) and dry (winter) season forms but within these there is a large amount of variation. When the adults settle amongst the leaf litter they are almost impossible to see. Even the shape of the wings changes with the seasonal forms. As the name suggests, this butterfly is most active at dusk.

Dry-season form.

Recorded Host Plants: Many species of grass are recorded as host plants but in reality they will lay on almost any species, native or introduced, that has a broad leaf, is not too hairy, and grows at least 30cm high, even Sugar Cane.

Wet-season form.

  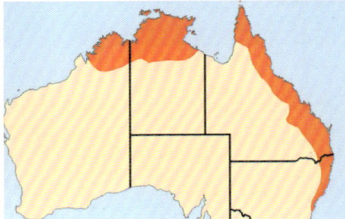

Two variations of the dry-season form.

Evening Brown *Melanitis leda*

Imperata cylindrica (Blady Grass) is found over most of Australia except the south-west. It is more common within a couple of hundred kilometres of the coast but does occur in the centre of the country in sheltered gorges. It is the main host plant for the Evening Brown and is also used by a number of other Browns. This grass has leaves with sharp edges that can cut your finger if rubbed over them the wrong way. When in areas that are burnt regularly (almost every year) it becomes the dominant grass and suppresses most other small plants. The heat from a Blady Grass fire is intense and can completely change the structure of a forest.

An example of a forest that is burnt every year where the Blady Grass and a species of introduced grass have completely taken over the understorey. While this may appear to be good for the species of butterflies that feed on these grasses it is actually not, as cool burns in late winter or early spring kill all the caterpillars of the Browns that are breeding there. Most of these species remain as a caterpillar from late summer until late spring or early next summer. As well as the butterfly species destroyed, numerous other insects that are hibernating are also wiped out, thus reducing the bottom end of the food chain, which impacts on the entire diversity of the forest.

Orange Bush-brown *Mycalesis terminus*

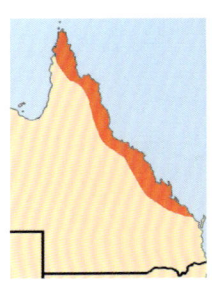

Size: Male 44mm, female 48mm.

Restricted to Qld from Cape York to about Maryborough. It prefers moist shady gullies and along streams but is quite at home in a garden with shade and some soft-leaved grass upon which to lay eggs. Adults tend to settle on low vegetation instead of on leaf litter as many other Browns do.

Recorded Host Plants: *Oplismenus*, *Dichanthium sericeum* (Queensland Bluegrass), *Imperata cylindrica* (Blady Grass), *Themeda triandra* (Kangaroo-grass).

Oplismenus aemulus is found most often in sunny areas near and in lowland rainforest. It also occurs along streams in shaded areas where there is constant moisture.

If you have a rainforest or generally shady garden you can grow this species. Don't try to grow it as a lawn as it will not tolerate mowing. It will creep over the ground in areas of light shade but will die out if the light level becomes too low. In the very dry times it can die down, but reappears after rains.

Cedar Bush-brown *Mycalesis sirius*

Size: Male 44mm, female 48mm.

Prefers wet lowland areas, being particularly common in shaded swampy situations, such as those found around permanent springs in sandstone areas over Cape York Peninsula, up to 200km from the coast. It is also found in the top end of NT and then in Qld from Cape York to the Kolan River, south of Gladstone.

Adults spend most of their time resting on grass and other low vegetation in these shaded areas. It is difficult to determine the size of these local populations unless you walk through the grass and disturb them. This is the largest of the Bush-browns and the rich red colour is very distinctive.

Recorded Host Plants: *Ischaemum australe* (Large Bluegrass), *Imperata cylindrica* (Blady Grass), *Themeda triandra* (Kangaroo-grass). They will use any grass with soft foliage that grows in their habitat; in the wet tropics most of these are introduced species.

Dingy Bush-brown *Mycalesis perseus*

Size: Male 40mm, female 42mm.

The name Dingy Bush-brown aptly describes this butterfly. It has a wide distribution, being found from the top end of NT, around the bottom of the Gulf and then from Cape York to south-east Qld. Records show a break in distribution on the lower western side of Cape York Peninsula but this is probably due to a lack of collecting records as there is no logical reason why the butterfly should be absent from this area.

Recorded Host Plants: *Aristida calycina* (Dark Wire-grass), *Brachiaria*, *Dichanthium sericeum* (Queensland Bluegrass), *Eriachne*, *Heteropogon contortus* (Black Speargrass), *H. triticeus* (Giant Speargrass), *Themeda triandra* (Kangaroo-grass).

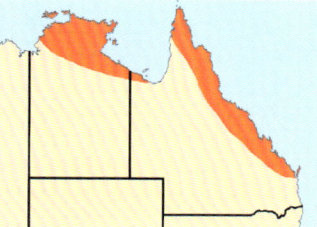

Northern Ringlet *Hypocysta irius*

Size: Male 40mm, female 45mm.

This species and the next two Ringlets are quite difficult to identify in the wild. The best method is by the markings on the underside of the hindwing. Luckily this is clearly visible when they rest with wings closed. The Northern Ringlet does not occur far from the coast, except in the sandstone areas west of Rockhampton such as Blackdown Tableland. Distribution ranges from Cape York to northern NSW.

Recorded Host Plants: Actual host plants are not recorded but like most of the Browns they would use grasses that are common in the area where they occur.

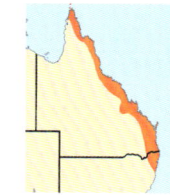

Common Ringlet *Hypocysta metirius*

Size: Male 38mm, female 40mm.

Has a wide distribution, from Cape York, Qld, to Vic, extending at least 200km inland in some areas. Habitat ranges from eucalypt forest to coastal heath.

Recorded Host Plants: *Cynodon dactylon* (Bermuda Grass), *Eriachne pallescens* (Wanderrie Grass), *Oplismenus hirtellus* (Basket Grass), *Alexfloydia repens* (Floyd's Grass) and most likely many other grasses.

Alexfloydia repens is quite restricted in distribution, being found mainly around Coffs Harbour and south to about Nambucca Heads in NSW. This is a typical host plant for this group of butterflies, with abundant soft foliage.

Dingy Ringlet *Hypocysta pseudirius*

Size: Male 38mm, female 40mm.

The distribution of the Dingy Ringlet overlaps with those of the previous two species; it ranges from the Atherton Tableland to southern NSW. Both images shown here are males and it is the markings on the underside of the hindwing of the male that separates this species from the Common Ringlet. The preferred habitat does somewhat separate this species from the other similar ones, as the Dingy Ringlet is more commonly found in lower rainfall areas, especially west of the Great Dividing Range.

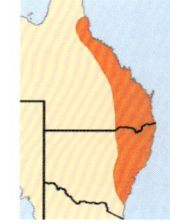

Recorded Host Plants: The only recorded host plant is *Themeda triandra* (Kangaroo-grass) but most likely a number of other grass species are utilised.

Orange Ringlet *Hypocysta adiante*

Size: Male 34mm, female 38mm.

There are two subspecies:
- *H.a. adiante* from Cape York, Qld, to southern NSW.
- *H.a. antirius* in the top end of WA and NT.

Found in a variety of habitats from open forest to coastal heathland. In the drier regions, grassy areas along streams are the preferred habitat.

Recorded Host Plants: *Aristida macroclada, Arundinella nepalensis* (Reed Grass), *Chloris, Digitaria didactyla* (Queensland Blue Couch), *D. gibbosa, Imperata cylindrica* (Blady Grass), *Ischaemum australe* (Large Bluegrass), *I. tropicum, Themeda triandra* (Kangaroo-grass).

H.a. adiante.

H.a. antirius.

Rock Ringlet *Hypocysta euphemia*

Size: Male 40mm, female 42mm.

The large eye-spot on the upperside of the forewing distinguishes this species from the other Ringlets. As the name suggests, this species prefers a habitat with rocky outcrops and is more common in areas above 600m amongst granite or sandstone.

Recorded Host Plants: No specific grass species are recorded as hosts.

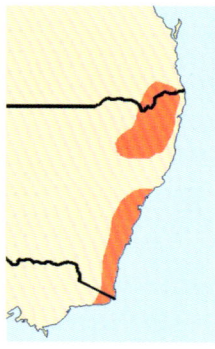

Helena Brown *Tisiphone helena*

Size: Male 60mm, female 64mm.

Distinctly different from the other species in the genus *Tisiphone* and is separated from them by a great distance. Generally found in upland rainforest in Qld from about Cooktown to just south of Townsville. This whole group (the Swordgrass Browns) does not feed on grass but on the sedge *Gahnia*.

Recorded Host Plants: *Gahnia sieberiana* (Swordgrass), occasionally just outside of the rainforest *G. aspera* is used.

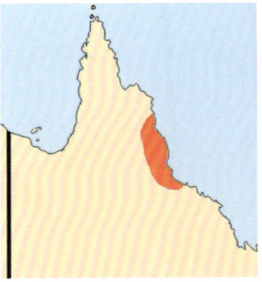

Gahnia sieberiana forms dense stands in swampy coastal areas and near springs. It is possibly the tallest of all *Gahnia* species reaching 3m in height including the flower spike. Occurs from Torres Strait, Qld, to SA. In the upland rainforests of north Qld it grows in open areas, especially along tracks where there is high light available. If a track closes over the *Gahnia* will eventually die.

Gahnia aspera is one species in the genus that does not grow in swampy areas, often being found in open forest or sometimes in vine thickets near the coast where there is constant high humidity but not necessarily high rainfall. It is a host plant for the Helena Brown when it grows just a short distance from upland rainforest.

Swordgrass Brown *Tisiphone abeona*

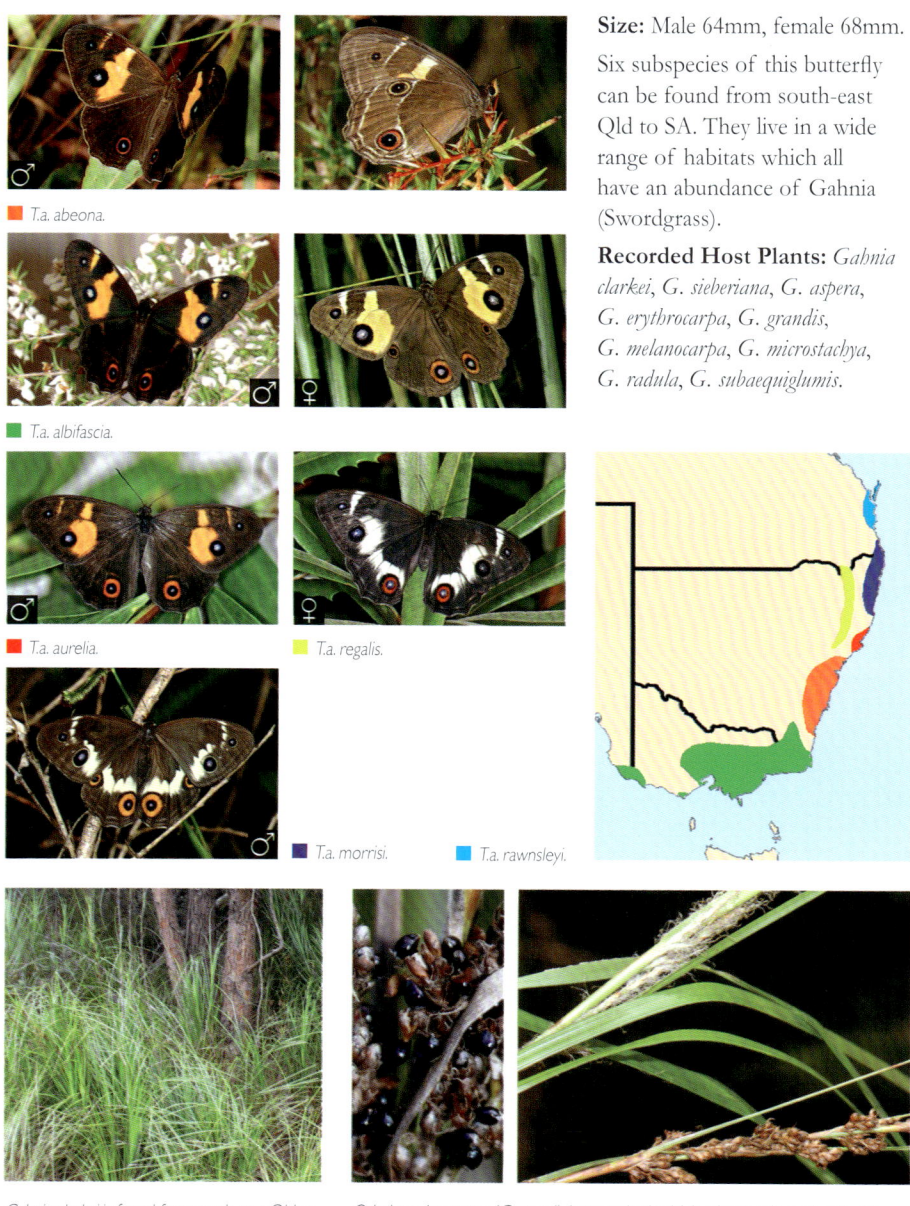

- T.a. abeona.
- T.a. albifascia.
- T.a. aurelia.
- T.a. regalis.
- T.a. morrisi.
- T.a. rawnsleyi.

Size: Male 64mm, female 68mm.

Six subspecies of this butterfly can be found from south-east Qld to SA. They live in a wide range of habitats which all have an abundance of Gahnia (Swordgrass).

Recorded Host Plants: *Gahnia clarkei, G. sieberiana, G. aspera, G. erythrocarpa, G. grandis, G. melanocarpa, G. microstachya, G. radula, G. subaequiglumis.*

Gahnia clarkei is found from south-east Qld to SA and is often used as a host by Swordgrass Browns, especially in coastal areas.

Gahnia melanocarpa (*G. grandis* in some herbaria) is a large, robust plant that forms large stands in permanently moist areas, occurring from the Richmond River, NSW, to Tas.

Spotted Alpine Xenica *Oreixenica orichora*

O.o. orichora.

O.o. paludosa.

Size: Male 34mm, female 35mm.

Two subspecies:
- *O.o. orichora* in southern NSW.
- *O.o. paludosa* in Tas.

This is a high-altitude butterfly, being found above 1,200m in NSW and above 750m in Tas.

Females have an unusual habit of dropping the eggs onto grass as they fly over.

Recorded Host Plants: *Poa fawcettiae* (Smooth Blue Snowgrass), *P. hiemata*.

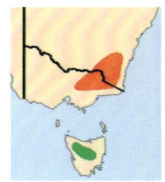

Small Alpine Xenica *Oreixenica latialis*

O.l. latialis.

Size: Male 29mm, female 29mm.

Another high-altitude butterfly occurring from 1,000–2,100m with similar egg-laying habits as the previous species. Restricted to the high areas of south-east Australia. There are two subspecies:
- *O.l. latialis* in NSW and Vic.
- *O.l. theddora* in northern Vic.

Recorded Host Plants: *Poa hiemata* (Soft Snowgrass).

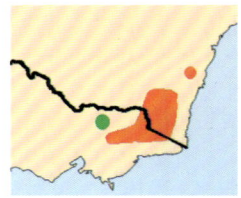

O.l. theddora

Tasmanian Alpine Xenica *Oreixenica ptunarra*

Size: Male 32mm, female 34mm.

This small butterfly is restricted to altitudes above 750m. Like most species in the cold southern regions, the adults fly only in the summer months.

Recorded Host Plants: *Poa gunnii* (Tasmanian Snow Grass), *P. labillardieri* (Common Tussock-grass), *P. rodwayi* (Velvet Tussock-grass) and probably other related species of grass. It is interesting to note that quite a few of these grasses are sold in nurseries and used in landscaping in south-east Australia and Tasmania.

Silver Xenica *Oreixenica lathoniella*

■ *O.l. lathoniella.*

■ *O.l. barnardi.*

■ *O.l. herceus.*

■ *O.l. laranda.*

Size: Male 36mm, female 36mm.

The most widespread member of the genus, ranging from the Qld border to Tas. On the mainland it is found between 700–1,500m, and in Tas from sea-level to 1,000m.

Recorded Host Plants: *Microlaena stipoides* (Weeping Grass), *Poa ensiformis* (Sword Tussock-grass), *P. labillardierei* (Common Tussock-grass). All these grasses are available from native plant nurseries.

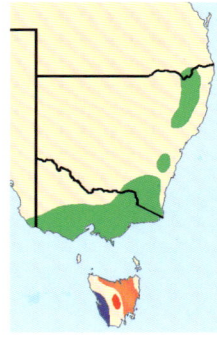

FAMILY NYMPHALIDAE – SUBFAMILY SATYRINAE   BROWNS

Orange Alpine Xenica *Oreixenica correae*

Size: Male 42mm, female 44mm.

Another butterfly that prefers high-altitude habitats, being found from 1,200–1,800m in southern NSW and Vic. Adults fly from December to April.

Recorded Host Plants: *Poa ensiformis*, *P. hiemata*.

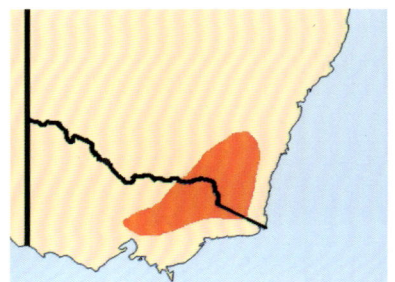

Striped Xenica *Oreixenica kershawi*

■ *O.k. kershawi*

■ *O.k. ella*

■ *O.k. kanunda*

Size: Male 42mm, female 44mm.

Found at altitudes from about 500–1,200m and usually in eucalypt forest. It is interesting to note that most of the Xenicas are in the uplands of southern NSW and Vic.

Recorded Host Plants: *Poa tenera* (Slender Tussock-grass), *Tetrarrhena juncea* (Wiry Rice Grass).

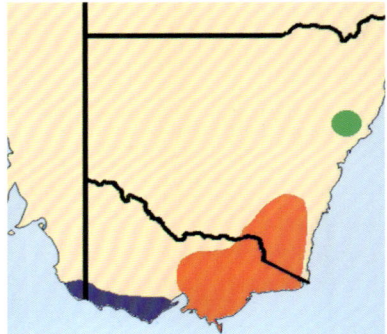

Ringed Xenica *Geitoneura acantha*

Size: Male 48mm, female 52mm.

The only member of the genus that ranges north, well into Qld, and is found on the Blackdown Tableland, west of Rockhampton. It occurs from there down the east coast (extending to tableland areas) to SA.

Recorded Host Plants: *Microlaena stipoides* (Weeping Grass), *Poa sieberiana* (Snow Grass), *P. tenera* (Slender Tussock-grass), *Themeda triandra* (Kangaroo-grass, possibly the most widespread grass in Australia).

Klug's Xenica *Geitoneura klugii*

Size: Male 45mm, female 49mm.

Favours a wide range of habitats from semi-arid areas in southern parts of the continent to an altitude of 1,400m in the northern end of its range in northern NSW and Qld. There are two forms – ■ dark and ■ pale – but the distribution of these forms does not match with the usual subspecies which are generally isolated by some geological barrier. With this species the dark form is in the east and the west of southern Australia, also Tas, and the pale form is in between these dark populations. Perhaps the pale form appeared in the Great Australian Bight and for some reason this colour favoured survival and it has spread out in both directions.

Recorded Host Plants: *Austrostipa flavescens* (Coast Spear-grass), *Poa labillardierei* (Common Tussock-grass), *P. morrisii* (Velvet Tussock-grass), *P. queenslandica*, *P. sieberiana* (Grey Tussock-grass), *P. tenera* (Slender Tussock-grass), *Joycea pallida* (Red-anther Wallaby-grass), *Themeda triandra* (Kangaroo-grass), *Ehrharta calycina*, *E. longiflora*, *Brachypodium distachyon*, *Vulpia*.

FAMILY NYMPHALIDAE – SUBFAMILY SATYRINAE BROWNS

Western Xenica *Geitoneura minyas*

Size: Male 36mm, female 40mm.

The Western Xenica, as the name suggests, is restricted to the south-west of WA. It is very common and is found in eucalypt and acacia woodland in both the high-rainfall and semi-arid locations. The native host plants are not known but it probably uses a number of species.

Recorded Host Plants: *Ehrharta longiflora* (Annual Veld Grass). This is a widespread introduced grass that is now found over most of southern Australia.

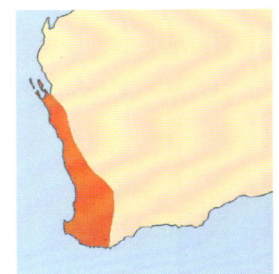

Leprea Brown *Nesoxenica leprea*

Size: Male 40mm, female 42mm.

Confined to Tas and has two subspecies. Habitat ranges from sea-level to over 1,200m. In the cool temperate beech forest the butterfly is usually seen in clearings and along streams.

Recorded Host Plants: *Uncinia tenella* (Delicate Hook-sedge).

  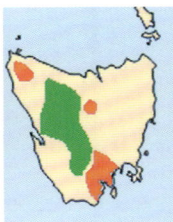

■ *N.l. leprea.*

■ *N.l. elia.*

Forest Brown *Argynnina cyrila*

Size: Male 42mm, female 44mm.

Adults fly swiftly, especially the males. Has a range of habitats from sea-level to about 1,500m. Males tend to settle 3–6m above the ground; females fly with the usual bobbing flight of Browns in general.

Recorded Host Plants: Larvae feed on various species of *Poa*.

Hobart Brown *Argynnina hobartia*

A.h. hobartia.

A.h. tasmanica.

A.h. montana

Size: Male 36mm, female 40mm.

Restricted to Tas. There are three subspecies:
- ■ *A.h. hobartia* in the east.
- ■ *A.h. tasmanica* in the west.
- ■ *A.h. montana*, which is an alpine butterfly and is larger than the others.

Overall this species ranges from sea-level to about 1,000m in a wide variety of habitats.

Recorded Host Plants:
Lolium perenne (English Ryegrass) and possibly *Poa labillardieri* and *Austrodanthonia*.

Wonder Brown *Heteronympha mirifica*

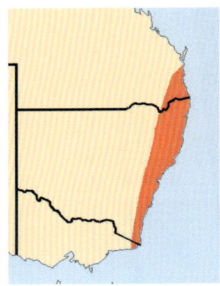

Size: Male 64mm, female 70mm.

The female is completely different from the male, which is very similar to the male of the Common Brown. This is the only butterfly in this group that shows these contrasting markings between the sexes. Habitat is along the edge of rainforest and adjacent eucalypt forest. Males

are seen first in October or November but females do not appear until later. Females live for quite a long time; they hatch in spring but do not start laying eggs until December or January and continue laying up to April.

Recorded Host Plants: *Oplismenus aemulus* (Basket Grass), *Oplismenus imbecillis* (Creeping Beard Grass), *Oplismenus undulatifolius* (Wavy Leaf Basket Grass), *Oplismenus*, *Ottochloa gracillima*, **Pennisetum clandestinum* (Kikuyu Grass).

Oplismenus compositus is a small, soft grass that grows in shade or part shade on the edge of rainforest or along streams. This is a typical host plant for many of the Browns.

Common Brown *Heteronympha merope*

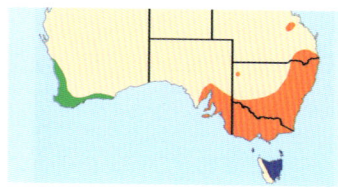

■ *H.m. merope* is found from the Blackdown Tableland in Qld to SA.

Size: Male 68mm, female 75mm.

Has a wide distribution, ranging from the Blackdown Tableland in Qld to SA, then also in south-west WA. Three subspecies have been named but as is obvious from the photographs there is not a great deal of difference between them.

Recorded Host Plants: *Cynodon dactylon*, *Microlaena stipoides*, *Poa labillardieri*, *P. poiformis*, *P. queenslandica*, *P. sieberiana*, *P. tenera*, *Themeda triandra*, **Brachypodium distachyon*, **Bromus catharticus*, *Ehrharta erecta, *Pennisetum.

■ *H.m. duboulayi* occurs in south-west WA.

■ *H.m. salazar* is found in the eastern half of Tas.

Shouldered Brown *Heteronympha penelope*

■ H.p. penelope.

Size: 68mm.

Found from the Border Ranges, Qld, to Tas. At the northern end of its range it occurs in the mountains up to 1,600m, but in Tas it can be found down to sea-level. Unlike most butterflies, the males of this species are similar in size to the females, sometimes larger; they stake out territories and pursue passing females. As well as the type species there are three smaller subspecies, two of which occur in Tas.

Recorded Host Plants: *Poa*, *Austrodanthonia penicillata* (Slender Wallaby-grass), *A. pilosa* (Velvet Wallaby-grass), *Themeda triandra* (Kangaroo-grass).

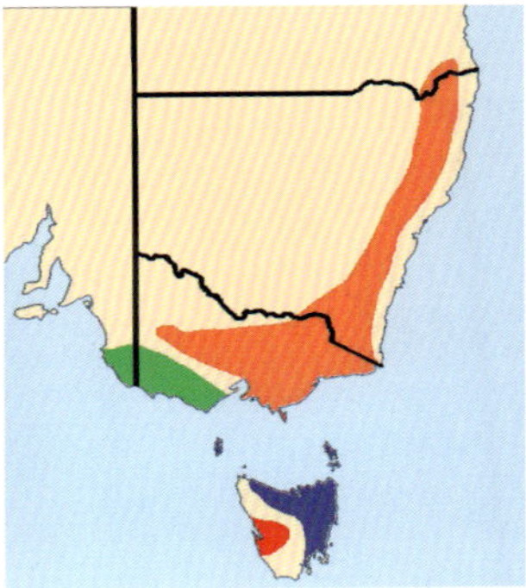

■ H.p. alope.

■ H.p. diemeni.

■ H.p. panope.

FAMILY NYMPHALIDAE – SUBFAMILY SATYRINAE — BROWNS

Spotted Brown *Heteronympha paradelpha*

Size: Male 52mm, female 58mm.

Found from the southern Border Ranges of Qld to central Vic. In the northern part of its range it is found in the mountains, but further south it occurs down to sea-level.

Recorded Host Plants: *Microlaena stipoides* (Weeping Grass), *Poa labillardierei* (Common Tussock-grass), *P. sieberiana*, *P. tenera*, *Sylvipoa queenslandica* (Queensland Poa).

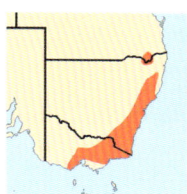

Banks's Brown *Heteronympha banksii*

Size: Male 54mm, female 58mm.

A common butterfly along the Great Dividing Range from about the Bunya Mountains in Qld to Vic. The larvae take all winter and spring to mature, changing into pupae in December. The adult butterflies emerge from January to April. There are three subspecies:

- 🟧 *H.b. banksii* in NSW and Vic.
- 🟩 *H.b. nevina* in Qld.
- 🟦 *H.b. mariposa* in western Vic.

H.b. banksii.

Recorded Host Plants: *Poa labillardierei* (Common Tussock-grass), *P. queenslandica*, *P. sieberiana* (Grey Tussock-grass), *P. tenera* (Slender Tussock-grass), *Tetrarrhena juncea* (Wiry Rice Grass), *Carex longebrachiata* (Drooping Sedge).

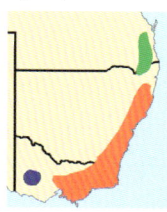

H.b. nevina.

FAMILY NYMPHALIDAE – SUBFAMILY SATYRINAE BROWNS 191

Solander's Brown *Heteronympha solandri*

Size: Male 56mm, female 60mm.

Common in the mountains and ranges of the south-eastern highlands of Australia from 300–1,600m. Found in subalpine woodland and montane eucalypt open forest with a grassy understorey. Adults are most abundant in January and February.

Recorded Host Plants: *Poa labillardieri* (Common Tussock-grass), *Tetrarrhena juncea* (Forest wire-grass).

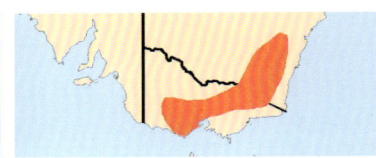

Bright-eyed Brown *Heteronympha cordace*

Size: Male 48mm, female 52mm.

Found from 600–1,800m in south-east mainland Australia and from sea-level to 1,000m in Tas. Usually occurs in swampy areas and along creeks where the sedge host plants grow.

Recorded Host Plants: *Carex appressa* (Tall Sedge), *C. gaudichaudiana* (Fen Sedge).

■ *H.c. cordace.*

■ *H.c. kurena.*

■ *H.c. legana.*   ■ *H.c. wilsoni.*

SKIPPERS, FLATS, AWLS and DARTS
Family Hesperiidae

Members of this group are the most difficult of all butterflies to identify because the majority of them are small, fly very fast and have similar black and orange markings. The few that stand out are the Flats and Awls, which are larger and generally have very distinctive markings.

One thing that stands out when observing these butterflies is that they have a very long proboscis, completely out of proportion to their size when compared to other butterflies. This enables them to feed on a wide range of flowers that have nectar not accessible to other groups.

Unlike most other butterfly larvae, those of the Hesperiidae family make shelters in which they hide when not feeding. This is a characteristic generally attributed to moths rather than to butterflies. Some taxonomists consider this group to actually fit somewhere between moths and butterflies. The fact that the vast majority of them fly during the day links them more to butterflies.

Many of the Skippers and Darts have a very distinctive way in which they hold their wings when resting; the hindwings are flat and the forewings slant up at an angle, rather like an F18 fighter jet, and they appear to move off at a similar speed. Getting a good photograph is definitely the best way to identify a member of this group.

Larval shelter of Regent Skipper opened up to view what is inside. In this case a pupa that is just about to hatch. The shelter is made using silk to bind the edges of the two leaves together.

Typical resting position of a Skipper.

Skippers feeding, showing the length of their proboscis in relation to their size.

Broad-banded Awl *Hasora hurama*

H.h. hurama.

H.h. hurama.

Size: Male 48mm, female 50mm.

Two subspecies:
- *H.h. hurama* from Torres Strait to about Sarina, Qld.
- *H.h. territorialis* in the top end of NT.

Most often found along the edge of mangroves where the main host plant grows.

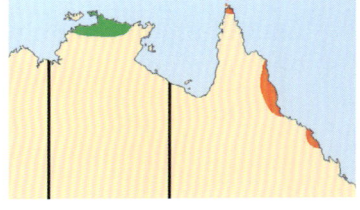

Host Plants: *Derris* sp. Tolga, *Derris rubrocalyx* Claudie River, *Derris trifoliata*.

Best Garden Host Plant: *Derris* sp. Tolga.

Derris trifoliata is the main host plant for the Broad-banded Awl. It is a coastal species that usually grows on the beach or just behind mangroves where it is only reached by saltwater during high tides. It occurs from South-East Asia to Australia where it is recorded from near Darwin, NT (and is most likely also in the Kimberley region, WA), then around the northern coast line almost to Rockhampton, Qld. When growing on the beach it forms a large prostrate plant that almost smothers other low beach vegetation. The flowers can be either pale pink or white or pink.

Broad-banded Awl *Hasora hurama*

Derris rubrocalyx Claudie River is found in monsoon and lowland rainforest from Cape York to about Cooktown, Qld. It can be easily recognised by the unusual corky spurs that cover the stems when they grow to 1cm or more in diameter. The flowers can be white or pale pink, new growth is always green. This is a large vine that requires some control when planted in a garden situation.

Derris sp. Tolga appears to be restricted to rainforests in the wet tropics of north Qld and mostly in the uplands. The flowers are a much brighter pink than the other two species and the new growth is bright red. This is a beautiful vine and makes a very attractive hedge when grown on a fence.

Common Banded Awl *Hasora chromus*

Size: Male 48mm, female 48mm.

Found from the top end of WA, around the coast and down to northern NSW. Inhabits coastal, monsoon and gallery rainforest.

Host Plants: *Pongamia pinnata, P. pinnata* var. *minor*

Best Garden Host Plant: *Pongamia pinnata* var. *minor*

Pongamia pinnata is a strand plant that occurs at least from near Darwin, NT, around the north coast and down to about Mackay, Qld. It usually grows as a large spreading tree on the beach or sometimes along the banks of streams within the tidal zone. Flowers can be white or pale pink.

Pongamia pinnata var. *minor* is a small tree that grows along streams on Cape York Peninsula and especially those that flow into the Gulf of Carpentaria, including the Mitchell River system. It is deciduous, the foliage turning golden-yellow in spring before falling and being replaced by copper-coloured new foliage.

Narrow-banded Awl *Hasora khoda*

Size: Male 48mm, female 50mm.

Confined to south-east Qld and most of eastern NSW. It is found in all types of rainforest where the host plant vines grow.

Host Plants: *Callerya australis*, *C. megasperma*, **Wisteria sinensis*.

Best Garden Host Plant: Either of the two species of *Callerya* mentioned above.

Callerya australis is a large vine that is found in low- to mid-altitude rainforest in south-east Qld and northern NSW. The flowers and the bright red seed make it quite a showy plant. It is readily available from native plant nurseries in the area where it grows.

Callerya megasperma is a large vine found from Fraser Island, Qld, to northern NSW in rainforest at all altitudes. It has huge seeds that can be 4cm across. It is readily available from native plant nurseries in southern Qld and northern NSW.

Green Awl *Hasora discolora*

Size: Male 48mm, female 50mm.

Found in low- to mid-altitude rainforest from Cape York, Qld, to northern NSW. Flies very swiftly but often visits flowers where it can be observed more closely. The larvae form shelters by cutting and folding leaves.

Host Plants: *Mucuna gigantea*, occasionally *M. novoguineensis*.

Best Garden Host Plant: *Mucuna gigantean*.

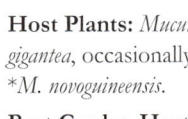
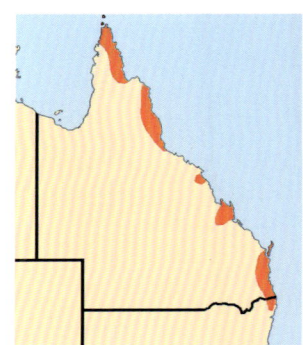

Mucuna gigantea is a very large vine that can develop stems more than 30cm thick, so if it is grown in a garden severe control needs to be employed. It is found in lowland rainforest from the Kimberley region of WA to northern NSW. The very large flowers are quite spectacular but beware of the seed pods, especially when ripe, as they are covered with sharp hairs and should never be touched with your hands.

Peacock Awl *Allora doleschallii*

Size: Male 45mm, female 50mm.

A spectacular skipper, especially the male which has iridescent green on the inside of the upper wing surface. It is found in coastal and monsoon rainforest as well as in vine thickets, where the host plant grows, from Torres Strait to about Townsville.

Host Plant: *Stigmaphyllon australiense*, (*Ryssopterys timorensis*).

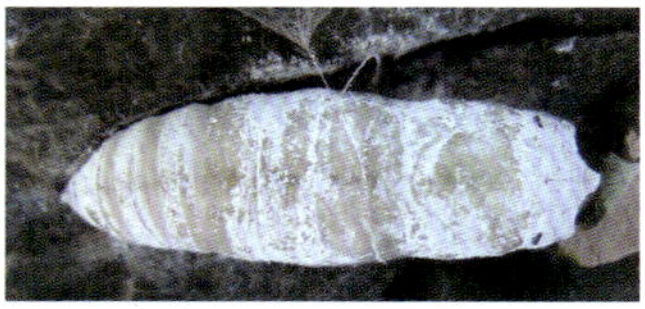

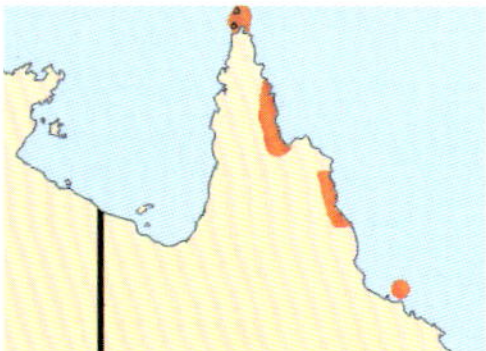

Peacock Awl *Allora doleschallii*

Stigmaphyllon australiense (*Rhyssopterys timorensis*) is a medium-sized vine that grows in coastal or monsoon rainforest but more commonly in vine thickets, both deciduous and semi-deciduous. It is quite a showy vine with bright yellow flowers and well worthy of cultivation. There are two forms; the one that grows in the vine thickets on the basalt flows around Mt Garnett has silver hairs on the leaves that glisten in the sun; the form from other areas tends to have almost no hairs on the upper surface and the leaves appear green, although the under surface has some silver hairs.

Greater Peacock Awl *Allora major*

Size: Male 50mm, female 55mm.

Recorded in Australia only in the Iron Range area of Cape York Peninsula, Qld, although its range probably extends from about the Pascoe River to the Rocky River, where the same habitat exists. It is larger than the Peacock Awl and the iridescent green on the upper surface of the wings is more intense.

Host Plants: In Papua New Guinea the larvae feed on *Corynocarpus cribbianus* so it is assumed that in Australia it will do the same. On Cape York Peninsula the range of *Corynocarpus* is from the Pascoe River to the Rocky River, including the McIlwraith Range.

Brown Awl *Badamia exclamationis*

Size: Male 48mm, female 52mm.

Has a very wide distribution, from the central coast of WA, across the top and down the east coast to Vic. Inhabits Brigalow forest (which is almost extinct now) and other acacia woodland, as well as coastal and monsoon rainforest. Large migrations occur from time to time.

Host Plants: *Terminalia catappa* (a strand plant), *T. oblongata* (an acacia forest plant), *T. sericocarpa* (a rainforest plant, and most likely many other species of *Terminalia*), occasionally *Pongamia pinnata*, *Stigmaphyllon australiense*.

Best Garden Host Plant: *Terminalia sericocarpa* as it will grow in almost any situation. It a medium to large tree and not suitable for suburban gardens.

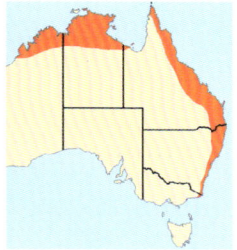

Terminalia catappa is a large spreading tree, occurring only along beaches above the high-tide mark. In spite of this it will grow well away from the coast and is commonly used as a street tree in north Qld and even on the Gold Coast. The leaves are very large and turn bright red in spring before they drop and are replaced almost immediately. The edible fruit are called Beach Almonds.

Regent Skipper *Euschemon rafflesia*

E.r. rafflesia.

Size: Male 58mm, female 65mm.

A very noticeable butterfly with bright yellow markings on a black background. Usually sits with wings spread so the wing patterns can be easily seen. Inhabits both lowland and upland rainforest where various species of their *Wilkiea* host plants grow. *Wilkiea pubescens* often grows just outside the rainforest and it is on these plants that the female prefers to lay. The subspecies *alba* occasionally has the yellow markings white or cream.

Host Plants: *Wilkiea austro-queenslandica*, *W. huegeliana*, *W. macrophylla* in southern populations, *W. angustifolia*, *W. cordata*, *W. pubescens* in north Qld.

Best Garden Host Plant: *Wilkiea macrophylla* or *W. pubescens*.

E.r. alba.

Larval shelter on *Wilkiea macrophylla*.

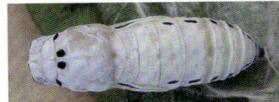

Wilkiea angustifolia is restricted to the wet tropical rainforest of north Qld where it grows in mid- to high-altitude very wet rainforest. Like most *Wilkiea* species the leaves are stiff and serrated, except on very old plants. It is a very common understorey shrub but for some unknown reason the Regent Skipper does not breed everywhere that it occurs.

Pupa about to hatch.

Regent Skipper *Euschemon rafflesia*

Wilkiea macrophylla is the most commonly used host of the Regent Skipper in low- to mid-altitude rainforest. The southern form has very stiff leaves with sharp serrations and grows to about 5m high. The north Qld form, the two images on the right, is quite different and is perhaps a different species.

Wilkiea pubescens is a small to medium shrub that has stiff foliage usually with a furry feel. It occurs in Qld from about Cooktown to Bowen in low- to mid-altitude rainforest. The leaves are quite sharply serrated and it is a much favoured host plant for the Regent Skipper when it grows just outside the rainforest in a fully exposed position. It has black fruit similar to that of all *Wilkiea* species.

Wilkiea huegeliana looks very similar to *W. pubescens* and is confined to an area between about Gympie, Qld, and southern NSW.

FAMILY HESPERIIDAE – SUBFAMILY PYRGINAE FLATS 203

Purple Dusk Flat *Chaetocneme porphyropis*

Size: Male 58mm, female 62mm.

Confined to the wet tropical rainforest in lowland and upland areas of north Qld from about Cooktown to Townsville. Females tend to lay their eggs on small saplings in the understorey of the rainforest.

Host Plants: *Neolitsea dealbata*, *Litsea leefeana*, *Cryptocarya grandis*, *Endiandra compressa*, **Cinnamomum camphora* and most likely many other species of laurels that occur in the rainforest within the butterfly's range.

Best Garden Host Plant: *Neolitsea dealbata*.

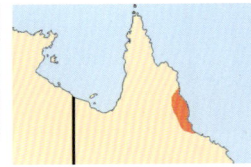

Larval shelter.

Small larva, shelter turned over so it can be viewed.

Neolitsea dealbata is a very common tree in the rainforests of eastern Australia, ranging from Cape York, Qld, to central NSW. The new growth is pendulous and covered with white hairs. As the leaves mature this white colouring remains on the underside. In a disturbed rainforest this plant can make up about a third of the seedlings and saplings in the understorey.

Rare Red-eye *Chaetocneme denitza*

Size: Male 52mm, female 60mm.

Found from the Kimberley region in WA to south-east Qld in open eucalypt forest, savannah woodland and along streams where its various host plants grow. The host plants for this butterfly are very common but it seems to breed only in selected areas.

Host Plants: *Eucalyptus, Lophostemon confertus, L. grandiflorus, L. suaveolens, Planchonia careya, Thespesia populnea, Xanthostemon chrysanthus.*

Best Garden Host Plant: *Planchonia careya.*

Planchonia careya (Cocky Apple) has a range that is almost identical to that of the Rare Red-eye, so it is highly likely that it is the main host plant. It grows in open eucalypt forest, forms colonies from suckers and has very showy flowers.

Lophostemon confertus is a medium to large tree that is found from near Cooktown, Qld, to southern NSW, usually in upland wet sclerophyll forest adjacent to rainforest or along streams.

Common Red-eye *Chaetocneme beata*

Size: Male 54mm, female 60mm.

A rainforest species that is found from about Cooktown, Qld, to southern NSW. From the number of unrelated host plants recorded for this butterfly you could expect it to be found on many more species of plants.

Host Plants: *Cryptocarya, Litsea, Neolitsea, Acmena, Commersonia, Croton, Eupomatia, Exocarpos, Glochidion, Lophostemon, Melicope, Melodorum, Smilax, Toechima, *Annona, *Cinnamomum, *Hibiscus.*

Best Garden Host Plant: *Cryptocarya, Litsea* or *Neolitsea.*

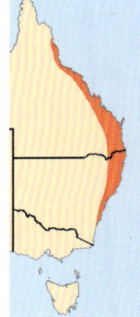

Larval shelter.

Cryptocarya cunninghamii is very widespread, being found from the Kimberley region in WA, across the top end of NT and from Torres Strait to Ingham, Qld, in low- to mid-altitude rainforest.

Banded Red-eye *Chaetocneme critomedia*

Size: Male 56mm, female 65mm.

Range restricted to Cape York Peninsula, Qld, where it is found from Torres Strait to Bathurst Bay inhabiting riparian or coastal rainforest. This species also has a wide range of host plants with perhaps those in the Lauraceae family being preferred.

Host Plants: *Blepharocarya, Macaranga, Cinnamomum, Cryptocarya, Endiandra, Litsea, Neolitsea, Syzygium, Commersonia, *Annona.*

Best Garden Host Plant: It is very difficult to nominate a special host plant but *Litsea breviumbellata* is often used.

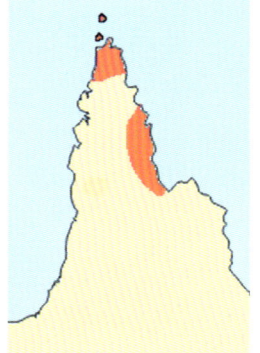

Litsea breviumbellata occurs in rainforest and nearby eucalypt forest in Qld from Torres Strait to about Townsville. It is a small tree usually less than 10m high. Flowering can occur when 2m or more high. Twigs and new growth are covered in short rusty hairs which is a fairly distinctive feature.

FAMILY HESPERIIDAE – SUBFAMILY PYRGINAE   **FLATS**   207

Eastern Flat *Netrocoryne repanda*

Size: Male 45mm, female 50mm.

Found from Iron Range on Cape York Peninsula, Qld, to Vic, extending inland to wherever rainforest occurs and sometimes in eucalypt forest where the *Brachychiton* host plant occurs. There are two subspecies:
- *N.r. repanda* from about Mackay, Qld, to Vic.
- *N.r. expansa* in Qld from Iron Range to about Townsville.

Host Plants: *Cryptocarya, Endiandra, Litsea, Neolitsea, Alectryon, Argyrodendron, Brachychiton, Callicoma, Elaeocarpus, Notelaea, Scolopia, *Prunus.*

Best Garden Host Plants: *Cryptocarya* or *Litsea* in the tropics, *Callicoma serratifolia* near Sydney, *Brachychiton populneus* in inland NSW.

N.r. repanda.

  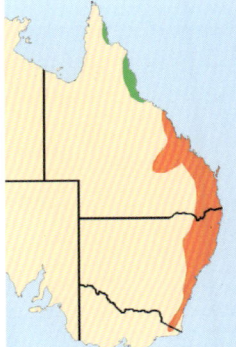

N.r. expansa.

Callicoma serratifolia is a small tree that is found in moist to wet rainforest from Kroombit Tops, west of Gladstone, Qld, to southern NSW. It is often available from native plant nurseries.

Pied Flat *Tagiades japetus*

Size: Male 38mm, female 42mm.

Occurs in Qld from Torres Strait to about Maryborough in lowland and monsoon rainforest. Male and females are almost identical. Records show it was first found as far south as Byfield in 1979 but the author observed it at Eurimbulah, north of Bundaberg, in the 1960s. This is always a problem with distribution maps produced only from official collections. If a species occurs in say three locations along the Qld coast and the host plant and suitable habitat in many more places in between, it is almost certain that the butterfly will be in some of these places as well, especially with species not dependent on ants.

Host Plant: *Dioscorea transversa*, (Native Yam).

Best Garden Host Plant: *Dioscorea transversa*.

Female flowers.
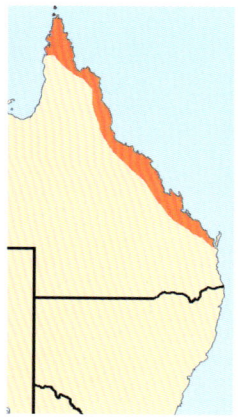

Male flowers.

Dioscorea transversa is a small vine that is widespread, occurring from the Kimberley region of WA around the coast and down to about Sydney, NSW. It is found in a wide range of rainforest types but usually at low to mid-altitudes. The triangular winged fruit are very distinctive and another feature is the very different male and female flowers.

Western Flat *Exometoeca nycteris*

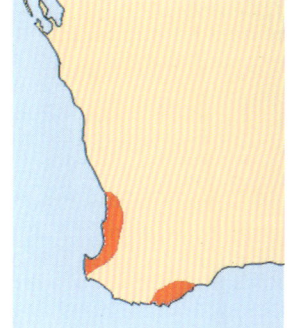

Size: Male 32mm, female 33mm.

Restricted to the south-west corner of WA. Found in mixed jarrah-sheoak forest and open woodland with a heath understorey.

Host Plants: *Tetratheca hispidissima* near Albany, *T. hirsuta* near Perth.

Best Garden Host Plant: Either of the above.

Tetratheca hirsuta is a small sprawling shrub that usually grows to only about 1m high. There are more than 30 species of *Tetratheca* in WA so it is likely that the Western Flat will breed on more than just the two recorded ones.

Montane Ochre *Trapezites phigalioides*

Size: Male 30mm, female 32mm.

Found from south-east Qld to western Vic in open forest usually above 300m altitude, extending into subalpine woodland in central and northern NSW, where it occurs up to 1,400m.

Host Plant: *Lomandra filiformis*.

Lomandra filiformis (Wattle Mat Rush) is widespread in eastern Australia, from northern Qld through NSW to Vic as far west as the Grampians. This species is generally found growing in open forest and woodland areas and will tolerate much drier conditions than *Lomandra longifolia*.

It is a compact perennial herb growing up to 50cm tall in sparse clumps up to 20cm in diameter with a semi-arching habit. The dull green to bluish-green leaves are stiff, approximately 3–5mm in width, with inrolled margins. Each leaf is tipped with one to three tiny pale brown points.

Heath Ochre *Trapezites phigalia*

Size: Male 32mm, female 34mm.

Range extends from about Gympie, Qld, to western Vic, with an outlying population in Qld on the Blackdown Tableland, west of Rockhampton. Found in eucalypt woodland and open forest as well as coastal heathland.

Host Plants: *Lomandra densiflora, L. fibrata, L. filiformis, L. glauca, L. multiflora, L. nana, L. obliqua, L. sororia.*

Best Garden Host Plant: Any of the above species that occur in a particular location.

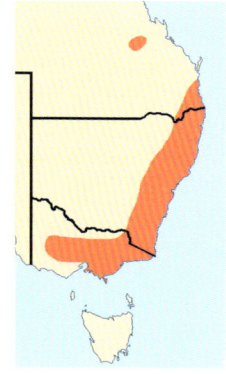

Silver-studded Ochre *Trapezites iacchoides*

Size: Male 33mm, female 38mm.

Occurs from south-east Qld to eastern Vic in open eucalypt forest in both coastal and montane areas. The host plant usually grows in damp areas or on banks of streams so this is where the butterfly will most often be seen.

Host Plant: *Lomandra longifolia*.

Lomandra longifolia is widely used in the landscaping industry. It forms a large dense plant that will choke out any competition. If you have planted it in the wrong place you will find it very difficult to remove after about 10 years. Very widespread, it occurs in eastern Australia from Cape York, Qld, to Tas.

It has beautifully perfumed flowers and in the right place makes a nice plant. It grows naturally on stream banks where it does a good job in preventing erosion.

Northern Silver Ochre *Trapezites maheta*

Size: 32mm.

Found from about Cooktown in Qld to central NSW in eucalypt forest, coastal heath and along the edge of rainforest.

Host Plants: *Lomandra hystrix*, *L. confertifolia*, *L. filiformis*, *L. multiflora*.

Best Garden Host Plant: *Lomandra hystrix*.

Lomandra filiformis occurs in the top end of NT, then from Cape York, Qld, to SA, but not in Tas. It is a fairly small *Lomandra* compared to *L. longifolia* and *L. hystrix*. The top right image shows typical coastal habitat for it in north Qld.

Southern Silver Ochre *Trapezites praxedes*

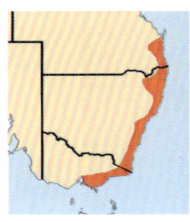

Size: Male 31mm, female 32mm.

Resembles Northern Silver Ochre so closely that it is virtually impossible to tell the difference between the two species in the field or from a photograph; even with pinned specimens it is very difficult.

Host Plant: *Lomandra obliqua* in NSW, occasionally *L. confertifolia*, *L. longifolia*.

Lomandra obliqua is found from about Rockhampton, Qld, to southern NSW, usually in heath-type country on sand or sandstone. It is a small plant with stiff blue/green foliage that grows to about 60cm high.

Sandstone Ochre *Trapezites taori*

Size: Male 38mm, female 42mm.

As the name suggests, found in sandstone habitats. Restricted to sandstone formations south-west of Rockhampton, Qld, including Blackdown Tableland. The host plant is a very fine-leaved *Lomandra* that grows in cracks and crevices and along ledges.

Host Plants: *Lomandra confertifolia*. Because of its very attractive form this plant was extensively cultivated by nurseries about 20 years ago. Like many plants from sandstone areas the water requirements are quite high (water seeps through sandstone and often provides a permanent supply, even in drought conditions). Many mass plantings were carried out but most were unsuccessful when the plants died from lack of water.

Best Garden Host Plant: *Lomandra confertifolia*.

Ornate Ochre *Trapezites genevieveae*

Size: Male 34mm, female 35mm.

Found in south-east Qld and northern NSW in rainforest, both lowland and upland.

Host Plant: *Lomandra spicata*.

Lomandra spicata is found in both lowland and upland areas, especially along the edges of rainforest where it forms large colonies. The large, bright orange fruit are a very distinctive feature of this species.

It is very easy to grow in the garden and available from native plant nurseries.

Mallee Ochre *Trapezites sciron*

T.s. scrion.

T.s. eremicola.

Size: Male 32mm, female 36mm.

Two subspecies:
- *T.s. scrion* in the south-west corner of WA.
- *T.s. eremicola* on the Vic-SA border.

Found in heathland and mallee heath, usually on or near sand dunes where the host plants grow.

Host Plants: *Lomandra collina* for *T.s. eremicola*; *Lomandra caespitosa*, *Acanthocarpus canaliculatus* for *T.s. scrion*.

Best Garden Host Plant: Any of the above, depending upon location.

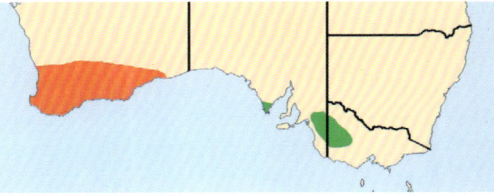

Atkins's Ochre *Trapezites atkinsi*

Size: Male 31mm, female 34mm.

Occurs in the south-west corner of WA, where it is found in wind-pruned coastal open heathland. The host plant is common along the coast from about Exmouth Gulf southwards, so there may be other populations further north than those recorded.

Host Plant: *Acanthocarpus preissii*.

Silver-spotted Ochre *Trapezites argenteoornatus*

Size: Male 26mm, female 29mm.

Occurs on the west coast of WA south of about Karratha in coastal heathland.

Host Plants: *Acanthocarpus preissii, A. robustus, A. verticillatus.*

Best Garden Host Plant: *Acanthocarpus preissii.*

Waterhouse's Ochre *Trapezites waterhousei*

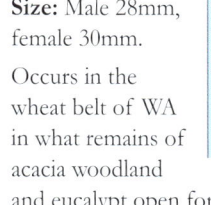

Size: Male 28mm, female 30mm.

Occurs in the wheat belt of WA in what remains of acacia woodland and eucalypt open forest. Because most of the habitat of this butterfly has been destroyed it is now found only in small scattered colonies.

Host Plant: *Xerolirion divaricata.*

Small Orange Ochre *Trapezites heteromacula*

Size: Male 29mm, female 32mm.

Restricted to the Qld tropics, ranging from Torres Strait to Townsville in eucalypt open forest and paperbark woodland in coastal areas.

Host Plants: *Lomandra filiformis*; rarely *L. longifolia.*

FAMILY HESPERIIDAE – SUBFAMILY TRAPEZITINAE   OCHRES   217

Yellow Ochre *Trapezites luteus*

T.l. leucon.

Size: Male 32mm, female 36mm.

Three subspecies:
- *T.l. luteus* is in SA.
- *T.l. glaucus* in eastern Tas.
- *T.l. leucon* from Blackdown Tableland, Qld, to Vic.

Found in eucalypt woodland, cypress-pine open woodland and grassland on the drier inland slopes and tablelands of the Great Dividing Range. In ACT occurs in subalpine woodland up to 1,700m.

Host Plants: Usually *Lomandra filiformis* in NSW and Vic, *L. longifolia* in Tas; also *L. confertifolia*, *L. densiflora*, *L. multiflora*.

Best Garden Host Plants: *Lomandra filiformis* in NSW and Vic, *L. longifolia* in Tas, *L. confertifolia* in SA.

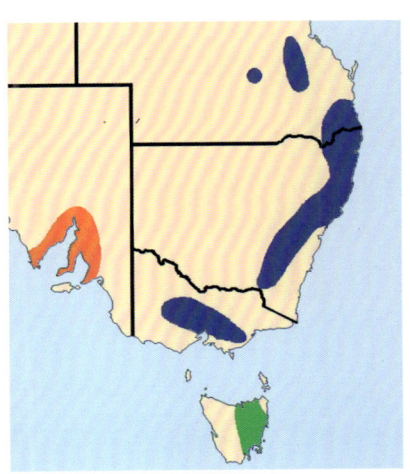

Macqueen's Ochre *Trapezites macqueeni*

Size: Male 32mm, female 35mm.

A tropical species that is found in Qld from about the Jardine River on Cape York Peninsula to a little south of Townsville in open eucalypt forest and woodland.

Host Plant: *Lomandra filiformis*.

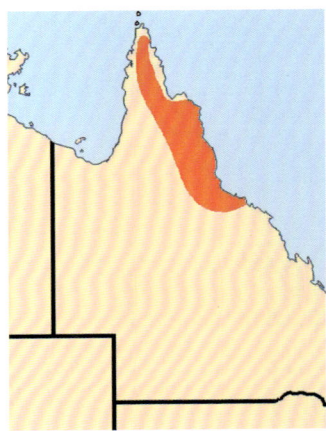

Black-ringed Ochre *Trapezites petalia*

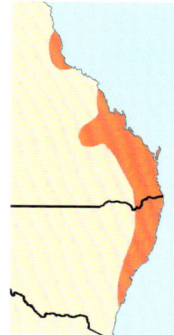

Size: Male 34mm, female 35mm.

Ranges from about Cooktown to Townsville then from central Qld to southern NSW in savannah woodland and eucalypt open forest with a heath understorey.

Host Plants: *Lomandra multiflora*; also *L. filiformis*, *L. longifolia*.

Best Garden Host Plant: *Lomandra multiflora*.

Lomandra multiflora is a small species that reaches about 50–80cm in height and usually grows as individual plants rather then forming large clumps. The flowers are very showy and occur in clusters from the base of the plant. This species is very widespread, ranging from the Gulf of Carpentaria to SA, where a smaller form grows.

OCHRES

Orange Ochre *Trapezites eliena*

Size: Male 38mm, female 42mm.

Widespread in eastern Australia, ranging from Torres Strait, Qld, to the SA border. Usually found in eucalypt woodland and open forest with a heath understorey, from low altitude to about 1,200m.

Host Plants: *Lomandra confertifolia*, *L. filiformis*, *L. longifolia*, *L. multiflora*.

Best Garden Host Plant: Any of the above.

Brown Ochre *Trapezites iacchus*

Size: Male 38mm, female 39mm.

Found from Torres Strait, Qld, to northern NSW and inhabits eucalypt open forest and savannah woodland, especially along streams where the host plant *Lomandra longifolia* grows.

Host Plants: *Lomandra hystrix*, *L. longifolia*, *L. multiflora*.

Best Garden Host Plant: *Lomandra longifolia*.

Splendid Ochre *Trapezites symmomus*

Size: Male 46mm, female 50mm.

Three subspecies:
- ■ *T.s. symmomus* from about Bundaberg, Qld, to eastern Vic.
- ■ *T.s. soma* in southern Vic.
- ■ *T.s. sombra* is a tropical subspecies that ranges in Qld from about Cooktown to Bowen.

Inhabits eucalypt woodland, open forest, tall open forest and rainforest edges in coastal areas.

Host Plants: *Lomandra longifolia*; occasionally *L. hystrix*, *L. filiformis*, *L. obliqua*, *L. spicata* and the related *Romnalda strobilacea*.

Best Garden Host Plant: *Lomandra longifolia*.

T.s. symmomus.

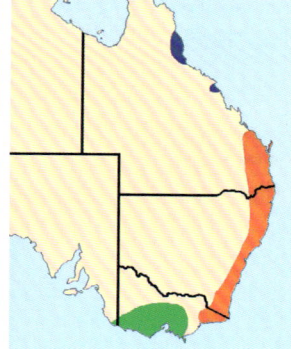

T.s. soma.

T.s. sombra.

FAMILY HESPERIIDAE – SUBFAMILY TRAPEZITINAE GRASS SKIPPERS 221

Barred Skipper *Dispar compacta*

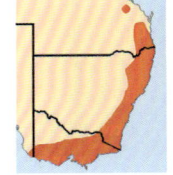

Size: Male 26mm, female 28mm.

Range extends from the Blackdown Tableland, west of Rockhampton, Qld, to SA in open forest and woodland where there are damp shady areas supporting the grass host plants.

Host Plants: *Poa labillardieri*, *P. queenslandica*, *P. sieberiana*, *P. tenera*; occasionally *Lomandra* or *Gahnia*.

Best Garden Host Plant: Any of the above *Poa* species.

Mottled Grass Skipper *Anisynta cynone*

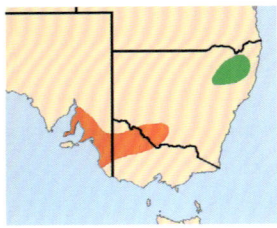

A.c. cynone.

Size: Male 26mm, female 28mm.

Two subspecies:
- ■ *A.c. gunneda* in northern NSW, away from the coast.
- ■ *A.c. cynone* from south-west NSW through north-west Vic to about Adelaide, SA.

Host Plants: *Austrostipa scabra*, *Cynodon dactylon*, *Poa sieberiana* in NSW; *Oryzopsis miliacea* in north-west Vic; *Brachypodium distachyon* in SA.

Best Garden Host Plant: Any of the above, depending upon location.

Chequered Grass Skipper *Anisynta tillyardi*

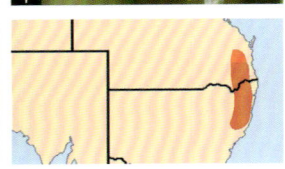

Size: Male 32mm, female 34mm.

Found in south-east Qld and northern NSW in eucalypt open forest up to 1,500m on or near the Great Dividing Range.

Host Plants: *Poa labillardieri*, *P. queenslandica*, *P. sieberiana*, *P. tenera*.

Best Garden Host Plant: Any of the above.

Mountain Grass Skipper *Anisynta monticolae*

Size: Male 24mm, female 28mm.

Confined to south-east Australia where it occurs in open eucalypt forest and subalpine woodland from about 600–1,070m on or near the Great Dividing Range.

Host Plant: *Poa tenera*.

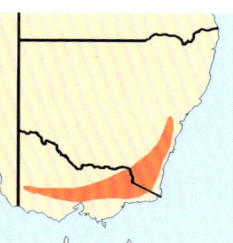

Two-brand Grass Skipper *Anisynta dominula*

A.d. dominula.

Size: Male 28mm, female 32mm.

Occurs in NSW, Vic and Tas, with two subspecies:
- *A.d. dominula* in NSW, Vic and eastern Tas.
- *A.d. pria* in western Tas.

Found in subalpine and alpine grassland and montane grassy open woodland, from about 600–1,600m on the mainland and from sea-level to 1,070m in Tas.

Host Plants: Large tussock-forming alpine snow grasses, *Poa* spp.

A.d. pria.

Two-spotted Grass Skipper *Pasma tasmanica*

Size: Male 26mm, female 28mm.

Found from south-east Qld to Tas in moist tall eucalypt forest and subalpine woodland.

Host Plants: *Microlaena stipoides* north-east NSW and Vic, *Poa labillardieri* in ACT.

Best Garden Host Plant: Either of the above, depending upon location. It is most likely other species are also used.

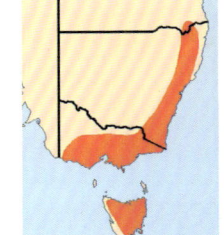

Spotted Grass Skipper *Neohesperilla senta*

Size: Male 26mm, female 29mm.

Occurs in the top end of WA, around Darwin, NT, and in Qld from Cooktown to about Townsville, in savannah woodland and eucalypt open forest where grassy areas occur.

 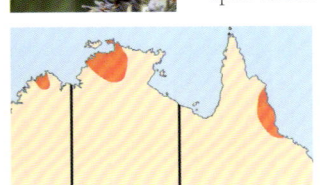

Host Plant: *Themeda triandra*, which is found over most of Australia.

Sword-brand Grass Skipper *Neohesperilla xiphiphora*

Size: Male 28mm, female 29mm.

A tropical species found from Darwin, NT, to about Townsville, Qld, in savannah woodland and open eucalypt forest, often in shaded areas along seasonal grassy creek beds.

Host Plants: *Sorghum intrans* in NT, *Schizachyrium perplexum* in Qld.

Best Garden Host Plant: Either of the above, but *S. perplexum* occurs in both NT and Qld so would be first choice.

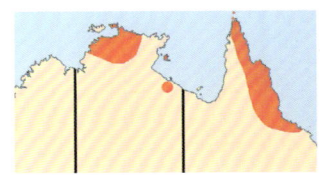

Narrow-brand Grass Skipper *Neohesperilla crocea*

Size: Male 28mm, female 32mm.

Another tropical species that is found around Darwin, NT, and then in Qld from Torres Strait to about Townsville. Occurs in paperbark swampland and tall open forest near rainforest in the uplands.

Host Plants: *Schizachyrium pachyarthron* on Cape York Peninsula, *Chrysopogon aciculatus* in north Qld.

Best Garden Host Plant: Either of the above, depending upon location.

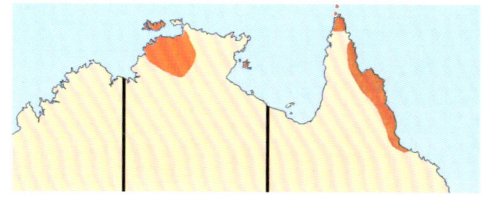

Yellow Grass Skipper *Neohesperilla xanthomera*

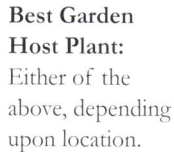

Size: Male 32mm, female 36mm.

Found from near Darwin, NT, sporadically through Qld to northern NSW in savannah woodland and open forest where the grass host plants grow.

Host Plants: *Heteropogon* in north Qld, *Andropogon virginicus* in south-east Qld.

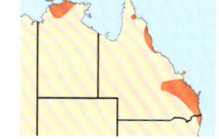

Small Grass Skipper *Toxidia parvula*

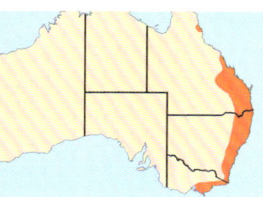

Size: Male 24mm, female 28mm.

Range extends from about Cairns, Qld, to southern Vic in open forest with a grassy understorey from the coast to about 900m.

Host Plants: *Poa labillardierei*, *P. queenslandica*, *P. sieberiana*, *P. tenera*.

Best Garden Host Plant: Any of the above.

Lilac Grass Skipper *Toxidia doubledayi*

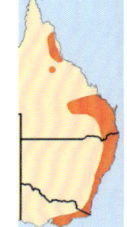

Size: Male 28mm, female 30mm.

Occurs in open eucalypt forest and woodlands from coastal areas to tableland regions, often in damp grassy gullies. Ranges from about Cairns, Qld, to southern Vic.

Host Plants: *Oplismenus*, *Ottochloa gracillima*, *Microlaena stipoides*.

Best Garden Host Plant: Any of the above.

Dusky Grass Skipper *Toxidia thyrrhus*

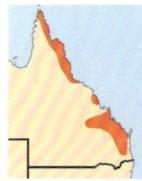

Size: Male 30mm, female 34mm.

Found from Torres Strait to south-east Qld in damp grassy areas in open forest, from coastal to upland regions.

Host Plants: Various grasses, including *Cenchrus echinatus*.

Best Garden Host Plant: No special preference recorded.

Anderson's Grass Skipper *Toxidia andersoni*

Size: Male 32mm, female 35mm.

Ranges from south-east Qld to southern Vic in tall open forest and along the edge of warm temperate rainforest up to 1,100m altitude.

Host Plants:
Poa labillardierei,
P. queenslandica,
P. sieberiana, *P. tenera*,
Tetrarrhena juncea.

Best Garden Host Plant: Any of the above.

Spotless Grass Skipper *Toxidia inornata*

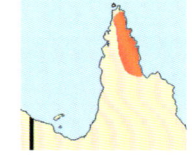

Size: Male 30mm, female 32mm.

Found in Qld on the eastern half of Cape York Peninsula down to about Bathurst Bay, in rainforest where the grass host plants grow.

Host Plants: No specific host plant is recorded.

Dingy Grass Skipper *Toxidia peron*

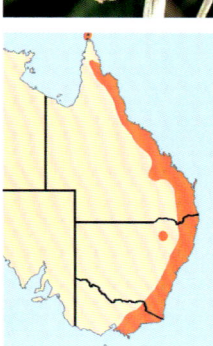

Size: Male 34mm, female 35mm.

Quite widespread, occurring from Torres Strait, Qld, to southern Vic in open eucalypt forest on the tablelands and east of the Great Dividing Range.

Host Plants: Mostly grasses, including **Stenotaphrum secundatum* but also *Gahnia sieberiana*, *Dianella caerulea* and *Lomandra*.

Best Garden Host Plant: No preferred species is recorded.

White-brand Grass Skipper *Toxidia rietmanni*

T.r. rietmanni.

T.r. parasema.

Size: Male 28mm, female 30mm.

Two subspecies:
- *T.r. rietmanni* from central Qld to southern NSW.
- *T.r. parasema* in north Qld from about Cairns to south of Townsville.

Usually found along rainforest edges or in tall open forest.

Host Plants: *Entolasia marginata*, *Oplismenus hirtellus*, *Ottochloa gracillima*, *Panicum pygmaeum*.

Best Garden Host Plant: Any of the above.

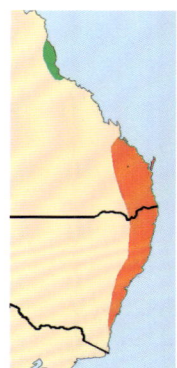

Dark Grass Skipper *Toxidia melania*

Size: Male 36mm, female 38mm.

A tropical species that is found in Qld from about Cairns to south of Townsville in both lowland and upland rainforest where there are grassy areas along the edges.

Host Plants: No specific host plant recorded.

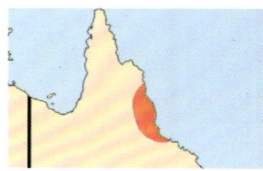

Bright Shield Skipper *Signeta flammeata*

Larval shelter.

Size: Male 32mm, female 34mm.

Found in tall open forest and subalpine woodland on or near the Great Dividing Range at altitudes up to 1,700m.

Host Plants: *Poa tenera*, *Tetrarrhena juncea*.

Best Garden Host Plant: Either of the above.

Dull Shield Skipper *Signeta tymbophora*

Size: Male 30mm, female 32mm.

Range extends from south-east Qld to southern NSW. Found in subtropical and warm temperate rainforest in upland areas of south-east Qld and northern NSW, and lowland areas and slopes of the Great Dividing Range in southern NSW.

Host Plants: Usually *Carex hubbardii* but also *Gahnia sieberiana* and *Entolasia marginata*.

Best Garden Host Plant: *Carex hubbardii*.

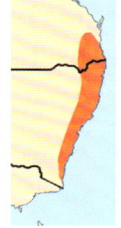

Alpine Sedge Skipper *Oreisplanus munionga*

O.m. munionga.

O.m. larana.

Size: Male 30mm, female 35mm.

Two subspecies:
- *O.m. munionga* from central coastal NSW to central Vic.
- *O.m. larana* in north-western Tas.

Host Plants: Usually *Carex appressa*; also *C. longebrachiata*, *Scirpus polystachyus*.

Best Garden Host Plant: *Carex appressa*.

Note: Sedges are in the family Cyperaceae. While they often look like grasses, which are in the family Poaceae, they are a separate entity. Some skippers use both families but usually it is one or the other.

Most of the Sedge Skippers feed on *Gahnia*. It is commonly called Swordgrass because of the sharply serrated edges to the leaves that can easily slice your finger.

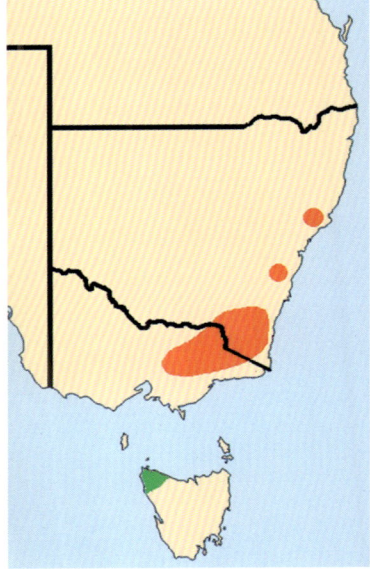

Mountain Sedge Skipper *Oreisplanus perornatus*

Size: Male 32mm, female 38mm.

Found from central eastern NSW to SA in open eucalypt forest with a heath understorey in coastal lowlands and uplands of the Great Dividing Range to an altitude of about 1,000m, usually below 600m.

Host Plant: *Gahnia sieberiana*.

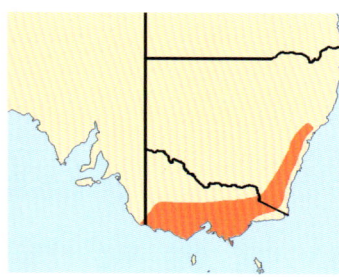

Painted Sedge Skipper *Hesperilla picta*

Size: Male 36mm, female 38mm.

Range in south-eastern Australia extends from about Gympie, Qld, to southern Vic in eucalypt and tall open forest in lowland areas. Damp shaded areas are preferred.

Host Plant: *Gahnia clarkei*.

Spotted Sedge Skipper *Hesperilla ornata*

Size: Male 32mm, female 36mm.

Two subspecies:
- ■ *H.o. ornata* from west of Townsville, Qld, to Vic.
- ■ *H.o. monotherma* in Qld on eastern Cape York Peninsula south to about Townsville.

Found in a range of habitats including open eucalyptus forest, heathland on sandstone and along the edge of rainforest.

Host Plants: *Gahnia aspera*, *G. clarkei*, *G. erythrocarpa*, *G. grandis*, *G. melanocarpa*, *G. radula*, *G. sieberiana*; also *Carex appressa*, *C. brunnea*, *C. longebrachiata*, *C. maculata*.

Best Garden Host Plant: Any of the above.

H.o. ornata.

H.o. monotherma.

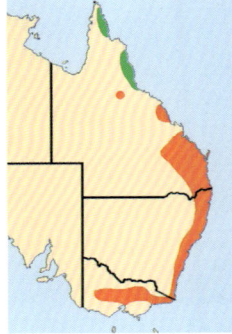

Gahnia aspera is a small sedge that grows to about 1m high and is mostly found in moist open eucalypt or melaleuca forest. The leaves have a saw-like edge and can cut your fingers if rubbed the wrong way.

Golden Sedge Skipper *Hesperilla hopsoni*

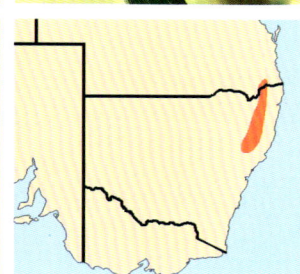

Size: Male 32mm, female 36mm.

Restricted to open eucalypt forest in montane areas of the Great Dividing Range from south-east Qld to northern NSW.

Host Plants: Usually *Gahnia sieberiana*, occasionally *G. grandis* at Barrington Tops, NSW.

Best Garden Host Plant: *Gahnia sieberiana*.

Silver Sedge Skipper *Hesperilla crypsargyra*

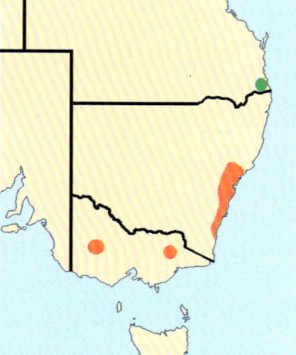

Size: Male 28mm, female 30mm.

Two subspecies:
- *H.c. crypsargyra* from eastern central NSW to western Vic in eucalypt forest with a heath understorey.
- *H.c. binna* restricted to the Lamington Plateau in montane heath.

Host Plants: *Gahnia insignis* in Qld, *G. microstachya* in NSW and Vic.

Best Garden Host Plant: Either of the above, depending on location.

SEDGE SKIPPERS

Chequered Sedge Skipper *Hesperilla mastersi*

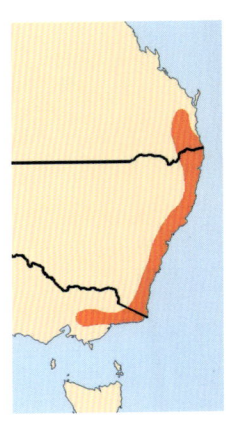

Size: Male 38mm, female 44mm.

Found from south-east Qld to central Vic in subtropical and warm temperate rainforest and open forest with a scattering of rainforest species in the understorey, from sea-level to about 900m.

Host Plants: Usually *Gahnia melanocarpa*; occasionally *Gahnia* sp. aff. *radula* in southern populations.

Best Garden Host Plant: *Gahnia melanocarpa*.

Golden-haired Sedge Skipper *Hesperilla chrysotricha*

H.c. chrysotricha.

Size: Male 36mm, female 40mm.

Ranges across southern Australia from north of Perth, WA, to southern NSW and eastern Tas. Two subspecies have been named:
- ■ *H.c. chrysotricha* in WA.
- ■ *H.c. cyclospila* in SA, Vic and Tas.

Host Plants: Usually *Gahnia trifida*, *G. filum* in coastal estuarine swamps; also *G. sieberiana*, *G. radula*, *G. microstachya* in near coastal areas in Vic, Tas and SA, *G. decomposita*, *G. deusta* in near coastal areas of WA.

Best Garden Host Plant: Any of the above, depending upon location.

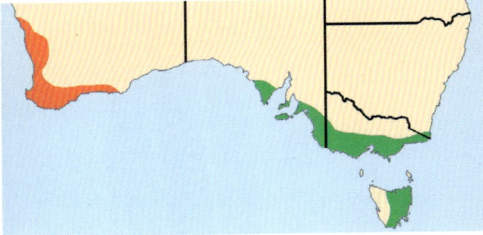

H.c. cyclospila.

Flame Sedge Skipper *Hesperilla idothea*

Size: Male 40mm, female 42mm.

Found from south-east Qld to SA, also in Tas, in open eucalypt forest from sea-level to the Great Dividing Range. Two subspecies:
- 🟧 *H.i. idothea* from south-east Qld to SA and Tas.
- 🟩 *H.i. clara* in SA.

Host Plants: *Gahnia sieberiana*, *G. radula*; also *G. aspera*, *G. clarkei*, *G. grandis*, *G. melanocarpa*, *G. subaequiglumis*, *G. trifida*.

Best Garden Host Plant: *Gahnia sieberiana*.

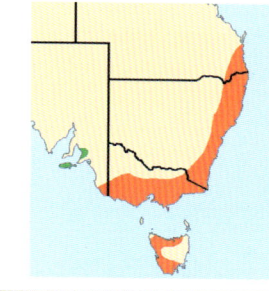

H.i. idothea.

H.i. clara.

Gahnia sieberiana is a large sedge and can grow to more than 3m high. It mostly occurs in swampy coastal areas or clearings in upland wet rainforest but can also be found around springs further inland, including sandstone gorges. In coastal swamps it forms virtually impenetrable colonies. The saw-edged leaves mean care needs to be taken when walking through these areas.

FAMILY HESPERIIDAE – SUBFAMILY TRAPEZITINAE   SEDGE SKIPPERS

Varied Sedge Skipper *Hesperilla donnysa*

H.d. donnysa.

Size: Male 34mm, female 40mm.

Has a wide distribution in southern Australia with four subspecies named:
- *H.d. donnysa* from about Maryborough, Qld, to southern SA.
- *H.d. galena* in a small coastal area north of Perth, WA.
- *H.d. albina* in south-west WA.
- *H.d. aurantia* in Tas.

Found in a variety of habitats from coastal sedgeland to subalpine woodland, usually in fairly exposed areas that the host plants favour.

Host Plants: At least 15 species of *Gahnia*.

Best Garden Host Plant: Probably any species of *Gahnia* if you are within the range of the butterfly.

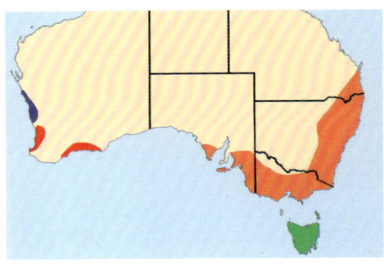

H.d. galena.

H.d. albina.

H.d. aurantia.

Yellow Sedge Skipper *Hesperilla flavescens*

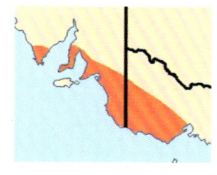

Size: Male 34mm, female 40mm.

Restricted to south-west Vic and south-east SA, where it is found in slightly saline swamps and along the edges of lakes where the sedge host plants grow.

Host Plants: *Gahnia filum*; occasionally *G. deusta*. **Best Garden Host Plant:** *Gahnia filum*.

Two-spotted Sedge Skipper *Hesperilla malindeva*

Size: Male 34mm, female 38mm.

Found from north Qld to northern NSW in woodland and monsoon forest on sandstone and granite.

Host Plant: *Gahnia aspera*.

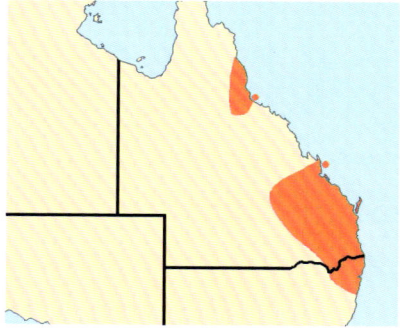

Gahnia aspera forms a small clump about 1m high by 1m wide. It is mostly found in open eucalypt or melaleuca forest and sometimes in disturbed areas in rainforest.

Riverine Sedge Skipper *Hesperilla sexguttata*

Size: Male 28mm, female 32mm.

Has quite a wide distribution, ranging from the Kimberley, WA, across the top and down to central Qld. It is usually found in eucalypt or paperbark woodland where there are swamps, lagoons or creek beds that support the host plant.

Host Plants: Usually *Cyperus javanicus*; also *C. decompositus* and *C. microcephalus*.

Best Garden Host Plant: *Cyperus javanicus*.

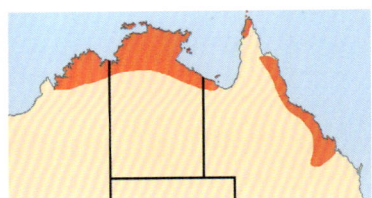

Grey Sedge Skipper *Hesperilla furva*

Size: Male 32mm, female 34mm.

Restricted to open eucalypt forest and brigalow woodland in south-east Qld. Often encountered on sandstone outcrops and ridges where the host plants are usually found.

Host Plants: *Scleria sphacelata*; occasionally *S. mackavienis*.

Best Garden Host Plant: *Scleria sphacelata*.

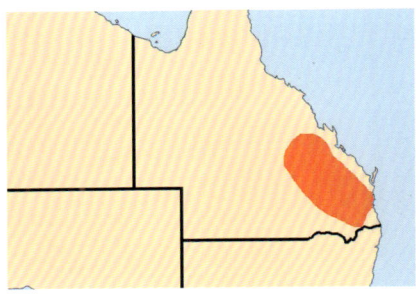

Wide-brand Sedge Skipper *Hesperilla crypsigramma*

Size: Male 28mm, female 29mm.

Has a population in the Darwin area, NT, then occurs from far north Qld to northern NSW where it is found in monsoon rainforest, vine thickets and savannah woodland. The host plants prefer to grow in gullies and on rocky slopes and ridges.

Host Plants: Usually *Scleria sphacelata*; also *S. mackaviensis* in central Qld.

Best Garden Host Plant: *Scleria sphacelata*.

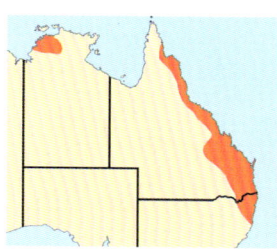

Swift Sedge Skipper *Hesperilla sarnia*

Size: Male 34mm, female 36mm.

Confined to Qld where it occurs in two widely separated areas: Cairns to about Bowen, then Rockhampton to south-east Qld. Found in vine thickets and tall open forests adjoining rainforest.

Host Plants: *Scleria levis* in north Qld, *S. sphacelata* in central and south-east Qld.

Best Garden Host Plant: Either of the above, depending on location.

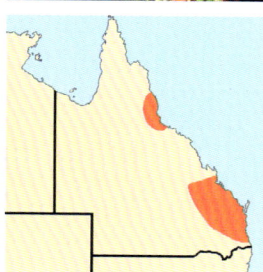

FAMILY HESPERIIDAE – SUBFAMILY TRAPEZITINAE   SAND SKIPPERS

Western Brown Skipper *Motasingha dirphia*

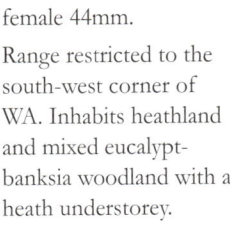

Size: Male 40mm, female 44mm.

Range restricted to the south-west corner of WA. Inhabits heathland and mixed eucalypt-banksia woodland with a heath understorey.

Host Plants: Not known.

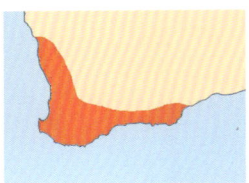

Heath Sand Skipper *Antipodia chaostola*

Size: Male 36mm, female 38mm.

Three subspecies:
- ■ *A.c. chaostola* in central eastern NSW.
- ■ *A.c. chares* in Vic.
- ■ *A.c. leucophaea* in Tas.

Usually found in heathy woodland and open eucalypt forest with a heath understorey. At 400–1,000m in the Blue Mountains, NSW, and in coastal lowlands and foothills of the Great Dividing Range below 300m in Vic.

Host Plants: Usually *Gahnia filifolia* in NSW, *G. radula* in Vic and Tas; also *G. sieberiana*, *G. microstachya*, *G. grandis*.

Best Garden Host Plant: Any of the above, depending on location.

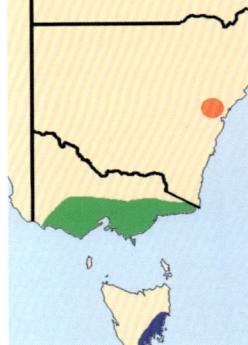

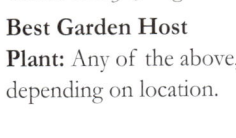

A.c. chares.

Large Brown Skipper *Motasingha trimaculata*

M.t. trimaculata.

M.t. dilata.

M.t. occidentalis.

Size: Male 40mm, female 44mm.

Three subspecies in the southern half of Australia:
- ■ *M.t. occidentalis* in south-west WA.
- ■ *M.t. trimaculata* in south-east SA and western Vic.
- ■ *M.t. dilata* in south-east Qld and central NSW.

Inhabits eucalypt open forest and heathy woodland on sandstone in NSW, heathland and mallee heath on sandy soils in Vic and SA, and heathland and mixed eucalypt-banksia woodland with a heath understorey on sand in WA.

Host Plants: *Lepidosperma viscidum* in NSW, Vic and SA; *L. carphoides* in north-west Vic and SA; and *L. angustatum*, *Phlebocarya ciliata* in WA.

Best Garden Host Plant: Any of the above, depending on location.

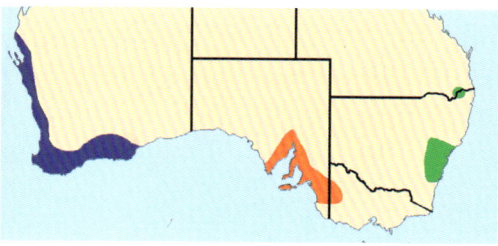

Diamond Sand Skipper *Antipodia atralba*

Size: Male 32mm, female 38mm.

Found in western Vic and south-east SA in heathland and mallee heath forests in the semi-arid zone.

Host Plants: Usually *Gahnia lanigera*; also *G. ancistrophylla*, *G. deusta*, *G. hystrix*.

Best Garden Host Plant: *Gahnia lanigera*.

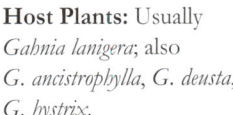
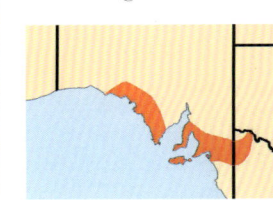

Western Sand Skipper *Antipodia dactyliota*

Size: Male 35mm, female 36mm.

Restricted to the southern and south-eastern parts of WA where it inhabits eucalypt woodland, mallee or acacia shrubland and mixed mallee-paperbark shrubland in drier coastal and near-coastal areas. Two subspecies:
- *A.d. dactyliota* in southern regions.
- *A.d. nila* in the Peron Peninsula area to the north.

Host Plants: *Gahnia lanigera*; also *G. ancistrophylla*, *G. australis*.

Best Garden Host Plant: *Gahnia lanigera*.

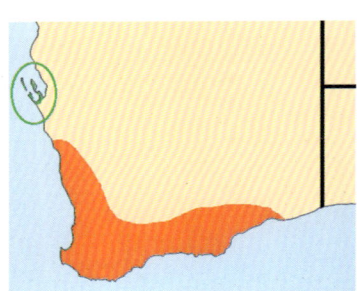

Yellow Sand Skipper *Croitana croites*

Size: Male 28mm, female 30mm.

Found in the south-west of WA in heathland, eucalypt and open acacia woodland on sand dunes. Two forms have been recognised:
- ■ a dark form and ■ a pale form.

Host Plants: *Austrostipa elegantissima, A. platychaeta, A. flavescens.*

Best Garden Host Plant: Any of the above species.

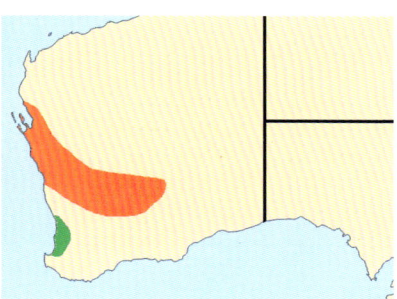

Inland Sand Skipper *Croitana arenaria*

Size: Male 25mm, female 26mm.

Two subspecies:
- ■ *C.a. arenaria* in southern NT and northern SA.
- ■ *C.a. pilepudla* in southern SA.

Inhabits a range of open woodland and sand dunes where it is often common but rather local.

Host Plants: *Enteropogon acicularis, E. ramosus* in southern NT and northern SA; *Austrostipa acrociliata, A. platychaeta, A. elegantissima* in southern SA.

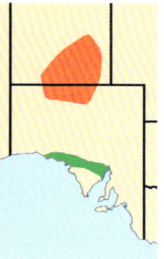

Best Garden Host Plant: Any of the above, depending upon location.

Spinifex Sand Skipper *Proeidosa polysema*

Size: Male 34mm, female 36mm.

Has two forms in northern Australia:
- ■ Large-spot form from the central coast of WA to inland northern Qld.
- ■ Small-spot form in a small area of central Qld.

Found where Spinifex grows on sand dunes, eucalypt open woodland and dry rocky sandstone.

Host Plants: *Triodia pungens* in the arid zone, *T. bitextura* in the semi-arid zone of the Kimberley, *T. microstachya* in NT and *T. mitchellii* in central Qld.

Best Garden Host Plant: Any of the above, depending upon location.

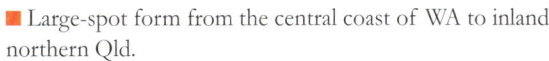
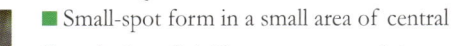

Large-spot form.

White-veined Sand Skipper *Herimosa albovenata*

Size: Male 30mm, female 34mm.
Three subspecies:
- ■ *H.a. albovenata* in south-west WA and around the bight to the Vic border, then in south-east NSW.
- ■ *H.a. weelma* in inland central NSW.
- ■ *H.a. fuscata* in a small area of southern WA.

Usually found in tussock-grassland on exposed rocky outcrops and low hills.

Host Plants: *Austrostipa scabra* in NSW and SA; also *A. eremophila*, *A. semibarbata* in south-east SA.

Best Garden Host Plant: Any of the above, depending on location.

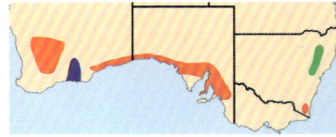

Desert Sand Skipper *Croitana aestiva*

Size: Male 28mm, female 30mm.

Restricted to a small area in the southern part of NT where it is found in low open woodland, usually in sheltered gullies where the larval host plant grows.

Host Plant: *Neurachne tenuifolia*.

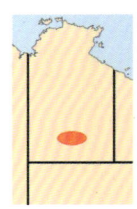

Mountain Iris Skipper *Mesodina aeluropis*

Size: Male 38mm, female 40mm.

Restricted to a small strip of eastern NSW, inland from the coast in subalpine open woodland and montane grassland from altitudes of about 800–1,270m.

Host Plant: *Patersonia sericea*.

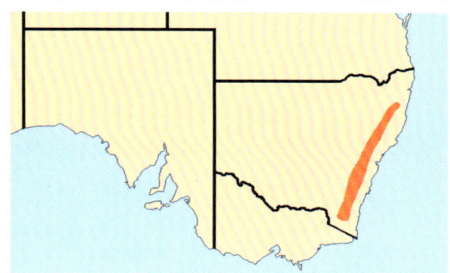

Patersonia sericea is a small herb that grows to about 60cm high with stiff upright foliage. It is found from central Qld to Vic in open forest where there is a heath understorey. The bright flowers are very showy so when in flower it is easy to identify.

Eastern Iris Skipper *Mesodina halyzia*

Size: Male 36mm, female 37mm.

Found from about Rockhampton, Qld, to Melbourne, Vic. Inhabits heathland, heathy woodland and moist open eucalypt forest.

Host Plants: *Patersonia fragilis*, *P. glabrata*, *P. sericea*, *P. occidentalis*.

Best Garden Host Plant: Any of the above.

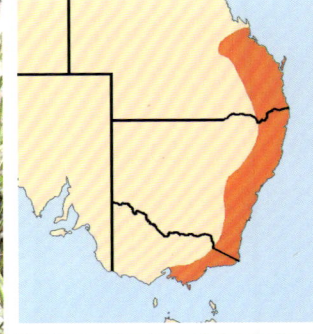

Patersonia fragilis is a small herb that grows to about 50cm high with mauve flowers. It is found from about Rockhampton, Qld, to SA, and is quite common in Tas.

Northern Iris Skipper *Mesodina gracillima*

Size: Male 30mm, female 32mm.

Restricted to the top end of NT where it is found in eucalypt woodland on well-drained sandy soils.

Host Plant: *Patersonia macrantha*.

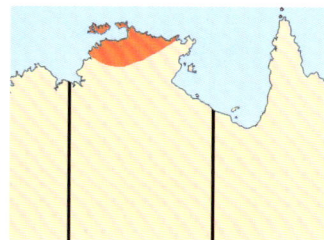

Small Iris Skipper *Mesodina hayi*

Size: Male 32mm, female 34mm.

Found in two isolated locations in the south-west of WA where it occupies sheoak heathland and shrubland.

Host Plant: *Patersonia drummondii*.

Blue Iris Skipper *Mesodina cyanophracta*

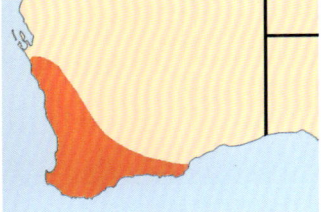

Size: Male 32mm, female 34mm.

Restricted to the south-west corner of WA where it is found in banksia and jarrah woodland.

Host Plants: *Patersonia juncea, P. lanata, P. occidentalis, P. umbrosa.*

Best Garden Host Plant: Any of the above.

Patersonia occidentalis is a small herb that grows to about 1.5m high. It is found in south-west WA, being quite common where it occurs.

Blue-flash Skipper *Rachelia extrusa*

Size: Male 36mm, female 38mm.

A tropical rainforest species that is found in north-east Qld, especially in the Iron Range area of Cape York Peninsula, usually occurring in lowland rainforest.

Host Plant: *Flagellaria indica*.

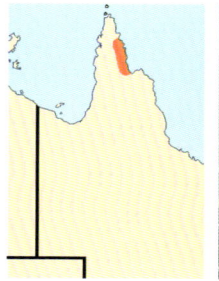

Flagellaria indica is a medium to large vine that is found in rainforest from the Kimberley region, WA, and around the north and east of Australia south to about Sydney, NSW. The very long and thin canes of this form that occurs on Cape York Peninsula and across the top end of Australia is suitable for weaving. This vine is unusual insomuch as the climbing tendrils are on the ends of the leaves. The small pink fruit are eaten by birds.

FAMILY HESPERIIDAE – SUBFAMILY TRAPEZITINAE　　SKIPPERS, DEMONS

Banded Demon *Notocrypta waigensis*

Size: Male 38mm, female 42mm.

Restricted to the tropical rainforest of north Qld, even though the range of the main host plant extends to northern NSW.

Host Plants: *Alpinia caerulea, Hornstedtia scottiana.*

Best Garden Host Plant: *Alpinia caerulea.*

Alpinia caerulea is very widespread, being found in rainforest from Cape York, Qld, to northern NSW. One of the very hardy gingers, this one will show stress only when in full sun and subjected to very long dry periods. With regular watering it performs well at all times. The lovely blue berries add a splash of colour among the greens of a rainforest planting. Often, forms are found with the underside of the leaves red.

Hyaline Swift *Parnara amalia*

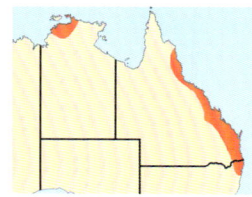

Size: Male 30mm, female 32mm.

Known from two disjunct populations: north-western NT, and then from about Cooktown, Qld, to northern NSW. The host plant (which is a grass) usually grows in swamps or bog areas so this is where the butterfly will mostly be seen.

Host Plants: *Leersia hexandra, *Oryza sativa*.

Best Garden Host Plant: *Leersia hexandra*.

Grey Swift *Parnara bada*

Size: Male 32mm, female 34mm.

Found from about Cooktown in Qld to northern NSW in swamps and on edges of freshwater lakes.

Host Plants: *Leersia hexandra, *Oryza sativa*.
Best Garden Host Plant: *Leersia hexandra*.

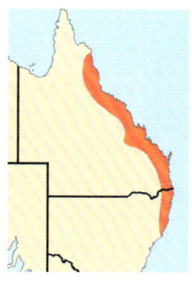

Rice Swift *Borbo cinnara*

Size: Male 35mm, female 37mm.

Confined to the top end of NT and some Torres Strait islands, Qld. Usually found in swampy areas close to rainforest where its grass host plant grows.

Host Plant: *Rottboellia cochinchinensis*.

Yellow Swift *Borbo impar*

B.i. lavinia.

B.i. tetragraphus.

Size: Male 36mm, female 38mm.

Two subspecies:
- *B.i. lavinia* in the top end of NT.
- *B.i. tetragraphus* restricted to some Torres Strait islands, Qld.

Both subspecies are usually found in flood plain wetlands where their native grass host plants grow.

Host Plants: *Hymenachne acutigluma*, *Whiteochloa airoides*, **Cenchrus pedicellatus*, **Megathyrsus maximus* in the NT and *Rottboellia cochinchinensis* in Torres Strait.

Best Garden Host Plant: Any of the above, depending on location, but the two introduced species are considered weeds.

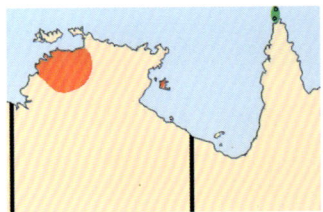

Dingy Swift *Pelopidas agna*

Size: Male 36mm, female 38mm.

Has a distribution ranging from Torres Strait, Qld, to northern NSW. Found in a wide range of habitats, including coastal paperbark, woodland and eucalypt open forest.

Host Plants: *Ischaemum australe*, **Oryza sativa*, **Paspalum paniculatum*, **Sorghum*.

Best Garden Host Plant: **Paspalum paniculatum*.

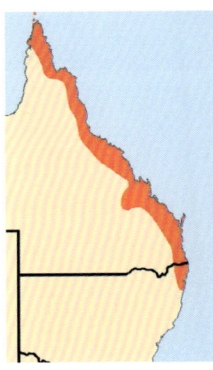

Lyell's Swift *Pelopidas lyelli*

Size: Male 35mm, female 37mm.

Found in northern Australia from the Kimberley, WA, across the top end and south to northern NSW. Occurs in a range of habitats from rainforest edges to savannah woodland, usually in areas with tall grass.

Host Plants: *Mnesithea rottboellioides, Chrysopogon elongatus, Eriachne triodioides, *Cenchrus pedicellatus, *Megathyrsus maximus, *Oryza sativa, *Sorghum.*

Best Garden Host Plant: Any of the above.

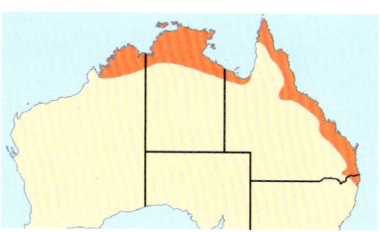

Large Yellow Grass Dart *Taractrocera anisomorpha*

Size: Male 24mm, female 28mm.

Has a wide distribution covering most of northern Australia, favouring eucalypt woodland and banks of dry stream beds. Prefers more sheltered areas where tussocks of the larval host plants grow.

Host Plants: *Eulalia aurea, Setaria paspalidioides, *Sorghum bicolor.*

Best Garden Host Plant: *Eulalia aurea.*

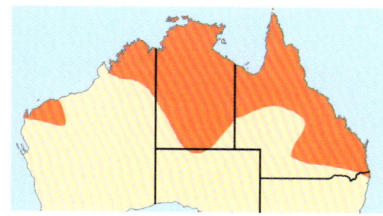

No-brand Grass Dart *Taractrocera ina*

Size: Male 24mm, female 27mm.

Found in northern and eastern Australia with disjunct populations in the inland as far south as Vic. Usually in open eucalypt forest and savannah woodland where there are open grassy areas. As a number of introduced grasses are used as host plants it is also found in suburban parks and gardens.

Host Plants: *Cymbopogon procerus*, *Sorghum* spp., **Cymbopogon citrata*, **Sorghum verticilliflorum*, **Cenchrus pedicellatus*, **Megathyrsus maximus*, **Paspalum conjugatum*, **P. dilatatum*, **P. urvillei*, **Oryza sativa*, **Brachiaria decumbens*.

Best Garden Host Plant: No preference for any species is known.

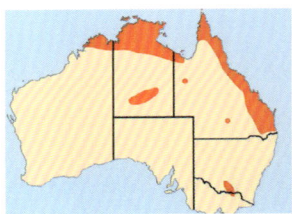

Small Dingy Grass Dart *Taractrocera dolon*

T.d. dolon.

T.d. diomedes.

Size: Male 20mm, female 24mm.

Two subspecies:
- *T.d. dolon* in the top end of NT.
- *T.d. diomedes* from about Cape Melville, Qld, to northern NSW.

Found in savannah woodland, eucalypt open forest and coastal wallum areas.

Host Plants: Various grasses including **Sorghum verticilliflorum*.

Best Garden Host Plant: No particular preference recorded.

Northern Grass Dart *Taractrocera ilia*

Size: Male 20mm, female 22mm.

Restricted to a very small area at the top end of NT where the host plants grow on sandstone.

Host Plants: *Micraira adamsii, M. compacta, M. multinervia, M. spinifera, M. tenuis.*

Best Garden Host Plant: No particular preference is known.

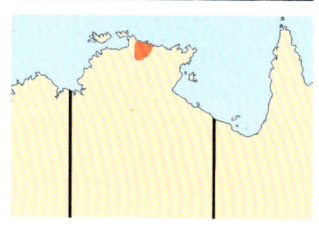

White-banded Grass Dart *Taractrocera papyria*

T.p. papyria.

Size: Male 20mm, female 22mm.

Two subspecies:
- *T.p. papyria* in north Qld then from inland central Qld to SA.
- *T.p. agraulia* in the south-west corner of WA.

Found in open woodland and grassland, also in suburban parks and gardens in WA.

Host Plants: *Austrodanthonia, Austrostipa, Cynodon, Echinopogon, Imperata, Microlaena, Phragmites, Poa, *Ehrharta, *Oryza, *Paspalum, *Pennisetum*; also on the sedge *Carex*.

Best Garden Host Plant: No particular preference is known.

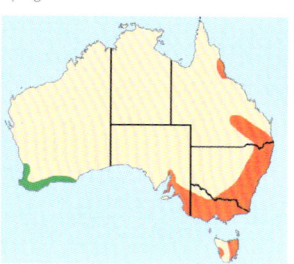

T.p. agraulia.

FAMILY HESPERIIDAE – SUBFAMILY HESPERIINAE GRASS DARTS

White-margined Grass Dart *Ocybadistes hypomeloma*

O.h. hypomeloma.

Size: Male 24mm, female 26mm.

Two subspecies:
- ■ *O.h. hypomeloma* from far north Qld to southern NSW.
- ■ *O.h. vaga* in northern WA and NT, just reaching Qld in the southern Gulf.

Savannah woodland, open woodland and grassland are the preferred habitats.

Host Plants: *Themeda triandra, Ischaemum australe, Microlaena stipoides, *Andropogon virginicus.*

O.h. vaga.

Best Garden Host Plant: *Themeda triandra.*

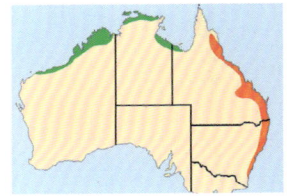

Common Grass Dart *Ocybadistes flavovittatus*

O.f. flavovittatus.

O.f. vesta.

Size: Male 20mm, female 22mm.

Two subspecies:
- ■ *O.f. flavovittatus* in eastern Australia from Torres Strait, Qld, to Vic.
- ■ *O.f. vesta* in the top end of WA and NT.

Occurs in savannah woodland and open eucalypt forest as well as suburban gardens.

Host Plants: Many grasses (Poaceae), including **Cynodon dactylon* in WA.

Best Garden Host Plant: No preference recorded.

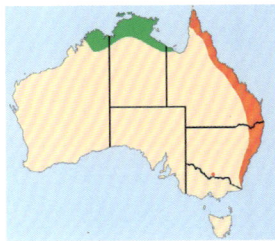

Walker's Grass Dart *Ocybadistes walkeri*

O.w. sothis.

Size: Male 22mm, female 24mm.

Found in northern, eastern and southern Australia and has three subspecies:
- *O.w. sothis* from Cape York, Qld, to Tas.
- *O.w. hypochlorus* confined to eastern SA.
- *O.w. olivia* in the top end of WA and NT.

Found in savannah woodland and open eucalypt forest as well as suburban gardens.

Host Plants: *Cynodon dactylon, Imperata cylindrica, Thuarea involuta, *Axonopus, *Brachypodium, *Bromus, *Ehrharta, *Lolium, *Megathyrsus, *Melinis, *Paspalum, *Pennisetum*; occasionally the sedge *Carex brunnea*.

Best Garden Host Plant: No preference recorded.

O.w. hypochlorus.

   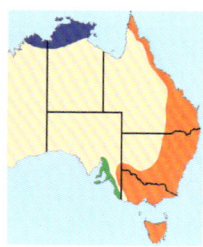

O.w. olivia.

Knight's Grass Dart *Ocybadistes knightorum*

Size: 20mm.

Confined to a small area of north-eastern NSW where it is found in open sheoak forest with a grassy understorey in the king tide zone above mangroves. Classified as Endangered.

Host Plant: *Alexfloydia repens*, which is also listed as Endangered.

Alexfloydia repens is quite restricted in distribution, being found mainly around Coffs Harbour and south to about Nambucca Heads in NSW. This is a typical host plant for this group of butterflies, with abundant soft foliage.

Dark-orange Grass Dart *Ocybadistes ardea*

Size: Male 20mm, female 20mm.

Has a wide distribution in northern and eastern Qld, south-eastwards from Torres Strait. Found along the edge of rainforest, especially along streams where the rainforest grasses grow in open sunny areas.

Host Plants: *Oplismenus aemulus, O. undulatifolius*.

Best Garden Host Plant: Either of the above.

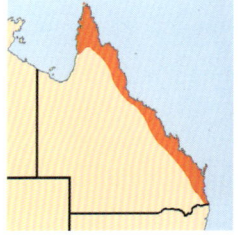

Orange Grass Dart *Suniana sunias*

S.s. rectivitta.

Size: Male 25mm, female 27mm.

Two subspecies:
- ■ *S.s. rectivitta* from Torres Strait, Qld, to central NSW.
- ■ *S.s. sauda* in a relatively small area of north-west NT.

Favours the edges of gallery and wet monsoon rainforest in open areas where grasses flourish.

Host Plants: *Leersia hexandra* in Qld; also **Megathyrsus maximus*, **Paspalum urvillei*, **Sorghum verticilliflorum*.

Best Garden Host Plant: No preference is recorded.

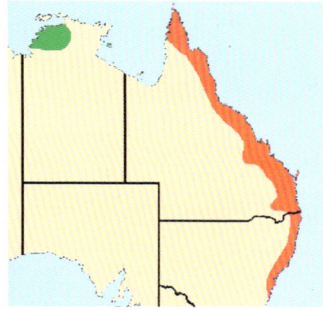

S.s. sauda.

Dark Grass Dart *Suniana lascivia*

Size: Male 24mm, female 26mm.

Range encompasses northern and eastern Australia. Four subspecies:
- ■ *S.l. lascivia* from about Mackay, Qld, to Melbourne, Vic, extending several hundred kilometres inland from coast.
- ■ *S.l. neocles* in Qld from Torres Strait to about Townsville.
- ■ *S.l. larrakia* confined to the top end of WA and NT.
- ■ *S.l. lasus* only on the Tiwi Islands, NT.

Grassy areas along creeks, paperbark swampland and open eucalypt forest are the preferred habitats.

Host Plants: *Imperata cylindrica, Ischaemum australe* in WA, **Megathyrsus maximus* in NT and Qld.

Best Garden Host Plant: No preference known.

S.l. lascivia.

S.l. neocles.

S.l. larrakia.

Swamp Darter *Arrhenes marnas*

Size: Male 26mm, female 28mm.

Found from about Iron Range, Qld, to northern NSW in melaleuca swamp areas where the host plant grows.

Host Plant: *Leersia hexandra* (Swamp Rice Grass).

Scrub Darter *Arrhenes dschilus*

Size: Male 28mm, female 30mm.

Occurs in open forest adjoining rainforest where its grass host plant grows. Ranges from Cape York to about Sarina, Qld.

Host Plants: *Imperata cylindrica*, *Megathyrsus maximus*, *Saccharum officinarum*.

Best Garden Host Plant: *Imperata cylindrica*.

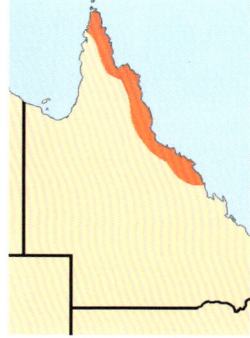

Northern Sedge Darter *Telicota eurotas*

Size: Male 30mm, female 34mm.

Found in north-eastern Qld from Cape York to about Townsville in lowland paperbark swamp areas.

Host Plants: *Scleria ciliaris, S. polycarpa, S. sumatrensis.*

Best Garden Host Plant: Any of the above.

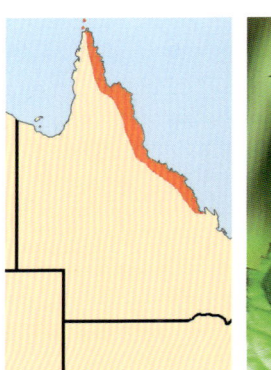

Southern Sedge Darter *Telicota eurychlora*

Size: Male 32mm, female 34mm.

Ranges from south-east Qld to Vic and found in coastal swampland, especially where there is brackish water. Also occurs in upland swamps near rainforest.

Host Plants: *Cladium procerum* in coastal lowlands, *Carex polyantha* in near-coastal uplands.

Best Garden Host Plant: Either of the above, depending on location.

Pale-orange Darter *Telicota colon*

Size: Male 30mm, female 33mm.

Very widespread, being found in northern and eastern Australia down to southern NSW. It has a wide range of habitats including open eucalypt forest with a grassy understorey, edges of creeks, mangroves and rainforest as well as gardens and parklands.

Host Plants: *Chrysopogon fallax, Ischaemum australe, Imperata cylindrica, Mnesithea rottboellioides, Ophiuros exaltatus, Phragmites australis,* *Andropogon, *Megathyrsus, *Miscanthus, *Paspalum, *Sorghum.*

Best Garden Host Plant: No preference is known.

Northern Large Darter *Telicota ohara*

Size: Male 35mm, female 38mm.

Occurs in Qld from Torres Strait to about Sarina in lowland and upland tropical rainforest.

Host Plant: *Flagellaria indica.*

Flagellaria indica is a scrambling vine that is unusual insomuch as the tendrils are on the ends of the leaves. The image shows the true *F. indica* that is found from India to Australia, and in Australia from the Kimberley region in WA and then in Qld from Cape York to about Cooktown. The form in the wet tropics of north Qld has very thick stems and large leaves – previously it was known as the variety *gracilicaulis*.

FAMILY HESPERIIDAE – SUBFAMILY HESPERIINAE   **DARTERS**

Southern Large Darter *Telicota anisodesma*

Size: Male 35mm, female 39mm.

Occurs from about Gladstone, Qld, to south of Sydney, NSW, in low- to mid-altitude rainforest.

Host Plant: *Flagellaria indica.*

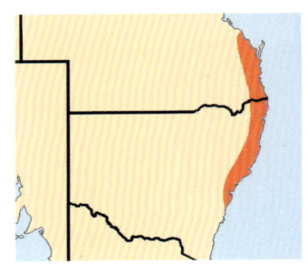

Greenish Darter *Telicota ancilla*

Size: Male 32mm, female 34mm.

Found in eastern Australia from Cape York, Qld, to southern NSW in open eucalypt forest and rainforest edges.

Host Plants: *Imperata cylindrica*; occasionally **Paspalum urvillei*, **Sorghum halepense, Gahnia aspera, Phragmites australis.*

Best Garden Host Plant: *Imperata cylindrica* (Blady Grass).

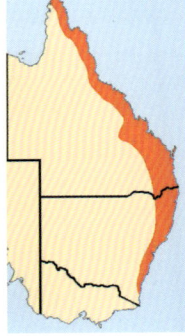

Bright-orange Darter *Telicota augias*

Size: Male 32mm, female 33mm.

A tropical species that is found from the Kimberley area of WA, across the top end of NT, and then in Qld from Torres Strait to about Rockhampton. Occurs in low- to mid-altitude rainforest.

Host Plant: *Flagellaria indica*.

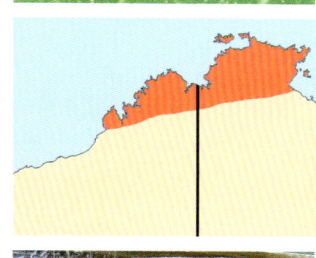
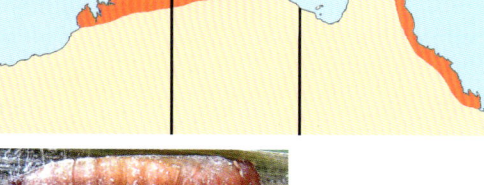

Flagellaria indica has very narrow leaves and slender canes with small bunches of flowers. It occurs across the top end of Australia from the Kimberley region of WA down to just south of Cooktown, Qld.

In the wet tropics of north Qld there is a different form that is a very large vine with thick canes and large leaves. This was originally named *Flagellaria indica* var. *gracilicaulis* but this name has been dropped and both varieties lumped into just one.

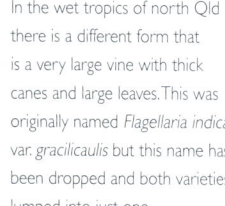

Small Darter *Telicota brachydesma*

Size: Male 26mm, female 28mm.

Confined to rainforest in Qld, in the Iron Range area and then from about Cooktown to Mackay, where the unusual rainforest grass host plant grows.

Host Plant: *Leptaspis banksii*.

The genus *Leptaspis* contains five species in the world, with one endemic in Australia. *Leptaspis banksii* was first collected at the Endeavour River, Qld, by Sir Joseph Banks and Dr Solander.

This attractive small rainforest grass has stems rising from a horizontal or shortly creeping rhizome. The plant grows to about 50cm, but the showy flowering spikes tower above the leaves, reaching 1m in height.

Narrow-brand Darter *Telicota mesoptis*

Size: Male 28mm, female 30mm.

Occurs in Qld from Torres Strait to about Sarina, extending down to about Weipa on the west coast of Cape York Peninsula. Prefers higher rainfall areas and is usually found along the edges of rainforest and gallery forest.

Host Plants: Various grasses (Poaceae), including *Megathyrsus maximus*, *Sorghum verticilliflorum*.

Best Garden Host Plant: No preference known.

Orange Palm Dart *Cephrenes augiades*

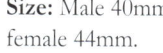

Size: Male 40mm, female 44mm.

Natural range extends across the top end of NT and from Torres Strait, Qld, to southern NSW. It has been accidentally introduced to other states through the movement of potted palm plants. There are plenty of naturally occurring palm species that grow from Broome to the Darwin area and all around the Gulf of Carpentaria so it is highly likely that this butterfly is also found there.

Host Plants: *Archontophoenix, Arenga, Calamus, Carpentaria, Hydriastele, Laccospadix, Licuala, Livistona, Ptychosperma, Rhopalostylis, Wodyetia*. The larvae are not restricted to native palms and will utilise most introduced species as well.

Best Garden Host Plant: In the author's garden *Archontophoenix* and *Livistona* palms are the most preferred, although smaller species belonging to genera such as *Ptychosperma* are suitable for suburban gardens.

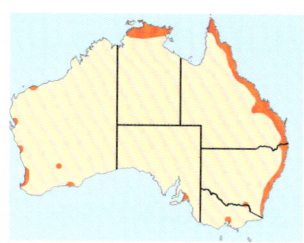

Like all *Archontophoenix* palms, *A. tuckeri* produces huge volumes of fruit, and can do so at any time of the year. Because they drop their old leaves with monotonous regularity, as do all Alexandra Palms, they should not be planted where the falling fruit and fronds will be a problem.

Butterflies that do not usually feed on nectar are attracted to the flowers of this group of palms. These are the Brown butterflies, such as the Evening Brown and Orange Bush Brown, that often feed on sap or rotten fruit. It is not actually the nectar that they are after, but a sticky exudate that is all over the flowering body.

Archontophoenix alexandrae is a tall, fast-growing palm that is found from north Qld to about Bundaberg, in rainforest along streams. In very wet areas it can form almost a monoculture with the ground completely covered with thousands of seedlings.

Archontophoenix maxima is a very large palm found in the high-rainfall rainforests on the Atherton Tableland in north Qld.

Ptychosperma elegans is found in lowland rainforest in Qld from Torres Strait to about Rockhampton. It is a slender palm that produces large bunches of bird-attracting seed. It will grow in most places east of the Great Dividing Range.

Yellow Palm Dart *Cephrenes trichopepla*

Size: Male 38mm, female 42mm.

Usually found in eucalypt forest or along the edges of rainforest where palm trees grow. Its natural range is in the northern half of Australia, usually not more than about 300km from the coast. The range has been extended due to the movement of potted palm plants with eggs or larvae on them.

Host Plants: *Archontophoenix, Livistona, Ptychosperma, Wodyetia.*

Best Garden Host Plants: *Archontophoenix, Livistona.*

Livistona muelleri is a small palm that is found all over Cape York Peninsula, extending south of Cooktown to about Cairns. In areas where the soil is poorly drained large stands can be found.

PALM DARTS

Livistona humilis is a very small palm that is found across the top end of NT in open eucalypt forest. The trunk is very hardy and when a few years old is able to survive fires.

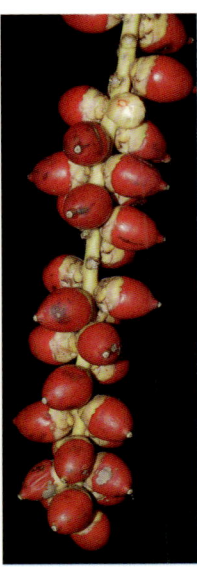

Ptychosperma macarthurii is a clumping palm that is found across Cape York Peninsula, Qld, and in NT along streams. It grows to about 6–8m. The NT form was previously called *P. bleeseri*.

Purple Swift *Mimene atropatene*

Size: Male 38mm, female 44mm.

Confined to the Iron Range area of Cape York Peninsula, Qld. This habitat extends from about the Pascoe River to the Rocky River.

Host Plants: Not known.

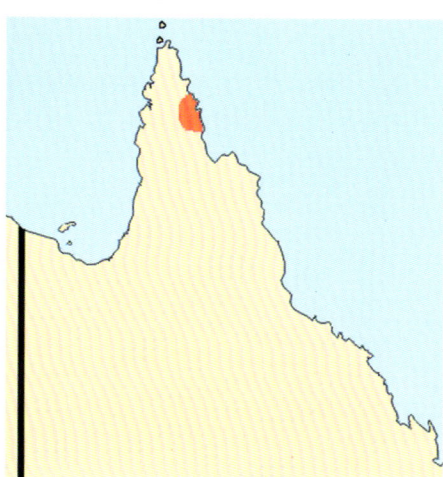

Black-and-white Swift *Sabera caesina*

Size: Male 32mm, female 33mm.

A rainforest species found in Qld from Torres Strait to about Townsville.

Host Plants: *Calamus caryotoides, Archontophoenix, Normanbya normanbyi.*

Best Garden Host Plant: *Archontophoenix.*

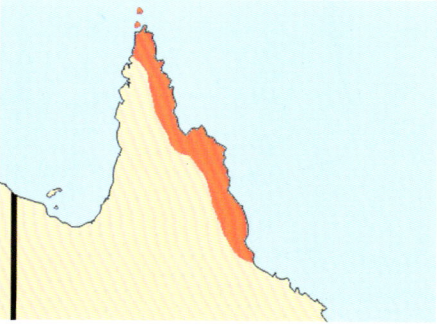

Orange Swift *Sabera dobboe*

Size: Male 34mm, female 36mm.

A tropical species, ranging in Qld from Torres Strait to about Rockhampton, in rainforest and gardens where the *Cordyline* host plants are grown. The larvae have an unusual habit of making a special 'packet' in which they make their pupae. It is cut from the *Cordyline* leaf, then drops to the ground and the final seal is made. These can even float on water without drowning the larva.

Host Plants: *Cordyline cannifolia, C. fruticosa, C. manners-suttoniae, C. stricta, *C. australis.*

Best Garden Host Plant: *Cordyline manners-suttoniae.*

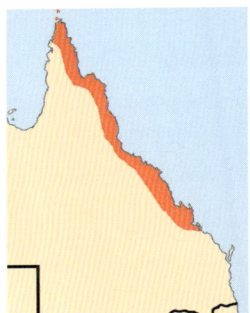

Pupal shelter lying on the ground.

Cordyline manners-suttoniae can be used as a palm substitute if a small plant is required. It looks best if it is pruned a few times when young, as it will then develop several trunks. The flower head is quite large, and the eye-catching bunches of brilliant red fruit are an asset in the garden. It is found from Iron Range to about Bundaberg in lowland rainforest. Some birds, especially the koel and the figbird, eat the fruit, but usually they remain on the bush for several months.

White-fringed Swift *Sabera fuliginosa*

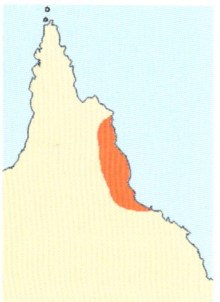

Size: Male 34mm, female 36mm.

Range is in the Qld wet tropics, from about Cape Flattery to Townsville, where the large and rather vicious Lawyer Cane host plant grows.

Host Plant: *Calamus moti*.

Calamus moti is a very large 'Lawyer Cane' vine that is armed with vicious yellow spines along the young canes. It is found in Qld from about Cooktown to Mackay in low- to mid-altitude rainforest.

BLUES, COPPERS and HAIRSTREAKS
Family Lycaenidae

While this family contains butterflies that are quite small, some have quite spectacular colours when viewed close up. They tend to fly fast and rather erratically so are difficult to see clearly or photograph well. Patience is required when photographing them, and early in the morning is a good time as they often rest with wings spread to absorb warmth from the rising sun. When feeding on nectar many continuously open and close their wings, giving the photographer an opportunity to snap a shot.

The majority of these butterflies have an association with ants and some species actually live in ant nests. A few species eat ant larvae rather than the usual plant parts. The larvae of the species that associate with ants have special glands on their back that exude nectar, thus rewarding the ants for tolerating or looking after them.

The larvae of the Azure group usually associate with the large sugar ants, hiding in the ants' nest during the day and moving up a tree to their mistletoe host plants at night, being accompanied by the ants at all times. The sugar ants take nectar from the mistletoe flowers when available.

Butterfly larvae being attended by ants.

Common Oak Blue larva attended by the usually vicious Green Tree Ants of the tropical lowlands. These ants usually destroy most butterfly larvae with the exception of a selected few that they attend.

Larva of the Black-and-white Tit being attended by extremely tiny ants. These are not native ants but the larva can still make use of them. The ants also stay with the pupa so long as it is alive.

Some of the Lycaenidae larvae rely on camouflage for protection. This larva of the Small Green-banded Blue rests near the main vein of the leaf when not feeding. The pupa is usually made in the same place.

If you look at the eggs of these butterflies – in this case those of the Black-and-white Tit – you will find many strange patterns and shapes. Perhaps this is camouflage but no one really knows.

Most brightly coloured butterflies have dark camouflaged markings on the underside of the wings like the Common Oak Blue (left), but one notable exception is the Jewel butterflies like this Copper Jewel (right); the underside, as well as the upper side is also marked with bright iridescent colours.

Bronze Ant-blue *Acrodipsas brisbanensis*

Size: Male 26mm, female 28mm.

Found in northern and eastern Australia in a wide variety of open forest types and in the south-west of WA in *Banksia* woodland with a heath understorey. Ant-blues do not have host plants and most of them are known to feed on larvae and pupae of the ants that they live with. The females lay their eggs near the ants' nest and when the tiny larvae hatch they resemble ant larvae and are collected and carried into the ants' nest. It is not known if they also have a chemical attractant that resembles that of ant larvae, but this is a possibility. Information on the ants listed in this text can be found on the Internet. Like many Lycaenidae the males of this species hilltop, and this is where most specimens have been taken.

Larval Food – Attendant Ants: The Bronze Ant-blue larvae feed on the immature stages of the host *Papyrius* ant species.

Copper Ant-blue *Acrodipsas cuprea*

Size: Male 28mm, female 30mm.

Has a similar distribution to that of the previous species except it does not extend to SA or WA. The butterfly is found in open eucalypt forest and coastal heath where the host ant occurs. It is common where it occurs but found in localised colonies.

Attendant Ants: *Crematogaster* sp.

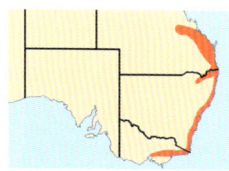

Brown Ant-blue *Acrodipsas mortoni*

Size: Male 25mm, female 27mm.

Very little is known about this species. It has been found in three relatively small areas: south-east Qld, north-eastern NSW and south-eastern NSW. Adults are usually seen on hilltops where they have been observed feeding on *Eucalyptus* flowers.

Attendant Ants: Not recorded
Host Plant: Not recorded.

FAMILY LYCAENIDAE – SUBFAMILY THECLINAE   **BLUES AND COPPERS**

Golden Ant-blue *Acrodipsas aurata*

Size: Male 26mm, female 28mm.

Found in eucalypt woodland, usually above 550m, from the Blue Mountains, NSW, to Pine Mountain near Corryong, Vic. The butterflies are mostly seen on hilltops where they are sometimes common.

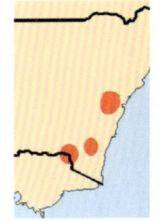

Larval Food – Attendant Ants: *Crematogaster* sp.

Small Ant-blue *Acrodipsas myrmecophila*

Size: Male 22mm, female 26mm.

Has a very wide but scattered distribution, being found in NT, Qld, NSW and Vic. Because these butterflies are rarely seen by anybody who can recognise them, there are most likely many more isolated colonies of them than those presently known. They are found in open eucalypt forest, grassy open woodland and mallee shrubland from sea-level to 1,500m and most often seen on hilltops. This species is rare to uncommon and very localised.

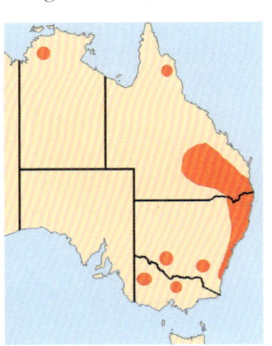

Larval Food – Attendant Ants: *Papyrius* sp.

Black-veined Ant-blue *Acrodipsas arcana*

Size: Male 25mm, female 29mm.

A rarely seen butterfly that is found on sandstone outcrops in open eucalypt forest from Mount Moffatt in the Carnarvon Range, Qld, to near Grafton, NSW.

Larval Food – Attendant Ants: Unknown.

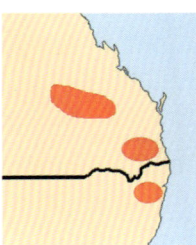

Small Copper *Lucia limbaria*

Size: Male 25mm, female 28mm.

Quite common and widespread, ranging from near Bowen, Qld, to SA. Usually found in open grassland or grassy woodland where the larval host plant grows. The larvae are attended by ants in the genus *Iridomyrmex*. When not feeding the larvae rest in the ants' nest, which is where they make their pupae.

Attendant Ants: *Iridomyrmex* sp.

Host Plants: *Oxalis perennans*, *O. exilis*, **O. corniculata*.

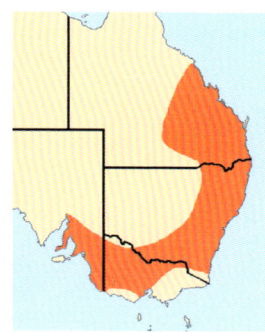

The images above are typical *Oxalis* species. They are small creeping plants that have a clover-like leaf and yellow flowers.

Oxalis perennans is very widespread, being found in all states of Australia.

Dull Copper *Paralucia pyrodiscus*

Size: Male 30mm, female 32mm.

Lives in open eucalypt forest where the host plant grows in conjunction with the attendant ant. Range extends from the Atherton Tablelands, Qld, to western Vic.

Attendant Ants: *Notoncus capitatus*, *N. gilberti*, *N. enormis* or *N. ectatommoides*.

Host Plants: *Bursaria spinosa*, *B. incana*, *Pittosporum spinescens*.

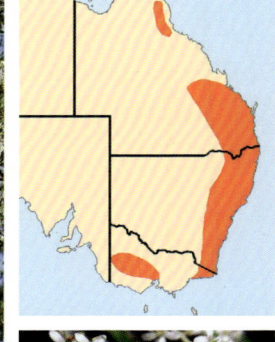

Bursaria incana is found in north-east NT, and from Cape York to south-east Qld, in open forest. It is a small tree that usually grows less then 10m tall. This is the most spectacular of all the *Bursaria* species. Although flowering can occur at any time of the year, the best displays are in spring or summer.

Dull Copper *Paralucia pyrodiscus*

Bursaria spinosa is well named. In the juvenile stage it has numerous very sharp spines; however, these gradually vanish as the plant matures. It is most unusual in that it flowers when very small; the bright white, perfumed flowers are very showy. Plant it in the full sun where you will not come into contact with the thorns.

Bright Copper *Paralucia aurifera*

Size: Male 28mm, female 29mm.

Widespread and locally common, occurring in open forests from south-east Qld to Vic and eastern Tas, where the host plants grow in association with the attendant ant. Young larvae stay on the host plant to feed but later they rest in the ants' nest and feed by night. Pupation takes place in the ants' nest.

Attendant Ants: *Anonychomyrma* sp.

Host Plants: *Bursaria spinosa*, *Pittosporum multiflorum*.

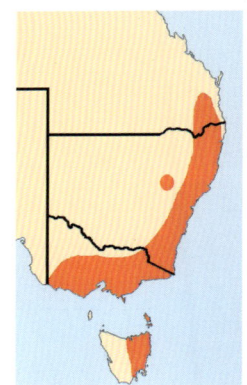

Bathurst Copper *Paralucia spinifera*

Size: Male 23mm, female 26mm.

Has a very limited distribution; it is restricted to open eucalypt woodland with a dense undergrowth in the central highlands of NSW from 800–1,200m altitude. This butterfly is a protected species which is classified as Endangered. Protection applies to private and public land.

Attendant Ants: *Anonychomyrma* sp.

Host Plant: *Bursaria spinosa* where the attendant ant occurs.

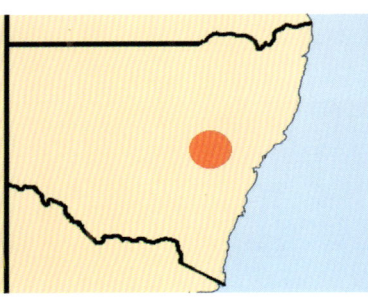

Dark Forest Blue *Pseudodipsas eone*

Size: Male 24mm, female 26mm.

Found in Qld from Cape York to about Townsville in low- to mid-altitude rainforest and nearby wet sclerophyll forest. The larvae are attended by the ant *Anonychomyrma gilberti*.

Host Plants: Mostly *Smilax australis*, sometimes *Guioa acutifolia*, *Clerodendrum costatum*, *Faradaya splendida*.

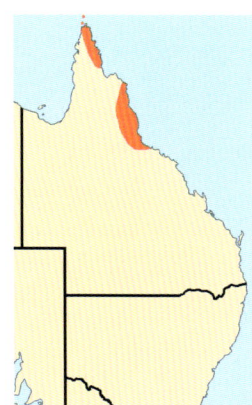

Smilax australis is a medium-sized vine that grows in a wide variety of rainforest types, usually at mid to low altitudes. The stem is very hard and has spines that can inflict a nasty wound. The bunches of berries turn black when ripe. One distinctive feature is the bright red new growth. It is this soft red foliage that the butterfly larvae use.

Guioa acutifolia is a very common small tree of lowland and mid-altitude rainforest. It usually grows in disturbed areas, along the edges of the rainforest or in nearby tall eucalypt forest. The branches are sometimes completely covered by the mass of small white flowers. The following abundance of small red fruit split open to show a bright orange aril surrounding the seed.

Bright Forest Blue *Pseudodipsas cephenes*

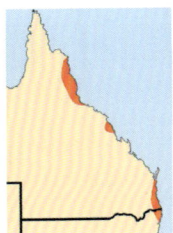

Size: Male 28mm, female 30mm.

Common in certain localised areas but not often seen. Found in littoral rainforest and along the edges of low- to mid-altitude rainforest in disjunct locations from about Cooktown in north Qld to northern NSW.

Attendant Ant: *Nonychomyrma gilberti*.

Host Plants: Mostly *Smilax australis*, sometimes *Guioa acutifolia*, *Acacia flavescens*, *A. sophorae*, *Diospyros fasciculosa*, *Halfordia kendack*.

Diospyros fasciculosa is a very widespread plant that is hardy but rather slow-growing. The beautiful glossy dark green foliage contrasts with the red, yellow, and black fruit. It is found in a variety of rainforest types, including coastal, and it handles salt spray. It ranges from Cape York, Qld, to northern NSW, usually in coastal rainforest, but further inland on Cape York Peninsula.

Apollo Jewel *Hypochrysops apollo*

H.a. phoebus.

■ H.a. apollo.

Size: Male 40mm, female 42mm.

Unusual as the larvae tunnel inside the host plant rather than eating the leaves. The host plants are species of Ant Plants (*Myrmecodia*), which are epiphytes that grow in the very humid lowlands of the wet tropics and Cape York Peninsula, Qld. The females lay their eggs on the tuber or foliage of the plants and the larvae move into ant tunnels, eating the fleshy tuber.

Attendant Ant: *Philidris cordatus* cohabits with them in the tunnels. The ants create the tunnels but the larvae of the Apollo Jewel enlarge them as they feed on the tuber. Sometimes at night the larvae move outside and feed on the leaves of the plant.

Host Plants: *Myrmecodia beccarii, M. platytyrea, M. tuberosa.*

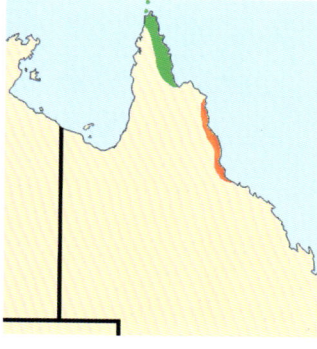
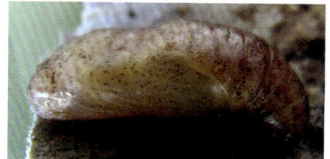

Apollo Jewel *Hypochrysops apollo*

Ant and larvae tunnels, with larva, in *Myrmecodia beccarii*.

Myrmecodia beccarii is restricted to an area from Hopevale (north of Cooktown) to about Ingham and is usually found in wet Melaleuca forests, swamps or mangroves. The spineless stems of *M. beccarii* distinguish it from *M. platytyrea* which also grows in the same area.

Myrmecodia platytyrea is quite widespread, occurring in north Qld from Torres Strait to Mossman in very moist locations from mangroves to about 600m altitude. The stems of this one are covered in spines.

Copper Jewel *Hypochrysops apelles*

Size: Male 32mm, female 34mm.

Unusual insomuch as it has an extremely varied habitat. Most commonly found in mangrove communities where it uses a number of species as host plants, but also occurs well inland in areas such as Georgetown (300km south-west of Cairns) in very dry, sparse forested habitat. This beautiful little butterfly is brilliantly coloured on both sides and often rests with wings spread.

Attendant Ants: *Crematogaster* sp.

Host Plants: Mangroves include *Avicennia, Bruguiera, Ceriops, Lumnitzera, Rhizophora*; away from mangroves *Acacia, Alphitonia, Angophora, Barringtonia, Commersonia, Petalostigma, Planchonia, Terminalia, Vandasina*. The fact that this butterfly uses so many unrelated host plants suggests it is linked to the attendant ant *Crematogaster* sp. rather than any particular plant.

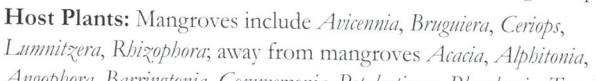

Ceriops tagal is a common mangrove found around the coastline of the northern half of Australia, south to northern NSW. Wherever it occurs it is most often used by the Copper Jewel as a host plant. The large soft leaves are ideal for the larvae to strip the flesh off as in the larva photo on the top right (this one is on *Terminalia catappa*) which is the usual way this species feeds. Skeletonised leaves on host plants are an indication of the butterfly's presence.

Elgner's Jewel *Hypochrysops elgneri*

Size: Male 40mm, female 44mm.

Restricted to Cape York Peninsula and Torres Strait, Qld. Two subspecies:
- ■ *H.e. barnardi* (illustrated here) on the mainland.
- ■ *H.e. elgneri* on the Torres Strait islands.

Adults fly high in the rainforest and adjacent open forest, rarely settling close to the ground.

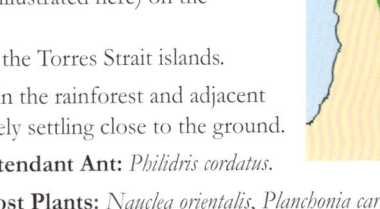

Attendant Ant: *Philidris cordatus*.

Host Plants: *Nauclea orientalis*, *Planchonia careya* and the mistletoes *Dendrophthoe glabrescens* and *Notothixos*.

Planchonia careya (Cocky Apple) is found in tropical Australia, rarely more then 200km from the coast, sometimes near rainforest but never in it. The large attractive flowers only last for the morning but do not wither immediately when they fall to the ground (see image).

Nauclea orientalis (Leichhardt Tree) is a large tree that grows to about 25m and is usually found along streams in tropical Australia north of about Bundaberg, Qld. There are two forms, the most common one has green new growth with hairless leaves and the other one has brown new growth which is covered in fine hairs.

Narcissus Jewel *Hypochrysops narcissus*

H.n. narcissus.

Size: Male 32mm, female 34mm.

A tropical butterfly that is found north of about Townsville, Qld. Two subspecies:
- ■ *H.n. narcissus* from Lakefield National Park to near Townsville.
- ■ *H.n. sabirius* from Torres Strait to Massy Creek (east of Coen).

The main habitat is mangroves and nearby melaleuca swamps where adults mostly fly high above the canopy, descending from time to time to feed on flowers.

H.n. sabirius.

Attendant Ant: *Philidris cordatus*.

Host Plants: Mangroves include: *Aegiceras corniculatum, Avicennia eucalyptifolia, Bruguiera exaristata, Ceriops tagal, Lumnitzera racemosa, Rhizophora stylosa*. Mistletoe host plants: *Dendrophthoe vitellina, Diplatia tomentosa, Notothixos incanus*. Other plants: *Lophostemon suaveolens, Terminalia catappa*.

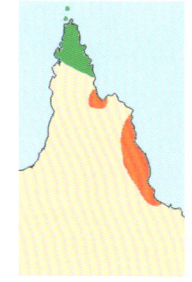

Aegiceras corniculatum is a very widespread mangrove, its range extending from the central coast of WA around to Vic. The white flowers are quite showy, perfumed, and attract many insects. As well as general coastal areas this species is also found along saltwater creeks and rivers.

Dendrophthoe vitellina is a mistletoe that is found predominantly in eastern Australia from Torres Strait, Qld, to Vic, extending well inland. It is a parasite, for the most part on Eucalyptus trees in the open forest but also on the edge of rainforest were there is ample light.

Miskin's Jewel *Hypochrysops miskini*

  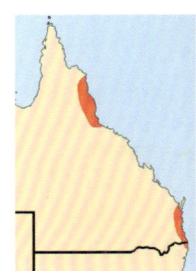

Size: Male 30mm, female 34mm.

Found in two widely separated locations: from about Maryborough, Qld, to northern NSW; and in Qld from about Hopevale, north of Cooktown, to Bowen. Inhabits moist to very wet rainforest where the host plant grows. Adults of this butterfly are rarely seen as they fly and settle quite high on foliage.

Attendant Ant: *Anonychomyrma gilberti*.

Host Plants: Mostly *Smilax australis*, also on *Commersonia, Eucalyptus, Faradaya, Glochidion, Guioa, Lophostemon, Maesa, Rhodomyrtus, Tetrasynandra*. This list of unrelated host plants suggests that the ant is more important than the plant.

Paradise Jewel *Hypochrysops hippuris*

Size: Male 34mm, female 36mm.

Another tropical butterfly that is restricted to the rainforest between the Rocky River and the Pascoe River on Cape York Peninsula, Qld. This is one of only two species that uses a fern as a host plant. Adults fly rapidly and males are often seen hilltopping.

Attendant Ant: *Philidris cordatus*.

Host Plant: *Pyrrosia lanceolata*.

 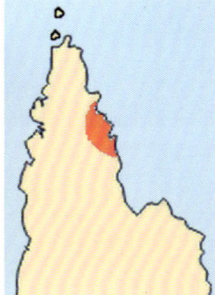

Pyrrosia lanceolata is in its element growing on rocks as well as on trees and is a common sight in the rainforests north of Coen on Cape York Peninsula, Qld.

Royal Jewel *Hypochrysops polycletus*

Size: Male 32mm, female 34mm.

A truly spectacular little butterfly of the tropics. The bright iridescent blue on the upper surface of the male's wings rivals that of the Ulysses Swallowtail and the bright red marks edged in blue/green on the underside add to its beauty. This butterfly is usually found in semi-deciduous or deciduous vine forest where the host plant grows. The larvae are very well camouflaged and blend in on the backs of the leaves.

Attendant Ants: Unlike most of the Lycaenidae butterflies the larvae of this species are only sometimes attended by ants, either *Iridomyrmex sanguineus* or *Camponotus* sp.

Host Plant: *Stigmaphyllon australiense (Rhyssopterys timorensis).*

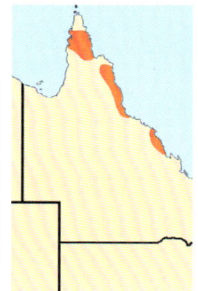

The almost invisible larvae.

Stigmaphyllon australiense (Rhyssopterys timorensis) is a medium-sized vine found in deciduous and semi-deciduous vine thickets in the eastern Australian tropics. In some areas the leaves are covered in silver hairs. The bright yellow flowers make this vine easy to identify.

Fruit.

Green-banded Jewel *Hypochrysops theon*

Size: Male 35mm, female 39mm.

Restricted to the northern part of Cape York Peninsula, Qld. Extremely localised and has three subspecies, each with a very limited distribution: ■ *H.t. medocus*, ■ *H.t. johnsoni* and ■ *H.t. cretatus*. Because the main host plant, *Drynaria*, usually grows on boulders in the rainforest the butterflies are found quite low down in the understorey.

Attendant Ant: *Philidris cordatus*.

Host Plants: Mostly *Drynaria quercifolia*. Also *Platycerium hillii* (Elk Horn).

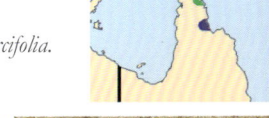

Spore frond.

Nest fronds.

Drynaria quercifolia is a lithophytic or epiphytic fern of the tropics. *Drynaria* ferns produce fronds of two distinct forms. The longer green fronds can be either fertile or sterile while the shorter fronds (nest fronds) are always sterile. The leaves of these nest fronds are thin and papery and persist on the plant for long periods. They shield the rhizome of the plant and as a unit they form a bowl effect by which the plant collects the fallen leaves and twigs of surrounding plants. These plant parts break down and supply the *Drynaria* with nutrients.

Platycerium hillii (Elk Horn) is a commonly cultivated garden plant. It usually grows as an epiphyte on the trunks or thick branches of rainforest trees. On Cape York Peninsula, Qld, it is regularly found growing on boulders (lithophytic), especially north of Coen, and this probably suits the butterflies more than the ones high up in trees.

Peacock Jewel *Hypochrysops pythias*

Size: Male 30mm, female 32mm.

Another tropical butterfly that occurs in Qld from about Cooktown to Townsville in well-developed rainforest. The adults usually fly high in the canopy and the populations are very local so it is not often seen.

Attendant Ants: None.

Host Plants: Usually *Commersonia bartramia*, also *Trichospermum pleiostigma*.

Trichospermum pleiostigma is restricted to the wet tropical lowland and foothill rainforest in north Qld from about Kuranda to Dunk Island. It is a medium-sized tree that is found commonly in disturbed rainforest. The flowers are quite attractive but rather small at about 1cm across. The leaves look somewhat like those of *Commersonia* but lack the pale, almost white underside.

Commersonia bartramia is a very widespread plant, its range extending from Cape York, Qld, to northern NSW, in moist to very wet rainforest. It can easily be identified by the mass of white flowers that are quite distinctive on the layered branches. It is interesting to note that the distribution of *C. bartramia* in north Qld matches almost exactly that of the Peacock Jewel. It is a large tree that is fast growing and for the most part found in re-growth rainforest.

Yellow-spot Jewel *Hypochrysops byzos*

Size: Male 30mm, female 32mm.

Found from south-east Qld to central Vic, then in an isolated colony on the Blackdown Tableland, west of Rockhampton. Adults fly rapidly, with both sexes seen frequently on the host plants. *Pomaderris* are usually small to medium shrubs so the butterflies are not very high up. Males establish territories by landing on leaves near the top of a host plant with wings partly spread (top left image). Usually found in moist eucalypt forest where the host plants grow as an understorey.

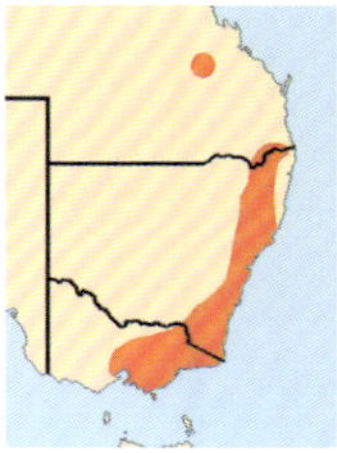

Attendant Ants: None.

Host Plants: *Pomaderris andromedifolia, P. aspera, P. cotoneaster, P. eriocephala, P. ferruginea, P. intermedia, P. lanigera, Rulingia salviifolia, Commersonia fraseri.*

The range of *Pomaderris lanigera* (Woolly Pomaderris) matches almost exactly that of the Yellow-spot Jewel; Rockhampton to Melbourne. It is a shrub that grows to about 3m high. Most species in this genus have either white or silver undersides to the leaves and yellow flowers. This one has rusty hairs on leaves and stems.

Diggles' Jewel *Hypochrysops digglesii*

Size: Male 33mm, female 36mm.

Quite widespread, occurring from Cape York, Qld, to northern NSW but is rarely seen and very local. Adults are very secretive although they are sometimes seen around the mistletoe host plants or feeding on flowers. They are usually found in open eucalypt forest but also in parks and gardens where their mistletoe host plants grow, often on *Eucalyptus* trees.

Attendant Ant: *Crematogaster* sp.

Host Plants: A wide range of mistletoe host plants includes: *Amyema bifurcata, A. congener, A. conspicua, A. miquelii, A. sanguinea, Dendrophthoe curvata, D. glabrescens, D. homoplastica.*

Dull Jewel *Hypochrysops epicurus*

Size: Male 30mm, female 32mm.

A mangrove butterfly. Its host plant is a mangrove so it will not be found far from the coast or saltwater sections of rivers. Occurs in south-east Qld and northern NSW; usually inhabits areas where *Casuarina* or *Melaleuca* trees provide shade nearby.

Attendant Ant: An *Anonychomyrma* species which colonises hollow branches of the host plant.

Host Plant: *Avicennia marina*.

Avicennia marina is a very widespread mangrove that is found around almost the entire Australian coastline. It is a large tree with spreading branches and roots. It is probably only the distribution of the attendant ant that limits the range of this butterfly.

Bright Purple Jewel *Hypochrysops cyane*

Size: Male 32mm, female 34mm.

Found from Cape York Peninsula, Qld, to southern NSW in isolated and localised populations. It is quite possible that there are more colonies as the adults fly high in the trees and quite fast so are very difficult to find. The attendant ants live in hollow branches of the host plants so the butterflies usually inhabit older trees that have developed suitable habitats for the ants. Because this species has a very wide range of unrelated host plants the ants are probably more important than the specific plant.

Attendant Ants: *Anonychomyrma* sp., *A. gilberti*.

Host Plants: *Acacia humifusa, Alphitonia pomaderroides (Alphitonia obtusifolia), Amyema miquelii, Angophora costata, Eucalyptus moluccana, Lophostemon grandiflorus, Melaleuca leucadendra*.

Alphitonia pomaderroides is a large shrub that is common in the open eucalypt forests of northern Qld. It is very hardy, and although it may show signs of stress during the dry season, it always springs back to life after the first rains. The underside of the foliage is white. It is found in north-eastern NT and in Qld from Cape York to about Townsville, in open eucalypt forest.

Fiery Jewel *Hypochrysops ignitus*

Size: Male 28mm, female 32mm.

Occurs in many isolated populations around mainland Australia, usually not more than 200km from the coast. There are four named subspecies: *H.i. chrysonotus*, *H.i. erythrina*, *H.i. olliffi* and *H.i. ignitus*.

Attendant Ants: *Papyrius* sp.

Host Plants: This butterfly has no specific host plant – the females will lay on almost any plant that the ants are on.

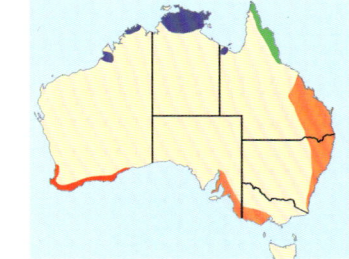

■ *H.i. chrysonotus.*

■ *H.i. erythrina.* ■ *H.i. olliffi.*

■ *H.i. ignitus.* *H.i. ignitus* – mallee form.

FAMILY LYCAENIDAE – SUBFAMILY THECLINAE   BLUES AND COPPERS

Blue Jewel *Hypochrysops delicia*

H.d. delicia.

H.d. duaringae.

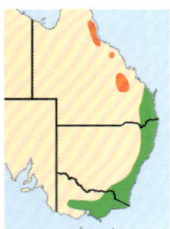

Size: Male 36mm, female 38mm.

Two subspecies:
- ■ *H.d. delicia* from west of Cairns to central Qld.
- ■ *H.d. duaringae* from south-east Qld to Vic.

Adults fly rapidly and are best observed when taking nectar. The usual habitat is open eucalypt forest. Preferred host plants are older trees with borer holes where the attendant ant can breed.

Attendant Ants: *Crematogaster* sp.

Host Plants: A wide range of *Acacia* species, sometimes *Alphitonia excelsa*.

Alphitonia excelsa covers an extremely wide range from the Kimberley region, WA, to southern Vic. It occurs in rainforest and eucalypt forest. The flowers attract numerous insects and is worth growing just for that. This plant varies so much when growing in different habitats and regions that three subspecies have been named.

Western Jewel *Hypochrysops halyaetus*

Size: Male 28mm, female 30mm.

Found in the south-west of WA in coastal heathland and mixed *Banksia* woodland where colonies of the attendant ant are established.

Attendant Ants: *Crematogaster* sp.

Host Plants: *Jacksonia sternbergiana, Acacia xanthina, Daviesia daphnoides, D. divaricata*. As there are numerous species of *Daviesia* in WA this butterfly very likely uses many of them.

Northern form.

Northern form.

Southern form.

Daviesia divaricata is a shrub that grows 1–3m high. The flowers vary from yellow to orange. *Daviesia* species are often called Bitter-peas.

Large Moonbeam *Philiris papuanus kerri*

Size: Male 28mm, female 30mm.

Two subspecies:
– *P.p papuanus* in Papua New Guinea.
■ *P.p. kerri* from Cape York to the Rocky River, Qld.

This butterfly is usually found along the edge of the rainforest where juvenile plants of the host plant are common.

Attendant Ants: None.

Host Plants: *Litsea breviumbellata*.

Best Garden Host Plant: *Litsea breviumbellata*.

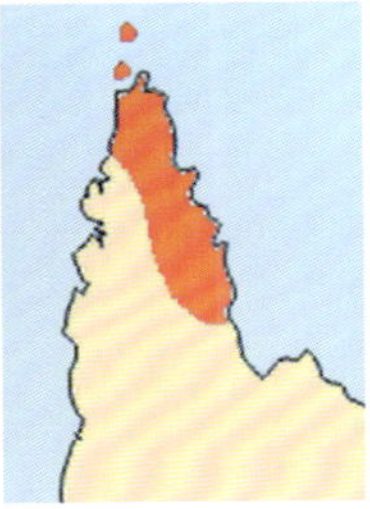

Female flowers.

Litsea breviumbellata is a medium to large shrub that is very hardy and should not require any special attention. The rusty leaves and flowers make it quite attractive, and as it produces separate male and female plants, several will be needed in order to guarantee fruit.

Male flowers.

Purple Moonbeam *Philiris fulgens kurandae*

Size: Male 28mm, female 32mm.

Found in Qld from Cape York to about Townsville in lowland rainforest, usually near the edge of forest or along streams, or in disturbed areas where juvenile host plants grow.

Attendant Ants: None.

Host Plants: *Litsea breviumbellata*, *L. leefeana*, *Cryptocarya mackinnoniana*, *C. murrayi*, *Endiandra hypotephra*.

Best Garden Host Plant: *Litsea breviumbellata* or *L. leefeana*.

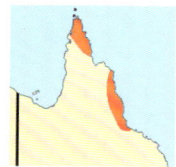

Litsea leefeana is a small to medium tree that grows in rainforest from about Cooktown, Qld, to northern NSW. The new growth is covered in rusty hairs. The black fruit attracts many birds. It can be heavily pruned to limit its size to a large shrub. The resulting new growth from regular pruning is ideal for the Purple Moonbeam females to lay on.

FAMILY LYCAENIDAE – SUBFAMILY THECLINAE   BLUES AND COPPERS

Common Moonbeam *Philiris innotata*

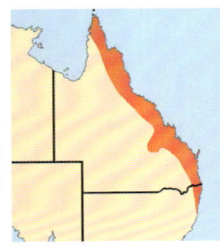

Size: Male 28mm, female 30mm.

Occurs from Cape York, Qld, to northern NSW in lowland rainforest, nearby open forest, gallery forest and vine thickets where the host plants grow.

Attendant Ants: Usually there are no attendant ants, but occasionally found with *Crematogaster* sp.

Host Plants: Mostly *Ficus opposita* (Sandpaper Fig), in southern areas *F. coronata*, less commonly on *F. congesta*, *F. benghalensis*, *F. carica*.

Best Garden Host Plant: *Ficus opposita*.

The larvae of the Common Moonbeam are almost impossible to see when resting along the leaf next to the main vein. Freshly chewed channels on the leaf betray their presence.

Ficus opposita (Sandpaper Fig) is a very common plant in dry rainforest, vine thickets and rocky outcrops across the northern half of Australia. It gets its common name from the very rough sandpapery surface of the leaves. The larvae live on the underside of the leaves, resting along the main vein when not feeding, and they make their pupae in the same place.

Blue Moonbeam *Philiris nitens*

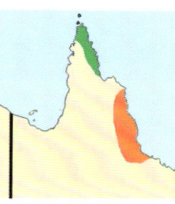

P. n. nitens.

Size: Male 26mm, female 28mm.

Two subspecies in Qld:
- ■ *P. n. nitens* from about Cape Melville to Townsville.
- ■ *P. n. lucina* from Cape York to about the Rocky River.

Found along the edges of lowland rainforest or in disturbed areas where the host plants grow.

Attendant Ants: None.

Host Plants: Usually *Macaranga involucrata*, also *M. tanarius*, *Glochidion philippicum*.

Best Garden Host Plant: *Macaranga involucrata*.

Macaranga tanarius (Blush Macaranga) is a very hardy, fast-growing tree which can be used as a quick screen or small shade tree. It has large, heart-shaped leaves which give the garden a 'tropical' look. Because it is such a fast-growing plant it tends to rob nearby plants of root-space and nutrients, so be prepared to see these plants suffer. This applies to all 'pioneer species' (trees that come up soonest after rainforest is cleared). Honeyeaters are fond of the small black seeds.

Sapphire Moonbeam *Philiris sappheira*

Size: Male 26mm, female 27mm.

Confined to a small area of Qld north of Cooktown centred around the McIvor River even though the larval host plant is very widely distributed. There is another subspecies of this butterfly in New Guinea.

Attendant Ants: None.

Host Plant: *Macaranga involucrata*.

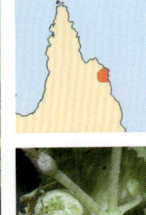

Macaranga involucrata is a large shrub or small tree that usually grows along the edge of rainforest or in disturbed areas within rainforest. It is widespread and occurs in Qld from Torres Strait to about Rockhampton.

White-margined Moonbeam *Philiris ziska*

Size: Male 24mm, female 24mm.

Restricted to a small area on the east coast of Cape York Peninsula, Qld, including Iron Range and the Rocky River. Males rest in sunlit areas on the tops of tall trees, while females fly in the same area for most of the day.

Attendant Ants: None.

Host Plant: *Trophis scandens* (see page 113 for more details).

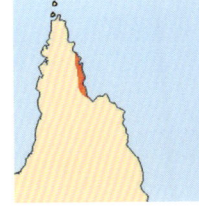

Trophis scandens is a large vine with milky sap and abrasive bark on the stems. It is found in most rainforest types in northern Australia.

Male flowers.

Dull Oak Blue *Arhopala eupolis*

Size: Male 50mm, female 50mm.

Two subspecies:
- ■ *A.e. eupolis* in Qld from Cape York to about Rockhampton.
- ■ *A.e. asopus* in the top end of WA and NT.

Attendant Ants: The larvae are attended by the Green Tree Ants, *Oecophylla smaragdina*, and are not tied to any specific host plants. The main requirement is that the Green Tree Ants have nests on the plant. Just south of Rockhampton is the southern limit of these ants.

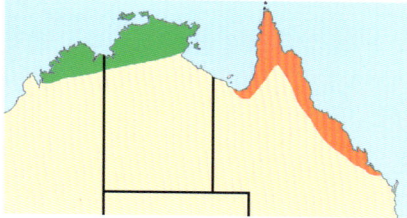

Host Plants: *Buchanania, Maranthes, Terminalia, Dendrophthoe, Eucalyptus, Corymbia, Melaleuca, Cupaniopsis, *Lagerstroemia.*

Best Garden Host Plants: *Buchanania, Maranthes, Terminalia.*

Buchanania obovata is found in the top end of WA, NT, and in Qld; the eastern extent of its range is about Mt Isa, in open forest. It has especially developed, very hard and stiff foliage to stand up to the blistering heat of the top end of Australia, in fully exposed situations.

Buchanania arborescens occurs in the top end of WA and NT, and then in Qld from Cape York to Cardwell, in lowland and gallery rainforest. It develops into a small tree which produces copious amounts of small black fruit, which are edible but give some people a sore throat if too many are consumed in one sitting.

Maranthes corymbosa occurs in the top end of NT, and in Qld from Torres Strait to about Coen, in coastal or gallery rainforest. It forms a dense tree with dark green foliage that will remain low to the ground if planted in the open. The large heads of small white flowers are quite showy.

Bright Oak Blue *Arhopala madytus*

Size: Male 48mm, female 50mm.

Like many iridescent blue butterflies around the world, the Oak Blues have dark camouflaged markings on the underside of their wings so that when they land they are very difficult to see. The adults of this species and others in the group can be seen flashing their bright blue colours in the sunlight as they dart around in the vicinity of the plant on which they are breeding. The Bright Oak Blue is found in Qld from Cape York to about Rockhampton.

Attendant Ant: Green Tree Ant, *Oecophylla smaragdina*. Most gardeners consider these ants a pest and try to exterminate them, so only avid butterfly enthusiasts would encourage the attendant ant of this species to live in their garden.

Host Plants: Recorded host plants are *Terminalia catappa*, *T. melanocarpa*, *T. sericocarpa*, *Hibiscus tiliaceus*.

Best Garden Host Plant: *Terminalia catappa*.

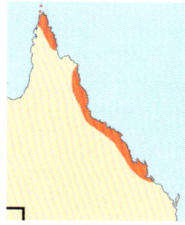

Terminalia microcarpa (sericocarpa) is a medium to large tree that spreads out when in the open. It is a tropical rainforest plant that is found from the Kimberley region in WA to about Rockhampton in Qld. Often grown as a street tree, it is readily available from native plant nurseries. The mass of small fruit attracts birds.

Common Oak Blue *Arhopala micale*

Arhopala micale northern form.

Size: Male 54mm, female 56mm.

Found in the top end of NT and in Qld from Cape York to about Rockhampton. The variation from NT is referred to as the 'northern form'.

Host Plants: *Buchanania, Cordia, Parinari, Calophyllum, Terminalia, Glochidion, Cryptocarya, Brachychiton, Hibiscus, Sterculia, Xylocarpus, Acmena, Ristantia, Syzygium, Cupaniopsis, Heritiera, Faradaya,* **Lagerstroemia.*

Best Garden Host Plant: *Syzygium tierneyanum.*

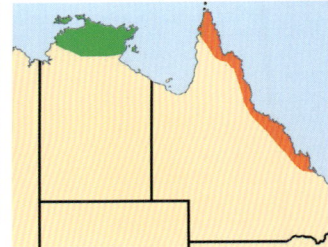

A.m. amytis.

Syzygium tierneyanum (River Cherry) is usually found along streams north of about Ingham, Qld. It makes the perfect windbreak or screen. With very dense foliage that is not bothered by winds, it can grow quite well without extra water. However, the more water it has the bigger and better it will grow. If the lower branches are trimmed it can be made into a small shade tree. Birds are attracted to the flowers. The fruit can be either red or white, white being most common.

Small Oak Blue *Arhopala wildei*

Size: Male 40mm, female 42mm.

Found in Qld from Cape York to about Townsville, and unlike the other Oak Blues its range extends further inland, quite some distance from rainforest.

Attendant Ants: *Polyrhachis queenslandica*, sometimes called Black Tree Ant.

Host Plants: *Ristantia pachysperma*, *Syzygium tierneyanum*, *Terminalia subacroptera*.

Best Garden Host Plants: *Syzygium* sp. or *Terminalia* sp.; attendant ants must be present.

Terminalia subacroptera is an extremely hardy plant that makes an ideal small shade tree in the drier areas of the tropics. The only problem is that it is deciduous and sheds most of its leaves near the end of winter (just before the dry season). When the new foliage appears it is a fresh pale green. The flowers have a strong honey scent and attract many insects, but not butterflies. Birds will flock to feast on the small purple to red fruit that is produced in large quantities.

Satin Azure *Ogyris amaryllis*

Size: Male 40mm, female 44mm.

Three subspecies, which when combined cover almost all of mainland Australia:
- *O.a. amaryllis* in south-east Qld and NSW, east of the Great Dividing Range.
- *O.a. meridionalis* occupies most of the inland, west of the ranges.
- *O.a. hewitsoni* in coastal Qld from about Cooktown to the Sunshine Coast.

Having such a wide distribution it occurs in a wide range of habitats from mangroves to the arid inland, but not usually in rainforest. The males are bright shimmering blue but you will be lucky to ever see one with wings spread.

Attendant Ants: As well as an extensive range of host plants the larvae are attended by a similar variety of ants, including *Anonychomyrma, Crematogaster, Iridomyrmex, Ochetellus, Tapinoma*.

Host Plants: They use a wide range of mistletoes including at least 17 species of *Amyema*, also *Diplatia grandibractea* and *D. furcata*.

Silky Azure *Ogyris oroetes*

Size: Male 42mm, female 44mm.

Two subspecies occur in widely scattered colonies in mainland Australia:
- *O.o. oroetes* is generally in coastal areas of WA and NT, but in Qld the range extends well inland. This could be simply be due to the fact that more collecting has been carried out in these areas and so there are more records.
- *O.o. apiculata* in south-west WA and SA.

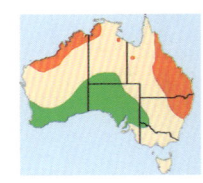

Principally found in eucalypt woodland and favours mistletoes that grow on smooth-bark gum trees.

Attendant Ants: The larvae are not always attended by ants but the following species have been recorded with them – *Anonychomyrma, Froggattella, Iridomyrmex, Ochetellus, Camponotus, Crematogaster, Meranoplus, Podomyrma, Rhytidoponera, Tetraponera, Tetramorium, *Technomyrmex*.

Host Plants: *Amyema bifurcata, A. miquelii, A. pendula*.

Broad-margined Azure *Ogyris olane*

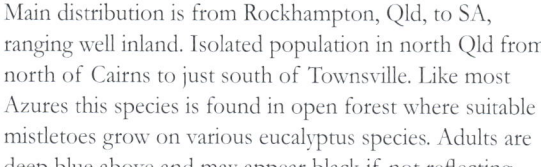

Size: Male 40mm, female 42mm.

Main distribution is from Rockhampton, Qld, to SA, ranging well inland. Isolated population in north Qld from north of Cairns to just south of Townsville. Like most Azures this species is found in open forest where suitable mistletoes grow on various eucalyptus species. Adults are deep blue above and may appear black if not reflecting sunlight when they fly.

Attendant Ants: The larvae are not always attended by ants but at times the following genera may be found with them – *Anonychomyrma, Froggattella, Iridomyrmex, Ochetellus, Camponotus, Crematogaster, Monomorium, Podomyrma*.

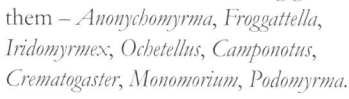

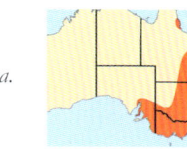

Host Plants: *Amyema miquelii, A. pendula*.

Barnard's Azure *Ogyris barnardi*

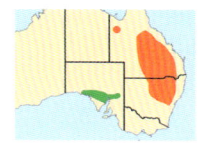

Size: Male 38mm, female 42mm.

Two subspecies:
- ■ *O.b. barnardi* in Qld and NSW.
- ■ *O.b. delphis* in southern SA.

Adults are deep blue to purple on the top of their wings but usually appear black when flying. This butterfly was once common in the Brigalow scrub belt but with that now all but wiped out, their colonies are very fragmented.

Host Plants: *Amyema quandang* or sometimes *A. maidenii* when growing on *Acacia* trees.

O.b. delphis.

Amyema quandang. var *quandang* is widespread, its range covering most of eastern Australia except for Cape York Peninsula, Qld. The blue/grey colour of the foliage is quite distinctive. It is mainly found growing on *Acacia* species.

Sydney Azure *Ogyris ianthis*

Size: Male 38mm, female 42mm.

Most unusual because even though the male is bright pale blue above, the female is golden-yellow. Has a fairly limited and patchy range from the Blackdown Tableland west of Rockhampton, Qld, to just south of Sydney, NSW. As with other Azures they are found in open eucalyptus forest where their mistletoe host plants grow.

Attendant Ant: *Froggattella kirbii.*

Host Plants: *Amyema linophylla, A. miquelii, A. quandang, Dendrophthoe glabrescens, D. vitellina, Muellerina eucalyptoides.*

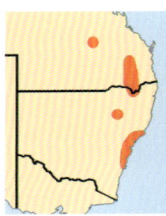

A.q. var. bancroftii.

A.q. var. bancroftii.

Amyema quandang has two varieties: *A.q.* var *bancroftii*, which is found over most of Qld and northern NSW; and *A.q.* var *quandang*, which is much more widespread, covering most of eastern Australia except for Cape York Peninsula, Qld. The blue/grey colouring of the foliage is quite distinctive, with variety *quandang* being more pendulous and having quite narrow leaves. It is mainly found growing on *Acacia* species.

A.q. var. quandang.

Orange-tipped Azure *Ogyris iphis*

♂

♀

O.i. iphis.

Size: Male 36mm, female 40mm.

Gets its name from the female, which has a small orange area near the top of the forewing (just visible in the image). The rest of the upper surface of the wings are bright blue, similar to the male. There are two subspecies:
- ■ *O.i. iphis* in north Qld, ranging from just north of Cooktown to west of Townsville.
- ■ *O.i. doddi* in NT on Melville Island and near Darwin.

An uncommon butterfly that is rarely encountered.

Attendant Ant: *Froggattella kirbii.*

Host Plants: *Amyema bifurcata, A. miquelii, A. quandang, A. sanguinea, Dendrophthoe glabrescens, D. vitellina.*

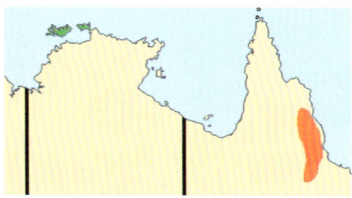

Amyema miquelii is found all over mainland Australia in the open forest, usually growing on eucalypts or acacias. It forms large pendulous clumps up to 3m long.

Cooktown Azure *Ogyris aenone*

Southern form female.

Size: Male 48mm, female 52mm.

The distribution covers a very wide area but the known populations are limited to the areas marked on the map. In north Qld this butterfly is found in moist coastal areas where *Melaleuca viridiflora* and *Lophostemon suaveolens* grow. These are the main host plants for the mistletoes upon which the larvae feed. In south Qld it lives in mixed open woodland. Both sexes are bright pale blue on the upper surface of the wings, with the female having a slightly wider black margin on the top, as is the case with most Azures.

Attendant Ant: *Philidris cordatus* in north Qld and *Anonychomyrma* sp. in south Qld.

Host Plants: *Dendrophthoe vitellina*, *Diplatia furcata*, *D. tomentosa* in north Qld, *Amyema linophylla* most often but also on *A. miquelii*, *Lysiana exocarpi*.

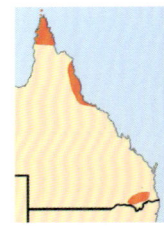

Lysiana exocarpi is very widespread, being most common in the central part of the southern half of the continent. Leaf width varies in different populations as do the flowers, which at times are bright red.

Dark Purple Azure *Ogyris abrota*

Size: Male 45mm, female 48mm.

Three isolated populations: in north Qld in upland open eucalyptus forest on the Atherton Tablelands; near Eungella, west of Mackay, Qld; and then from south-east Qld to SA where it also is found at lower altitudes. Males are deep blue on the upper surface of the wings and females are brown with a large yellow patch in the forewing. The host plant mistletoes for this butterfly are found on *Eucalyptus*, *Banksia* and *Allocasuarina*.

Attendant Ants: Sometimes attended by ants of the genera *Anonychomyrma*, *Crematogaster*, *Froggattella*, *Iridomyrmex*, *Rhytidoponera*, *Technomyrmex*, *Linepithema.

Host Plants: *Amyema congener*, *Dendrophthoe vitellina*, *Muellerina celastroides*, *M. eucalyptoides*.

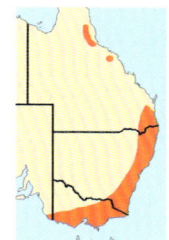

Amyema congener subsp. *congener* is widespread in eastern Australia, being found from Torres Strait, Qld, to Vic in open or monsoon forest, also in coastal rainforest. It has many host plants including *Casuarina*, *Acacia* and many rainforest species including *Geijera*. The foliage is mostly glossy, upright and rather rigid except for the new growth which has fine hairs.

Southern Large Azure *Ogyris genoveva*

Size: Male 52mm, female 58mm.

Range extends from central Qld to SA in eucalypt woodland where the larval host plant mistletoes grow on *Eucalyptus* and *Acacia* trees. Males are deep blue on the upperside. Females are pale blue with a yellow band on the forewing, which also shows up on the underside.

Attendant Ant: *Camponotus*.

Host Plants: *Amyema, Dendrophthoe, Muellerina*.

Muellerina eucalyptoides is found in eastern Australia, from about Mackay, Qld, to eastern SA in open forest. It is usually found growing on eucalypt trees but occasionally on introduced trees in gardens. Has a pendulous habit that makes it blend in with many eucalypt leaves.

Northern Large Azure *Ogyris zosine*

Size: Male 52mm, female 56mm.

Has a very wide distribution across the northern half of Australia. Most common in tall eucalypt forest but also occurs in coastal wallum and *Acacia* scrubland in the dry interior. Adults similar to those of the Southern Large Azure except most females are purple rather than blue.

Attendant Ant: *Camponotus*.

Host Plants: *Amyema, Decaisnina, Dendrophthoe, Diplatia, Muellerina.*

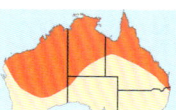

Diplatia furcata is found from the Kimberley region, WA, across the top end of Australia and down the east coast to northern NSW. It has an upright growth habit and is usually fairly open. The flowers are encased between special bracts that part as the flowers develop. These bracts remain until the fruit is mature, then fold back. Host plants include melaleucas, eucalypts and acacias.

Small Bronze Azure *Ogyris otanes*

■ *O.o. arcana.*

■ *O.o. sublustris.*

Size: Male 40mm, female 45mm.

Three subspecies have been named, all in southern and south-western Australia. The host plants are not actually mistletoes, but are related plants in the Santalaceae family which are root parasites. The butterfly is found in heathland, open eucalypt woodland and mallee shrubland. This is a very localised and uncommon species.

Attendant Ant: *Camponotus terebrans.*

Host Plants: *Choretrum spicatum* in north-west Vic, *C. glomeratum* in SA and *Leptomeria preissiana* in WA.

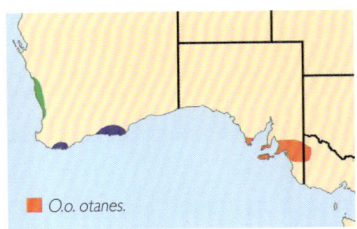

■ *O.o. otanes.*

Leptomeria preissiana is a shrub that usually grows from about 1–2m high. It has a mass of white flowers that makes it quite conspicuous and is widespread in the south-west of WA in open forest with a heath understorey.

Arid Bronze Azure *Ogyris subterrestris*

■ *O.t. subterrestris.*

■ *O.t. petrina.*

Size: Male 38mm, female 45mm.

Another extremely rare butterfly. Declared extinct in NSW and is listed as Critically Endangered in WA and Vulnerable in Vic. Found in mallee woodland and hop-bush shrubland in the semi-arid zone. A very unusual Azure butterfly as the larvae do not feed on mistletoe or related plants. They are believed to either feed on regurgitations of the attending sugar ants or their larvae. The female lays her eggs near the base of smooth bark trees and shrubs and the larvae live in the ants' nest underground, which is where they pupate.

Attendant Ant: *Camponotus terebrans.*

Host Plants: None.

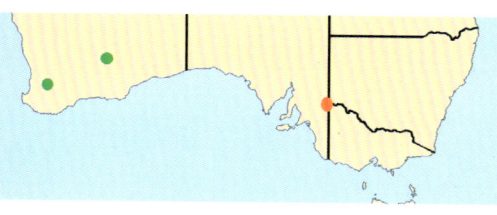

Large Bronze Azure *Ogyris idmo*

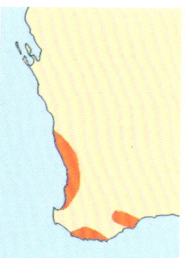

Size: Male 50mm, female 54mm.

Occurs in south-west WA in mallee open woodland and jarrah woodland.

Attendant Ant: Another species that does not have a host plant and observational evidence suggests that the larvae live in the nests of sugar ants, but how they feed is not known. Adults have been seen flying rapidly within 1–2m of the ground and laying eggs at the entrance of an ants' nest.

Host Plants: None.

Common Imperial Blue *Jalmenus evagoras*

Size: Male 38mm, female 42mm.

Found in eastern south-east Qld, NSW and Vic, in open forest where its *Acacia* host plants grow. Adults tend to congregate around the host plants where their attendant ants are abundant.

Attendant Ant: *Iridomyrmex* sp.

Host Plants: Numerous *Acacia* host plants have been recorded so more than likely the ants are more important than the specific Wattle. Host plants include the following: *Acacia irrorata, A. melanoxylon* in south-east Qld; *A. mearnsii* near Sydney, Canberra and Melbourne.

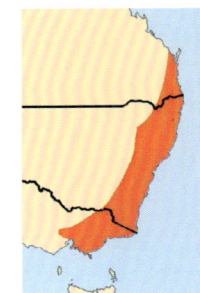

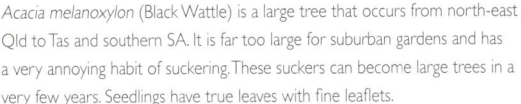

Acacia melanoxylon (Black Wattle) is a large tree that occurs from north-east Qld to Tas and southern SA. It is far too large for suburban gardens and has a very annoying habit of suckering. These suckers can become large trees in a very few years. Seedlings have true leaves with fine leaflets.

Stencilled Imperial Blue *Jalmenus ictinus*

Size: Male 36mm, female 40mm.

The main distribution is from about Rockhampton to central Vic, with several isolated populations in north Qld and western NSW. Information on range is based on collections, so there may be many more populations in between. Found in open eucalypt and acacia woodland where host plants and the attendant ants are abundant.

Attendant Ants: *Iridomyrmex purpureus*, *I. spadicus*.

Host Plants: *Acacia bidwillii*, *A. concurrens*, *A. dealbata*, *A. decurrens*, *S. harpophylla*, *A. implexa*, *A. irrorata*, *A. leiocalyx*, *A. mearnsii*, *A. melanoxylon*, *A. melvillei*, *A. pendula*, *A. rubida*, *Alectryon diversifolius* (only one record).

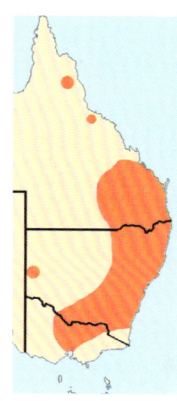

Acacia decurrens is endemic to central and southern NSW. Due to the fact that it is widely cultivated and grown in gardens, parks and forestry areas, it is now found from south Qld to SA, Tas and south-west WA. It is a medium-sized tree that grows to about 10–15m high, with bright yellow flowers. It has also naturalised in New Zealand, Africa and United States of America.

Macqueen's Imperial Blue *Jalmenus pseudictinus*

Size: Male 36mm, female 40mm.

Restricted to Qld with the main population being in the north, inland from Cairns, extending to south of Townsville in open eucalypt forest. Like many species in this group it is locally common, usually occurring where there are high populations of the attendant ants.

Attendant Ant: *Froggattella kirbii*.

Host Plants: *Acacia flavescens, A. humifusa, Alectryon connatus* in north Qld; *Acacia harpophylla, A. melvillei* in south Qld; and occasionally *Alectryon diversifolius*.

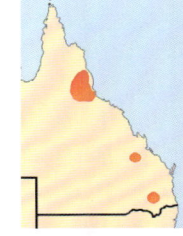

Acacia humifusa is a very widespread tropical plant that occurs from the Kimberley region to about Mackay in open eucalypt forest. It is a semi-prostrate shrub that grows to about 2m high and up to 5m wide. The small yellow flowers are not very conspicuous.

Northern Imperial Blue *Jalmenus eichhorni*

Size: Male 34mm, female 38mm.

Occurs in Qld from Cape York to about Greenvale (south-west of Cairns) in open eucalypt forest and along the edges of vine thickets. Fires in the winter can virtually wipe out populations as all the eggs, which are laid on *Acacia* shrubs, are destroyed. There used to be a very large colony near Mt Garnett but the species is hard to find there now. This problem exists for most *Jalmenus* butterflies as they usually spend the winter as eggs.

Attendant Ants: *Iridomyrmex reburrus*, *I. sanguineus*, *I. pallidus* and *Camponotus confusus* at night (the sugar-ants come out at night to feed from the nectar glands of acacias).

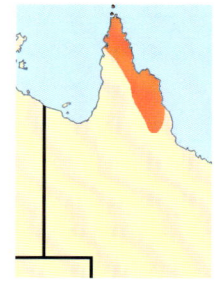

Host Plants: *Acacia crassicarpa*, *A. flavescens*, *A. holosericea*, *A. humifusa*, *A. leptocarpa*.

Acacia holosericea is a medium to large shrub. It has distinctive silver-blue foliage and bright yellow flowers. Its habitat ranges from wet coastal lowlands to the dry inland throughout tropical Australia.

Acacia crassicarpa is a large shrub or small tree that is very hardy and will grow in a wide range of situations. It is found in Qld from Torres Strait to about Gladstone in open eucalypt forest, being more common north of about Townsville.

The very large phyllodes and red new growth of *Acacia flavescens* (Red Wattle) make it an attractive tree. Fluffy cream flowers produced in great profusion are very showy. Flowering usually occurs within two years, but like many *Acacia* species it has a short life of less than 15 years. The common name comes from the colour of the wood.

Daemel's Imperial Blue *Jalmenus daemeli*

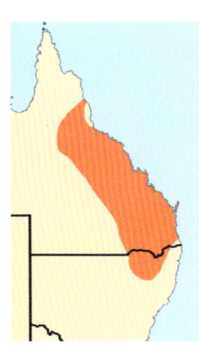

Size: Male 34mm, female 38mm.

Distribution extends from about Cairns, Qld, to northern NSW in open forest, including well inland, at least as far as Hughenden, Qld.

Attendant Ant: *Iridomyrmex* sp.

Host Plants: *Acacia bancroftii, A. bidwillii, A. concurrens, A. decurrens, A. glaucocarpa, A. harpophylla, A. irroata, A. leiocalyx, A. leucoclada, A. macradenia, A. melvillei, A. neriifolia, A. pendula, A. podalyriifolia*, as well as *Eucalyptus melanophloia, Corymbia, Alectryon diversifolius*.

Originally confined to south-east Qld, *Acacia podalyriifolia* is now found from about Cairns, Qld, to SA, Tas and south-west WA. Widespread planting as an ornamental has allowed it to become naturalised in many areas, including South-East Asia, East Africa and California in the USA. The blue/green (glaucous) foliage is a distinctive feature of this plant. This colour is due to a powdery substance that can be rubbed off when the leaf is touched.

Waterhouse's Imperial Blue *Jalmenus lithochroa*

Size: Male 34mm, female 36mm.

Only found in a small area of southern SA, in open shrubland and woodland in the open plains of the high-rainfall areas of the Mount Lofty and Flinders Ranges. In spite of this restricted distribution the species is quite common where it occurs.

Attendant Ants: *Iridomyrmex purpureus, I. viridiaeneus.*

Host Plants: *Acacia victoriae, A. pycnantha.*

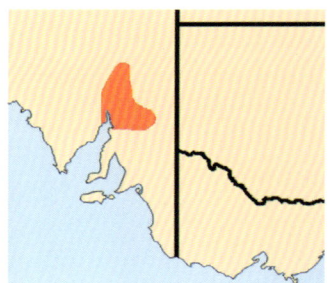

Acacia victoriae is a very widespread small to medium tree that grows 3–7m high and is found in all mainland states of Australia. It has very narrow 'leaves' (known as phyllodes – like many acacias it does not have true leaves) and spines on the branches, especially when juvenile. It often occurs in poorly drained soil where water is slow to drain away after rain.

Turquoise Imperial Blue *Jalmenus clementi*

Size: Male 28mm, female 32mm.

Found in the Pilbara district of WA in acacia open woodland. Adults usually remain close to the host plants where the attendant ants occur.

Attendant Ant: *Iridomyrmex*.
Host Plants: *Acacia inaequilatera, A. alexandri, A. tetragonophylla*.

Varied Imperial Blue *Jalmenus inous*

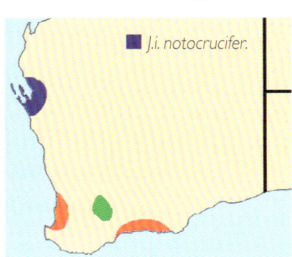

Size: Male 34mm, female 36mm.

Three subspecies named, all from south and west WA. The underside markings of all three are variable.

Attendant Ants: *Iridomyrmex conifer, I. turbineus* in coastal areas, *Iridomyrmex* sp. in inland areas.

Host Plants: *Acacia rostellifera, A. saligna, A. ligulata* in coastal areas; *Daviesia divaricata, Gastrolobium microcarpum* in near-coastal areas; *Daviesia benthamii* in inland areas.

■ *J.i. inous.*

■ *J.i. bronwynae.*

Amethyst Imperial Blue *Jalmenus icilius*

Size: Male 30mm, female 34mm.

Occurs in arid central Australia and south-west WA in grassy open woodland and acacia shrubland. Quite localised but common in the areas where it breeds. Has a big range of host plants so the presence of the associated ant is probably more important than the specific plant.

Attendant Ant: *Iridomyrmex* sp.

Host Plants: A big range of *Acacia* spp. as well as *Senna artemisioides* in the arid areas; *Daviesia benthamii* in WA.

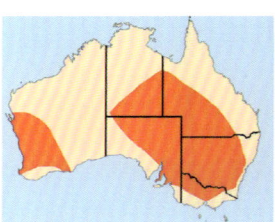

There are numerous subspecies of *Senna artemisioides*, all of which are in the arid parts of Australia. All are shrubs with yellow flowers but the foliage varies enormously.

Senna artemisioides subsp. *helmsii*.

Australian Hairstreak *Pseudalmenus chlorinda*

Size: Male 32mm, female 34mm.

Like no other Australian butterfly with its beautiful red/orange markings on the wings. Populations are very localised and even though the distribution is only from northern NSW to Tas there are six subspecies named. In the northern part of the range it occurs in open forest and subalpine woodland up to 1,500m, but down to sea-level in Tas.

Attendant Ant: *Anonychomyrma biconvexa*.

Host Plants: *Acacia melanoxylon, A. dealbata* in NSW, ACT and Vic; *A. dealbata* in Tas; and less commonly *A. decurrens, A. elata, A. irrorata, A. mearnsii, A. obtusifolia, A. preissiana, A. terminalis, A. trachyphloia*.

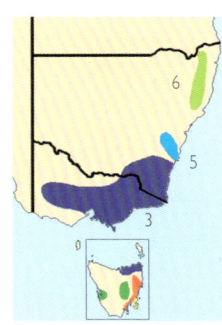

1 ■ *P.c. chlorinda*.

2 ■ *P.c. conara*.

   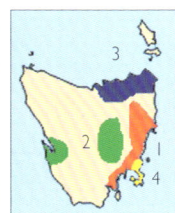

3 ■ *P.c. zephyrus*.
4 ■ *P.c. myrsilus*.
5 ■ *P.c. chloris*.
6 ■ *P.c. barringtonensis*.

FAMILY LYCAENIDAE – SUBFAMILY THECLINAE — BLUES AND COPPERS

Seedlings and saplings of *Acacia* species usually have 'true' leaves made up of very small leaflets. Like most wattles the mature plants have modified stems called 'phyllodes' that act as leaves.

Acacia melanoxylon (Black Wattle) is a large tree that is found in eastern Australia from about Cooktown, Qld, to SA and Tas. It can grow to 30m tall so is certainly too large for a suburban garden. Another problem is that it suckers and over the years can produce a large stand from these suckers.

Sword-tailed Flash *Bindahara phocides*

Size: Male 34mm, female 36mm.

Occurs in Qld from Torres Strait to about Bowen in low- to mid-altitude rainforest, most commonly in coastal areas where their mangrove host plant grows. The very long tails of this butterfly make it really stand out from all others.

Host Plants: Fruits of *Salacia chinensis*, *S. disepala*, *Celastrus subspicata*, *Pittosporum revolutum*, *Prunus turneriana*.

Best Garden Host Plant: *Salacia disepala*; the main host plant *S. chinensis* is a mangrove vine and will survive in a limited range of habitats.

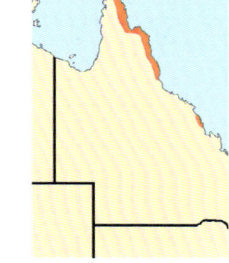

Larva on *Salacia chinensis* fruit.

Salacia chinensis is very cold-sensitive and does not survive very well when planted away from the coast. It is a medium-sized vine that grows in mangroves and along the banks of estuaries, where the base of the plant is usually submerged in water at high tide. The larvae of the Sword-tailed Flash eat the seed of the bright red fruit.

Blue Flash *Deudorix democles*

Size: Male 36mm, female 40mm.

Found in monsoon and wet tropical lowland rainforest as well as vine thickets where its *Strychnos* host plants grow. The larvae live in the fruit, eating the seed. Males are blue above with wide black margin; females are paler blue.

Host Plants: *Strychnos lucida*, *S. minor*.

Best Garden Host Plant: *Strychnos minor* – this is a large vine. The main host plant *S. lucida* is extremely slow-growing and most people find it impossible to grow.

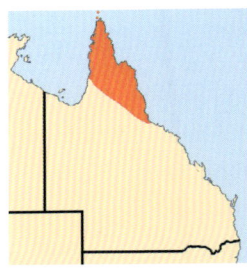

Strychnos minor a very large and extremely slow-growing vine; after more than 20 years plants in the author's garden are nowhere near mature. Because it occurs in lowland rainforest it should be grown at low altitudes where the higher temperatures will speed up the growth a bit. It is found on Melville Island, NT, then in Qld from Torres Strait to Ingham, in lowland rainforest. The large glossy leaves are quite attractive.

Darwin Blue Flash *Deudorix smilis*

  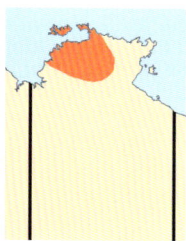

Size: Male 40mm, female 45mm.

Confined to the north-west area of NT where it occurs in vine thickets and monsoon rainforest. The larvae live inside the fruit of the host plant, eating the seed.

Attendant Ant: Very occasionally *Crematogaster*, *Oecophylla smaragdina*.

Host Plants: *Strychnos lucida*.

Best Garden Host Plant: *Strychnos lucida*.

Strychnos lucida is a small tree that grows in deciduous and semi-deciduous vine thickets in the top end of Australia, north of about Townsville, Qld. It is extremely slow growing and attempts to grow it in cultivation are usually unsuccessful. The leaves are very stiff and the three main veins are very distinctive. Bright orange/red fruit when mature.

Dull Cornelian *Deudorix epijarbas*

Size: Male 34mm, female 36mm.

A tropical species that is found in Qld from Torres Strait to about Townsville. Occurs in low- to mid-altitude rainforest.

Attendant Ants: None.

Host Plants: Fruits of *Caryota albertii* (native Fish-tail Palm), *Connarus conchocarpus*, *Salacia chinensis*, *Salacia disepala*, *Sarcopteryx martyana*, **Litchi chinensis*.

Best Garden Host Plant: *Connarus conchocarpus*.

Connarus conchocarpus is a very large but slow-growing vine, which has beautiful new growth and attractive bright red fruit. It should be planted in semi-shade from where it can climb into the sun. The Dull Cornelian larvae live in the fruit, eating the seed.

Bright Cornelian *Deudorix diovis*

Size: Male 34mm, female 35mm.

Occurs from the Pascoe River on Cape York Peninsula, Qld, to southern NSW in low- to mid-altitude rainforest and gardens where suitable host plants grow.

Attendant Ants: Very occasionally *Iridomyrmex, Paratrechina, Polyrhachis, Crematogaster, Tetramorium, Rhytidoponera, *Pheiodole*.

Host Plants: The list of host plants is large and most likely many more species are utilised. Recorded hosts are: *Connarus, Diploglottis, Elaeocarpus, Pittosporum, Macadamia, Alectryon, Arytera, Cupaniopsis, Harpullia, *Eriobotrya, *Litchi*. The Proteaceae plants *Buckinghamia* and *Stenocarpus* are also recorded but this is extremely doubtful as the seed of these is not suitable for the larvae.

Best Garden Host Plant: *Harpullia ramiflora*.

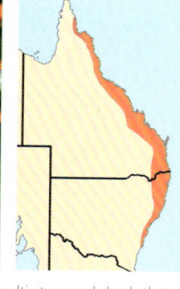

Harpullia ramiflora is a large multi-stemmed shrub that produces a mass of beautifully perfumed flowers and then fruit from the stems and branches. Fruiting will occur when it is only a couple of years old and Bright Cornelian butterflies will immediately be attracted. It is readily available from native plant nurseries.

Indigo Flash *Rapala varuna*

Size: Male 34mm, female 35mm.

Quite widespread, ranging from Torres Strait to south-east Qld. Found in rainforest, open forest and savannah woodland.

Attendant Ant: Very occasionally *Technomyrmex*.

Host Plants: Flower buds and flowers of *Acacia, Albizia, Alectryon, Buckinghamia, Alphitonia, Cupaniopsis, Dendrolobium, Elaeagnus, Eriobotrya, Jagera, Millettia, Paraserianthes, Pipturus, *Albizia, *Eriobotrya, *Litchi*.

Best Garden Host Plants: *Alphitonia excelsa, A. oblata*.

Alphitonia excelsa is found from the Kimberley region, WA, to southern NSW. There are three subspecies named and the plant varies from a large rainforest tree in north Qld to a small shrub in the eucalypt forest in south-east Qld. It is also found in sheltered sandstone gorges in inland Australia and the Kimberley region. The larvae of the Indigo Flash are perfectly camouflaged on the flowers of the host plants and almost impossible to see.

Indigo Flash *Rapala varuna*

Alphitonia oblata (incana) is very widespread, ranging from the Kimberley region, WA, all the way round to northern NSW. Usually in lowland rainforest or rainforest in sheltered gorges in the drier areas. It grows larger than *A. excelsa* and the leaves are furry to touch.

Black-and-white Tit *Hypolycaena danis*

Size: Male 30mm, female 34mm.

Range in Qld extends from Torres Strait to about Townsville in low- to mid-altitude rainforest. This butterfly is the bane of orchid-growers in this area as the larvae will eat the flowers of all orchids and the leaves and stems of those species soft enough for them to chew.

Attendant Ants: Occasionally small ants.

Host Plants: All orchid flowers, sometimes stems and leaves if they are fleshy.

Best Garden Host Plant: *Spathoglottis* – on this group the larvae eat only the flowers.

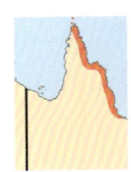

Spathoglottis paulinae is a tropical species with scattered populations in the top end of NT and in Qld on Cape York Peninsula, being more abundant between Cooktown and Ingham. It grows in moist situations among grass, in soaks and depressions in open forest. Sometimes becomes deciduous during drought.

Spathoglottis plicata is widely cultivated because of its spectacular flowers, which are favourites of this butterfly for egg-laying. Various colour forms are in cultivation but the typical bright pink one is the most showy. It is easy to grow if kept permanently moist and in high light.

Common Tit *Hypolycaena phorbas*

Size: Male 32mm, female 36mm.

Found in northern and eastern Australia from the Kimberley region of WA to central Qld, south of Rockhampton. It has a wide variety of habitats from coastal rainforest to open forest and savannah woodland, with an equally wide selection of host plants.

Attendant Ants: Usually *Oecophylla smaragdina*, very occasionally *Paratrechina*, *Tetramorium*.

Host Plants: *Aegiceras, Acmena, Breynia, Ceriops, Cupaniopsis, Castanospermum, Clerodendrum, Decaisnina, Dendrophthoe, Faradaya, Flagellaria, Lumnitzera, Planchonia, Ristantia, Senna, Smilax, Syzygium, Terminalia,* *Cassia.

Female laying on *Ristantia waterhousei*.

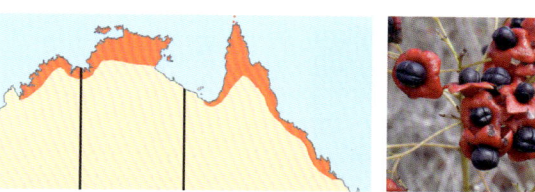

Best Garden Host Plant: Females seem to prefer different host plants in different areas and do not appear to have a favourite.

Clerodendrum floribundum is widespread over the northern half of Australia, with a range extending down the east coast to Vic. It is usually found in open forest and forms colonies along roads when roadworks cut the roots and cause the plants to sucker. It is a shrub that grows from about 2–4m.

Clerodendrum longiflorum is found in Qld from Torres Strait to about Bundaberg and also in the Tiwi Islands off NT, usually growing along the edge of rainforest. It is a large shrub that grows to about 8m high. The flowers are very long, hence the specific name.

Clerodendrum tomentosum var. *lanceolatum* is a tall shrub or small tree with narrow, slightly weeping foliage and showy heads of white flowers. It is found over most of tropical Australia in the lower rainfall areas, usually in vine thickets amongst boulders where it is protected from fire.

Clerodendrum grayi has bright white flowers and very attractive foliage; the new growth is smothered in purple hairs. It is confined to the upland rainforest of the wet tropics of north Qld. It is a medium-sized shrub that grows to about 4m high.

Pale Ciliate Blue *Anthene lycaenoides*

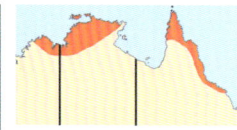

Pupae are very difficult to see on the host plant. Usually the only evidence of their presence is the hatched out shells.

Size: Male 30mm, female 32mm.

A tropical species that is found in lowland and monsoon rainforest from the Kimberley, WA, to north-east NT, then in Qld from Cape York to about Mackay.

Attendant Ants: Occasionally *Iridomyrmex, Ochetellus, Camponotus, Oecophylla, Opisthopsis, Paratrechina, Crematogaster, Odontomachus.*

Host Plants: Flower buds, flowers and new shoots of *Caesalpinia, Senna, Briedelia, Dendrolobium, Pongamia, Flagellaria, Barringtonia, Rhyssopterys, Acacia, Cupaniopsis, Clerodendrum, Faradaya,* **Caesalpinia,* **Senna,* **Calliandra,* **Lychi.*

Best Garden Host Plants: *Pongamia pinnata* var. *minor, Senna gaudichaudii.*

Pongamia pinnata var. *minor* is a small tree with weeping foliage that is usually found in rainforest along streams, occurring from the Kimberley region, WA, to about Bundaberg, Qld. It is deciduous, the foliage turning gold and yellow before falling (top left image).

Dark Ciliate Blue *Anthene seltuttus*

Size: Male 30mm, female 32mm.

A tropical species found in the top end of NT and then in Qld from Torres Strait to south of Rockhampton in the east and to about Kurumba on the western side of the peninsula. Inhabits lowland and gallery rainforest and vine thickets.

Attendant Ant: *Oecophylla smaragdina*.

Host Plants: *Millettia, Cryptocarya, Corymbia, Syzygium, Arytera, Cupaniopsis, Brachychiton, *Cassia, *Delonix, *Saraca, *Schotia, *Lagerstroemia*. From this varied list of unrelated plants it is obvious that the attendant ant is the most important factor.

Best Garden Host Plant: *Millettia*, if the ant is present.

Cupaniopsis anacardioides (Beach Tamarind) is a very common plant in gardens throughout Australia. Although it does grow on the beach in coastal rainforest, it is also found in dry rainforest and vine thickets over much of northern and eastern Australia. It usually develops into a well-shaped small tree with dense foliage. The form from Cape York is more open and grows much taller. The fruit are orange when ripe. When they open a bright orange/red aril is exposed surrounding a shiny black seed.

Shining Pencilled Blue *Candalides helenita*

♂

♀

Size: Male 36mm, female 37mm.

The male cannot be confused with any other small butterfly because of the bright pale blue colouring. The female however, looks similar to other species in this genus. A tropical species with a range that extends south to about Bowen in Qld.

Attendant Ants: None.

Host Plants: New soft leaves of *Arytera pauciflora, Austrosteenisia mollitricha, Brachychiton acerifolius, Glochidion ferdinandi, Cryptocarya hypospodia, Ventilago ecorollata, V. pubiflora.*

Best Garden Host Plant: *Brachychiton acerifolius.*

Ventilago pubiflora is a large vine that grows in well-developed rainforest from Cape York to south-east Qld. It has very glossy leaves and winged fruit. New flushes of growth attract the Shining Pencilled Blue females for laying.

Trident Pencilled Blue *Candalides margarita*

C.m. margarita.

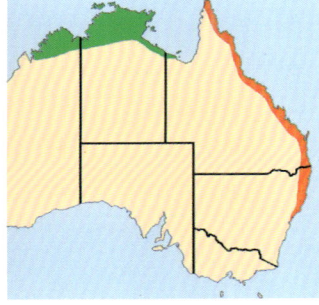

C.m. gilberti.

Size: 36mm.

Two subspecies:
- *C.m. margarita* from Cape York, Qld, to central NSW.
- *C.m. gilberti* in the top end of WA and NT, extending into Qld in the central gulf.

Found in a wide range of habitats where the larval host mistletoes grow.

Attendant Ants: Very occasionally *Crematogaster, Iridomyrmex, Polyrhachis, Technomyrmex.*

Host Plants: *Amyema, Amylotheca, Benthamina, Decaisnina, Dendrophthoe, Muellerina.*

Amyema biniflora is a large pendulous mistletoe that grows mostly on eucalypts which the mistletoe foliage resembles. It is restricted to Qld, being found from Cape York to about Maryborough in open eucalypt forest.

Common Pencilled Blue *Candalides absimilis*

Size: Male 34mm, female 36mm.

Three subspecies:
- ■ *C.a. absimilis* from about Cape Flattery, north Qld, to southern Vic in tropical and subtropical rainforest, especially along streams where *Castanospermum* (Black Bean) grows in abundance.
- ■ *C.a. edwardsi* in north-east Vic.
- ■ *C.a. eastwoodi* in Qld on Cape York Peninsula from about the Olive River to the Rocky River.

Attendant Ants: Very occasionally *Crematogaster, Technomyrmex*.

Host Plants: Soft new growth of *Alectryon, Atalaya, Brachychiton, Castanospermum, Callerya, Cupaniopsis, Erythrina, Harpullia, Millettia, Flagellaria, Macadamia, Stenocarpus, *Cassia, *Robinia, *Senna, *Wisteria, *Koelreuteria*.

C.a. absimilis.

Best Garden Host Plant: *Castanospermum australe* (Black Bean). As a garden plant it can be pruned each year to keep it as a large shrub and the new flush of foliage will attract the females.

C.a. edwardsi.

Castanospermum australe (Black Bean) is one of Australia's most spectacular flowering rainforest trees. Unfortunately it is far too large to allow it to grow to full size in a suburban garden. Like most rainforest trees it can be heavily pruned each year and by doing this it can be kept to a safe size. The flushes of new growth following pruning will attract Common Pencilled Blues for egg-laying.

Dark Pencilled Blue *Candalides consimilis*

C.c. consimilis.

Size: Male 35mm, female 36mm.

Populations occur from Iron Range on Cape York Peninsula, Qld, to southern Vic, usually along the edge of rainforest or in nearby open eucalypt forest. Three subspecies:
- *C.c. consimilis* from about Cooktown in Qld to southern NSW.
- *C.c. goodingi* from southern NSW to southern Vic.
- *C.c. toza* from about the Pascoe River to the Rocky River on Cape York Peninsula.

Attendant Ants: None,

Host Plants: Flower buds and flowers of *Alectryon coriaceus*, *Alphitonia excelsa* in south-east Qld; *Ceratopetalum gummiferum*, *Polyscias elegans*, *Hedera helix* near Sydney; *P. sambucifolia* in southern NSW and eastern Vic.

Best Garden Host Plant: *Alphitonia excelsa* or *Polyscias sambucifolia*, depending on location.

C.c. goodingi.

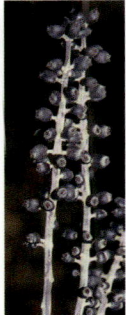

Polyscias elegans is a slender, mostly single-stemmed tree that grows to about 10m high. The first flowering is from the crown of the plant and after the fruit mature the tree then branches and forms an umbrella shape. The vast number of tiny fruit are eaten by just about every fruit-eating bird so this is an added attraction.

Copper Pencilled Blue *Candalides cyprotus*

C.c. cyprotus.

C.c. pallescens.

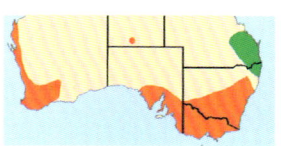

Size: Male 32mm, female 34mm.

Two subspecies:
- *C.c. cyprotus* in widely separated colonies from WA to NSW.
- *C.c. pallescens* in south-east Qld and northern NSW.

Found in heathland or in heathy woodland on sandstone and in coastal areas.

Attendant Ants: None.

Host Plants: Flowers and flower buds of *Jacksonia scoparia* in south-east Qld; *Conospermum taxifolium* in central coastal NSW; *Grevillea juniperina* in southern NSW; *G. huegelii*, *G. pterosperma*, *Hakea leucoptera* in SA; and *G. bracteosa* in WA.

Best Garden Host Plant: Any of the above, depending on location.

Golden-rayed Blue *Candalides noelkeri*

Size: 30mm.

Restricted to a very small area of western Vic where it inhabits open grassland along the edges of salt lakes. Classified as Critically Endangered.

Attendant Ants: None.

Host Plant: *Myoporum parvifolium*.

Best Garden Host Plant: This butterfly is unlikely to be attracted to a garden, although *Myoporum parvifolium* is widely cultivated as a ground-cover plant.

Common Dusky Blue *Candalides hyacinthinus*

C.h. hyacinthinus.

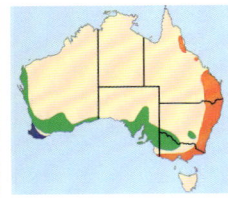

C.h. simplex.

Size: Male 32mm, female 34mm.

Very widespread, occurring from the central coast of WA around the south of Australia through SA, Vic, NSW and Qld north to about Cooktown. Found in a range of habitats from the edges of coastal rainforest to inland heathland, wherever the parasitic host plant vine Dodder grows. Three subspecies:

■ *C.h. hyacinthinus* from about Cooktown, Qld, to SA.
■ *C.h. simplex* from northern Vic to central coastal WA.
■ *C.h. gilesi* in south-west WA.

Attendant Ant: Very occasionally *Ochetellus* sp.

Host Plants: *Cassytha pubescens* in coastal areas; *C. melantha* in inland areas; *C. peninsularis*, *C. flindersii* in drier areas of SA; *C. racemosa* in south-west WA; *C. aurea* around North West Cape, WA.

Best Garden Host Plant: Very few people would deliberately grow Dodder as it is generally considered to kill its host plants. This may be the case with small herbs, but not so with large shrubs or trees.

Cassytha pubescens is a leafless, parasitic twining vine that grows in a wide range of habitats, being very common along the edge of coastal rainforest. *Cassytha* vines are collectively known as Dodder-laurel (they are actually in the Laurel family) and all species look quite similar.

Twin Dusky Blue *Candalides geminus*

Size: Male 32mm, female 34mm.

Has a very wide but patchy distribution ranging from the top end of NT to central NSW. Usually found in heath country or in forest with heath understorey. From collection records they are known to exist in widely separated colonies, but further investigation may show other populations in between these areas.

Attendant Ants: None.

Host Plants: Usually *Cassytha filiformis* in NT and Qld, *C. pubescens* in NSW, occasionally *C. capillaris* in NT.

Best Garden Host Plant: *Cassytha pubescens*, although most people do not welcome Dodder plants in their garden as they can affect the growth of their host species and overall they give a very messy appearance.

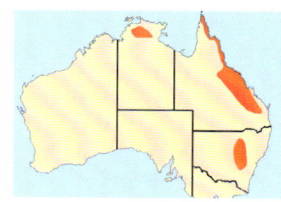

Small Dusky Blue *Candalides erinus*

Size: Male 26mm, female 28mm.

Range extends around the north of Australia from the central coast of WA to northern NSW, usually no more than a few hundred km from the coast. Again this species inhabits heath areas where the parasitic Dodder plants grow.

Attendant Ant: Very occasionally *Iridomyrmex* species.

Host Plants: *Cassytha filiformis*, *C. capillaris* in WA and NT; occasionally *C. aurea* in WA.

Best Garden Host Plant: Any of the above species that grow in the area.

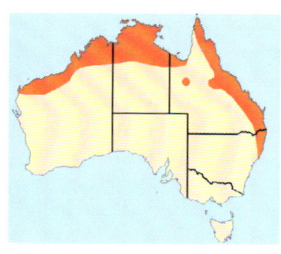

Blotched Dusky Blue *Candalides acasta*

Size: Male 24mm, female 26mm.

Found in coastal and desert heathlands, as well as woodlands with a heath understorey. Occurs in south-west WA, and through SA, Vic, Tas and NSW north to about Bundaberg, Qld.

Attendant Ants: None.

Host Plants: *Cassytha pubescens, C. peninsularis, C. filiformis.*

Best Garden Host Plant: Any of the above that grow in a particular area.

Spotted Dusky Blue *Candalides delospila*

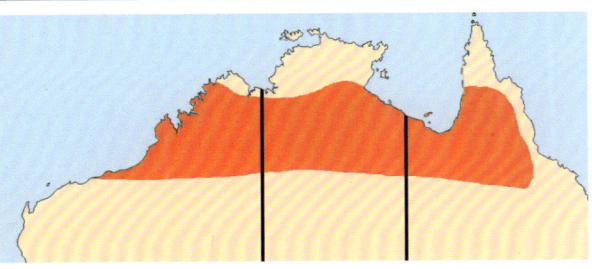

Size: Male 20mm, female 22mm.

Occurs in northern Australia north and inland of a line from about Bowen, Qld, but absent from the top end of NT and Cape York Peninsula, Qld. Preferred habitat is open eucalypt woodland and sandstone escarpments where the larval food plant grows. On the upperwing surface the male is dark purple and the female brown.

Attendant Ant: Very occasionally *Iridomyrmex* species.

Host Plant: *Cassytha capillaris.*

Best Garden Host Plant: *Cassytha capillaris.*

Yellow-spot Blue *Candalides xanthospilos*

Size: 28mm.

Range extends from about the Palmer River, north Qld, to Vic. Favours tall open eucalypt forest where the *Pimelea* host plants grow. There are only a few species recorded as host plants but as there are numerous different *Pimelea* plants occurring within the range of this butterfly many other species are likely to be host plants.

Attendant Ants: Very occasionally small black ants.

Host Plants: *Pimelea linifolia*, *P. latifolia*, *P. ligustrina*, *P. stricta*.

Best Garden Host Plant: *Pimelea linifolia*.

Pimelea linifolia is an extremely widespread plant ranging from mountains west of Mossman, north Qld, to SA, including hundreds of kilometres inland. Habitats range from the edge of upland rainforest to sandstone escarpments and gorges. It is a very attractive small plant that grows to about 1m high with heads of white flowers.

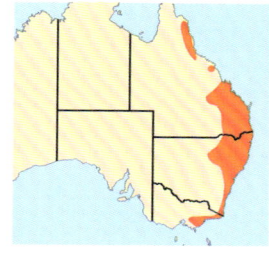

Pimelea latifolia subsp. *latifolia* is a small shrub that grows to about 1.5m, usually on the edge of rainforest or vine thickets from about Ravenshoe, eastern Qld, to northern NSW. It has small white flowers and quite large leaves for this genus.

The undersides of mature leaves are very pale, while those of the juvenile plants have a purple tinge.

FAMILY LYCAENIDAE – SUBFAMILY POLYOMMATINAE BLUES AND COPPERS

Common Rayed Blue *Candalides heathi*

C.h. heathi.

C.h. doddi.

Size: Male 32mm, female 34mm.

Four named subspecies:
- *C.h. heathi* widespread in WA, NT, SA, Qld, NSW and Vic.
- *C.h. doddi* restricted to montane areas of the northern tablelands of NSW.
- *C.h. alpinus* in the southern tablelands of NSW.
- *C.h. aeratus* on islands off the central coast of WA.

This butterfly occurs in a very wide range of habitats and uses an unusual mix of host plants. At times large migrations occur when breeding conditions have been favourable.

Attendant Ant: Very occasionally *Iridomyrmex* species.

Host Plants: *Eremophila deserti, E. gilesii, E. longifolia, E. maculata, Pimelea, Plantago debilis, P. lanceolata, Prostanthera nivea, Stemodia florulenta, Veronica derwentiana, V. perfoliata, Westringia fruticosa, W. rigida.*

Best Garden Host Plant: *Westringia fruticosa, Plantago debilis.*

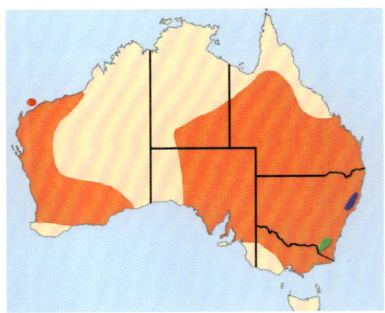

Westringia fruticosa is a shrub that grows in coastal heath areas from south-east Qld to Vic. It is readily available from native plant nurseries.

Satin Blue *Nesolycaena albosericea*

Size: 35mm.

Found in south-east Qld from about the Blackdown Tableland to the Gold Coast in sandstone heath or coastal Banksia forest.

Attendant Ants: None.

Host Plants: *Boronia obovata*, *B. glabra*, *B. rosmarinifolia*.

Best Garden Host Plant: *Boronia rosmarinifolia*, but only in coastal wallum country within the range of the butterfly.

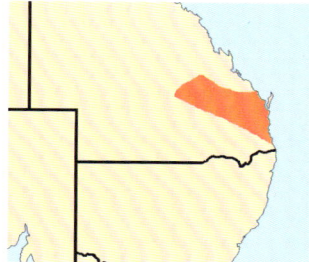

Boronia glabra ranges from central Qld to about Sydney, NSW, usually in sandstone areas or sometimes on old sand dunes near the coast. It is a small shrub that grows to about 1.5m high. The flower colour varies, even on plants in the same location.

Satin Blue *Nesolycaena albosericea*

Boronia rosmarinifolia is a small shrub that is found from central Qld to central NSW. It usually occurs in sandstone areas or on old coastal sand dunes. The flower colour varies quite a lot as shown in the images.

Kimberley Spotted Opal *Nesolycaena caesia*

Size: Male 28mm, female 30mm.

Confined to the top end of WA and usually found in eucalypt forest with a heath understorey growing on sandstone.

Attendant Ant: Very occasionally *Iridomyrmex* sp.

Host Plants: *Boronia wilsonii*, *B. kalumburuensis*.

Best Garden Host Plant: Not applicable.

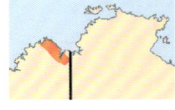

Dark Opal *Nesolycaena medicea*

Size: Male 32mm, female 36mm.

Another butterfly that has a very limited distribution. It is restricted to the White Mountains region of north Qld, occurring in sandstone gorges where its *Boronia* host plant grows.

Attendant Ant: Very occasionally *Dolichoderus scobiculatus*.

Host Plant: *Boronia eriantha*.

Best Garden Host Plant: Not applicable.

Spotted Opal *Nesolycaena urumelia*

Size: Male 32mm, female 34mm.

Range extends from the top end of NT to about Lawn Hill in Qld. Usually found in various forests with a heath understorey, especially on sandstone.

Attendant Ants: Very occasionally *Monomorium* sp., *Polyrhachis* sp.

Host Plants: *Boronia lanceolata, B. lanuginosa, B. laxa, B. wilsonii*.

Best Garden Host Plant: Any of the above.

Large Green-banded Blue *Danis danis*

Size: Male 40mm, female 42mm.

Found in north Qld from Torres Strait to just south of Townsville in well-developed rainforest at low to mid-altitudes. The female seeks out the soft, pink new growth of the host to lay her eggs on. Two subspecies have been named:
- ■ *D. d. serapis* from the wet tropics.
- ■ *D. d. syrius* from Cape York Peninsula.

Attendant Ants: Very occasionally small brown ants.

Host Plants: *Connarus conchocarpus, C.* sp. Bamaga, *Rourea brachyandra*.

Best Garden Host Plant: *Connarus conchocarpus*.

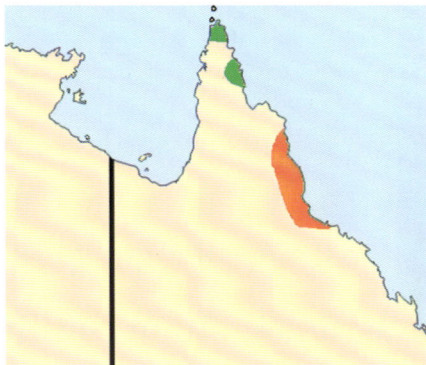

Rourea brachyandra is a small to medium vine that is confined to tropical lowland rainforest in Qld from about Cooktown to south of Mackay. The female butterflies lay on the soft red new growth.

Connarus conchocarpus is a medium to large vine that is found from about Cooktown to Ingham in low- to mid-altitude rainforest. Female **Large Green-banded Blues** lay on the soft pink to brown new growth. The vine has bunches of bright red fruit.

Small Green-banded Blue *Psychonotis caelius*

Size: 34mm.

Easterly distribution in Australia from Torres Strait, Qld, to southern NSW in rainforest and eucalypt forest where the host plant *Alphitonia* grows. The brightly coloured underside makes them easy to identify.

Attendant Ants: Usually none, very occasionally *Technomyrmex* species.

Host Plants: *Alphitonia excelsa*, *A. oblata*, *A. petriei*, *Alphitonia* sp. Selwyn Ranges.

Best Garden Host Plant: *Alphitonia excelsa*.

Young larvae tend to skeletonise the leaves and this gives their presence away.

Alphitonia excelsa covers an extremely wide range from the Kimberley region of WA to southern Vic. It occurs in rainforest and eucalypt forest. The flowers attract numerous insects and it is worth growing just for that.

This plant varies so much when growing in different habitats and regions that three subspecies have been named.

Alphitonia oblata (*Alphitonia incana*) grows in well-developed rainforest at various altitudes as well as in rainforest along streams well inland. The juvenile plants have large very furry leaves which distinguish them from other species of *Alphitonia*. It is a large tree and not suitable for suburban gardens. It is found across the top end of Australia from the Kimberley, WA, to north Qld.

Alphitonia petriei is a large, fast-growing rainforest tree that springs up after disturbance. It has a short life, less than 20 years, and is not really suitable as a garden plant. It is best used sparingly in rainforest revegetation plantings.

Alphitonia sp. Selwyn Ranges occurs in vine thickets on basalt, limestone and sandstone in Qld, from near Mt Garnett in the north, west to at least Mt Isa and south to Winton.

Tailed Green-banded Blue *Nacaduba cyanea*

N.c. arinia.

N.c. manto.

Size: Male 40mm, female 42mm.

Inhabits lowland rainforest in tropical Qld from Cape York to about Bowen. The tails distinguish it from the Small Green-banded Blue. There are two subspecies:
- ■ *N.c. arinia* on the mainland.
- ■ *N.c. manto* on Torres Strait islands.

Attendant Ants: Usually none, occasionally small black or brown ants.

Host Plants: *Entada phaseoloides*, *E. rheedii*.

Best Garden Host Plant: The host plants of this butterfly are massive vines and not suitable for most gardens. One vine can cover more than a hectare of rainforest.

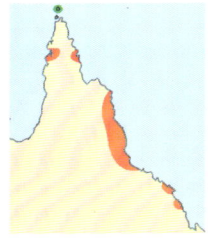

Entada rheedii is one of the largest vines in the Australian rainforest. Stems can reach 40cm in diameter and usually have a corkscrew habit. The whole vine can reach out to cover more than a hectare of rainforest. The huge seed pods can attain almost 1m in length. It is found from Cape York to central Qld in lowland and monsoon rainforest.

Northern Lineblue *Petrelaea tombugensis*

Size: 28mm.

Patchily distributed in the top end of Australia from the Kimberley, WA, to about Townsville, Qld, usually in lowland rainforest, especially coastal.

Attendant Ants: None.

Host Plants: *Terminalia catappa* (Beach Almond or Sea Almond) is the only recorded host plant but as there are three or four other species of *Terminalia* in the same habitat these are also likely host plants.

Best Garden Host Plant: *Terminalia catappa*. This is widely grown as a street tree in tropical coastal towns. It is too large for most gardens.

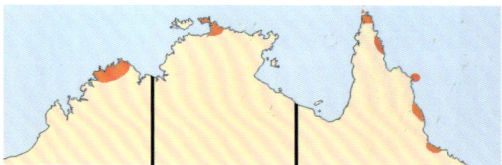

With its wide spreading branches, *Terminalia catappa* forms a magnificent shade tree in the tropics, especially on the coast – the only place it grows naturally. It is cold-sensitive and will not tolerate frost. It will grow on the Gold Coast but does so very slowly.

The huge leaves provide dense shade at the hottest time of the year. Old leaves turn bright red before falling in early summer, after which the new foliage rapidly appears.

As a bonus the nuts are quite tasty and have a distinctive coconut flavour.

White-banded Lineblue *Nacaduba kurava*

Size: Male 28mm, female 30mm.

Two subspecies:
- ■ *N.k. parma* from Cape York, Qld, to northern NSW.
- ■ *N.k. felsina* around and to the east of Darwin, NT.

Habitat includes all types of low- to mid-altitude rainforest.

Attendant Ants: Occasionally a few black ants.

Host Plants: *Maesa haplobotrys, M. dependens* in NT. In the wet tropics *Myrsine (Rapanea) variabilis, Aegiceras corniculatum*, also *Cupaniopsis anacardioides*, new shoots and flowers of *Embelia curvinervia*.

Best Garden Host Plant: *Myrsine variabilis*.

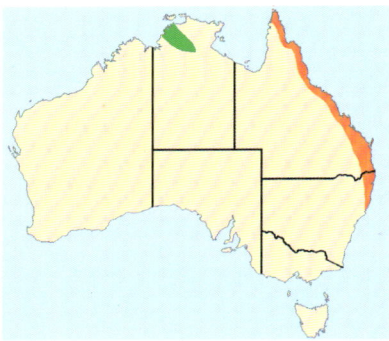

N.k. parma.

N.k. parma laying eggs.

N.k. felsina.

Myrsine variabilis is a small to medium-sized suckering shrub that usually grows in coastal or dry rainforest, often forming thickets. All the species in this genus have masses of small flowers along the branches, followed by purple to black fruit which is eaten by small birds. The female White-banded Lineblue lays eggs on the soft new shoots.

Common Lineblue *Nacaduba berenice*

Size: 28mm.

Found along the east coastal strip of Australia from Torres Strait, Qld, to southern NSW. Occurs in low- to mid-altitude rainforest and nearby eucalypt forest into which rainforest plants are spreading. Many of the host plants for this butterfly are grown in gardens so it is a common butterfly in these situations. The images of the female are from north Qld, where the colours on the underside seem to be paler than those in southern areas.

Attendant Ants: *Tapinoma, Camponotus, Oecophylla, Paratrechina, Polyrhachis, Crematogaster, *Pheidole megacephala, *Technomyrmex.*

Host Plants: Usually soft new growth of leaves, flowers or developing young fruit of *Alectryon, Arytera, Atalaya, Cupaniopsis, Elattostachys, Jagera, Guioa, Macadamia, Aphananthe.*

Best Garden Host Plant: *Arytera* or *Cupaniopsis.*

   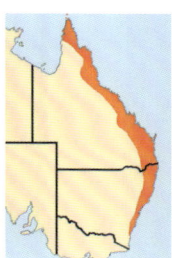

Arytera divaricata is found from Cape York, Qld, to northern NSW, in moist to wet rainforest, usually at low altitudes. The brilliant pink to red new growth of this plant demands that it should be placed in a prominent position in the garden. In spite of its delicate new growth, it is a very hardy plant.

Common Lineblue *Nacaduba berenice*

Arytera pseudofoveolata occurs in gallery rainforest in Qld from Torres Strait to the Rocky River on Cape York Peninsula. It has a very striking flush of new growth and is a hardy plant but very slow-growing. Very few plants have blue new growth; as the leaves mature they change to almost white or pale green, becoming dark green when they mature.

Arytera bifoliolata (Cape Coogara) is found in the top end of WA, north-west NT, and in Qld on Cape York Peninsula, in dry to moist rainforest. This very hardy plant has spectacular bright pink new growth. The leaves are very glossy, and the new growth provides a better display than many flowers.

It can be grown in part shade or full sun. When planted in a rainforest plot it is usually left behind by the other species and becomes an understorey plant. Birds eat the seeds when the fruit split open.

Twin-spotted Lineblue *Nacaduba biocellata*

Size: 24mm.

Occurs throughout the Australian mainland, just making it to Tas where it has been found in the north-east. The larvae feed on the flowers of acacias, which means that the species can breed almost anywhere.

Attendant Ants: Occasionally *Iridomyrmex*, *Technomyrmex*.

Host Plants: Flower buds and flowers of *Acacia* – more than 40 species recorded.

Best Garden Host Plant: Any *Acacia* suitable for a particular area.

Short-tailed Lineblue *Prosotas felderi*

Size: Male 22mm, female 23mm.

Found in eastern Australia from about Gladstone, Qld, to south of Sydney, NSW, inhabiting both coastal and inland areas.

Attendant Ants: Very occasionally *Dolichoderus*, *Crematogaster*.

Host Plants: Buds and flowers of *Acacia*, *Buckinghamia celsissima*, *Macadamia integrifolia*, *M. tetraphylla*, *Cupaniopsis anacardioides*, *Alectryon coriaceus*, *Harpullia pendula*, *Pararchidendron pruinosum*, *Albizia lebbeck*, *Litchi chinensis*.

Best Garden Host Plant: With such a wide range of host plants it is not possible to say if any one would be better than the others.

 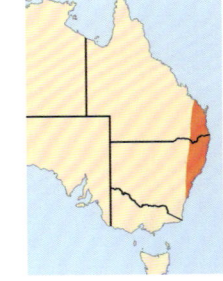

Long-tailed Lineblue *Prosotas nora*

Size: Male 22mm, female 23mm.

A tropical species that is confined to Qld, ranging from Torres Strait to about Mackay. Little is known about this butterfly, which has been collected in rainforest and seen only occasionally.

Attendant Ants: None.

Host Plant: Bob Miller found the larvae on flower buds of *Guioa acutifolia*.

Best Garden Host Plant: *Guioa acutifolia*.

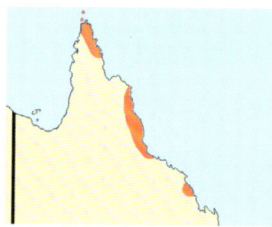

Guioa acutifolia is a fast-growing hardy small to medium tree that is found in rainforest from Torres Strait to south-east Qld. It often occurs along the edge of the rainforest and in nearby eucalypt forest and volunteers in gardens from seed distributed by birds. The flowers appear along the branches and while they are rather small they make quite a spectacular display when a plant flowers well.

Tailless Lineblue *Prosotas dubiosa*

Size: Male 22mm, female 23mm.

Found from about Broome, WA, across the top end and from Torres Strait, Qld, to northern NSW in savannah woodland and rainforest where its many host plants grow.

Attendant Ants: None.

Host Plants: Buds and flowers of *Acacia, Albizia, Cajanus, Dalbergia, Millettia, Archidendron, Pararchidendron, Buckinghamia, Macadamia, Alectryon, Harpullia, Cupaniopsis, Semecarpus, *Albizia, *Leucaena, *Litchi.*

Best Garden Host Plant: With such a varied list of host plants it is impossible to select the most suitable one.

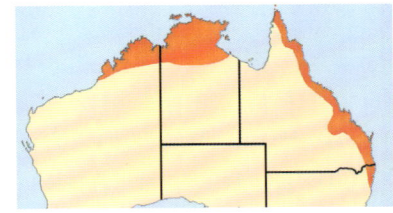

When in flower or fruit, *Archidendron grandiflorum* makes a wonderful spectacle. In south-east Qld the flowers attract large numbers of Richmond Birdwing butterflies and in some areas it is known as 'The Butterfly Tree'. In the north, however, the Cairns Birdwing pays little attention to it.

Because of its wide range, the hardiness of this plant will depend on the area from which the seed came. The Cape York form is extremely hardy, but the one from the mountains of south-east Qld will require water during dry periods. It is found from Torres Strait to northern NSW in rainforest.

Bronze Lineblue *Ionolyce helicon*

Size: 22mm.

Range extends from Torres Strait to about Rockhampton, Qld, in lowland rainforest, including coastal.

Attendant Ants: None.

Host Plants: *Allophylus cobbe, Entada phaseoloides*.

Best Garden Host Plant: *Allophylus cobbe*.

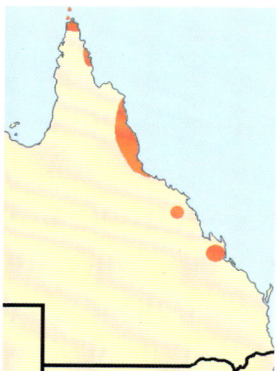

Allophylus cobbe is a small tree that grows to about 10m high in monsoon rainforest in Qld from Cape York to just south of Cooktown. The leaves are soft and furry to touch.

Papuan Lineblue *catopyrops ancyra*

Size: Male 28mm, female 30mm.

In Australia found only on islands in Torres Strait, where it occurs along rainforest edges and in clearings within the rainforest. On the upperwings the males are completely dark blue, while the females have a pale blue centre with brown border.

Attendant Ants: Occasionally *Crematogaster* species.

Host Plants: Flowers of *Pipturus argenteus, Caesalpinia bonduc*.

Best Garden Host Plant: *Pipturus argenteus*.

Pipturus argenteus is a large shrub or small tree that is found in the top end of NT then from Torres Strait, Qld, to northern NSW, usually in moist to wet rainforest or along streams and near springs in lower-rainfall rainforest.

Speckled Lineblue *Catopyrops florinda*

C.f. estrella.

Size: Male 28mm, female 29mm.

Two subspecies:
■ *C.f. estrella* from the Kimberley region, WA, across northern Australia and south to about Sarina, Qld.
■ *C.f. halys* from about Rockhampton, Qld, to southern NSW.

Almost all the host plants are rainforest species, so this is the habitat where the Speckled Lineblue will most likely be seen.

Attendant Ants: Occasionally *Polyrhachis, Crematogaster, Iridomyrmex, Paratrechina, Tetramorium, *Technomyrmex*.

C.f. halys.

Host Plants: Flower buds, flowers and young leaves of *Caesalpinia bonduc, Dodonaea hispidula, Harpullia pendula, Trema tomentosa, Adriana urticoides, Mallotus nesophilus, Pipturus argenteus*.

Best Garden Host Plant: *Pipturus argenteus*.

Trema tomentosa is a small tree that is found in northern and eastern Australia, in moist to dry rainforest or protected areas in gorges and sandstone escarpments, or amongst large granite boulders. When ripe, the small black fruit attract many fruit-eating birds. The foliage has a rough sandpapery feel to the touch.

Hairy Lineblue *Erysichton lineatus*

Size: 30mm.

Found from Cape York, Qld, to southern NSW along the edge of low- to mid-altitude rainforest. With such a wide range of host plants it is likely to be seen in gardens that are a reasonable distance from regular breeding sites.

Attendant Ant: Very occasionally *Polyrhachis pilosa*.

Host Plants: Flower buds and flowers of *Alectryon, Cupaniopsis, Elattostachys, Harpullia, Jagera, Mischarytera, Brachychiton, Ehretia, Syzygium*.

Best Garden Host Plants: *Alectryon, Cupaniopsis, Elattostachys*.

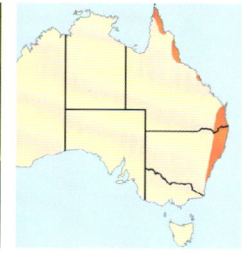

Elattostachys microcarpa is fast-growing and hardy and makes an excellent screen or edge-plant in a rainforest planting. The bright red new growth is attractive, as is the ripening fruit. It can be pruned as often and as hard as necessary if you want to restrict its size. It is found in rainforest in Qld from Torres Strait to about Ingham.

Glistening Lineblue *Sabulana scintillata*

Size: Male 28mm, female 29mm.

Occurs from near Darwin, NT, to southern NSW in woodland or coastal rainforest. The host plant range of this butterfly has enabled it to breed all year round in warmer regions by availing itself of the currently flowering host plant.

Attendant Ants: None.

Host Plants: Flower buds and flowers of *Alectryon coriaceus, Cupaniopsis anacardioides, Acacia aulacocarpa, A. concurrens, A. disparrima, A. leiocalyx, A. maidenii, *Albizia lebbeck.*

Best Garden Host Plant: *Cupaniopsis anacardioides.*

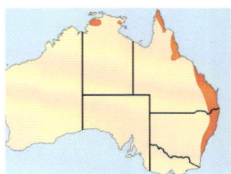

Fringed Heath Blue *Neolucia agricola*

Size: Male 25mm, female 26mm.

Three subspecies:
- *N.a. agricola* from central Qld to SA.
- *N.a. insulana* in northern and eastern Tas.
- *N.a. occidens* in south-west WA from sea-level to about 1,700m.

The host plants are heath plants so the butterfly is found in heathland or woodland with a heath understorey.

Attendant Ant: Very occasionally *Iridomyrmex* sp.

Host Plants: Flower buds and flowers of *Aotus, Bossiaea, Daviesia, Dillwynia, Eutaxia, Jacksonia, Pultenaea.*

Best Garden Host Plant: It is unlikely that this butterfly could be attracted to a garden. A property with suitable habitat within the range of the Fringed Heath Blue will probably already have it.

N.a. agricola.   N.a. occidens.

Mountain Heath Blue *Neolucia hobartensis*

Size: 20mm.

Two subspecies:
- *N.h. hobartensis* in south-east NSW, ACT, Vic and Tas.
- *N.h. monticola* in the eastern highlands of NSW.

Found in subalpine woodland with heath understorey, and alpine heathland. Male and female are very similar.

Attendant Ants: None.

Host Plants: *Epacris breviflora*, *E. petrophila* in ACT. *E. petrophila*, *E. paludosa* in Vic.

N.h. hobartensis.

Best Garden Host Plant: Any of the above within the range of the butterfly.

N.h. monticola.

Dull Heath Blue *Neolucia mathewi*

Size: 22mm.

Confined to eastern NSW, southern Vic and northern Tas, where it occurs in coastal heath and banksia coastal woodland as well as subalpine heathland on granite outcrops in montane areas.

Attendant Ants: None.

Host Plants: Flower buds of *Monotoca elliptica* in coastal NSW, *M. oreophila* in Vic.

Best Garden Host Plant: Either of the above.

Cycad Blue *Theclinesthes onycha*

T.o. onycha.

T.o. capricornia.

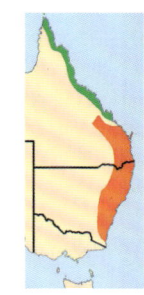

Size: Male 30mm, female 32mm.

Two subspecies:

■ *T.o. onycha* from the Blackdown Tableland, west of Rockhampton, Qld, to southern NSW.

■ *T.o. capricornia* from Torres Strait to Rockhampton.

The butterfly is found wherever suitable host plants grow, including in suburban gardens, and it is considered a pest by gardeners who grow cycads. However, a lot of the damage done to cycads and zamias is by beetle larvae and not by the Cycad Blue butterfly.

Attendant Ants: Occasionally *Iridomyrmex*, *Ochetellus*, *Calomyrmex*, *Camponotus*, *Notoncus*, *Paratrechina*, *Polyrhachis*, *Monomorium*.

Host Plants: Young soft fronds of *Cycas* and *Macrozamia* including the following species: *Cycas media*, *C. megacarpa*, *C. ophiolitica*, **C. circulus*, **C. revoluta*, **C. robusta*, *Lepidozamia peroffskyana*, *Macrozamia communis*, *M. douglasii*, *M. lomandroides*, *M. longispina*, *M. lucida*, *M. macleayi*, *M. moorei*, *M. pauli-guilielmi*, *M. spiralis*.

Best Garden Host Plants: *Cycas media* for *T.o. capricornia*; any of the above host plants that is local to the area for *T.o. onycha*.

Cycad Blue *Theclinesthes onycha*

Cycas media is one of the most common of all the Cycads, often occurring in very large populations. Although it is a plant of open eucalypt forest, the foliage can burn if exposed to full sun during the dry months. Best results will be obtained if it is grown in light shade. There are three subspecies and the overall range in Qld is from Iron Range to about Rockhampton. This is a deciduous species so do not be alarmed when all the leaves die. Soon after, the plant will flush with beautiful new foliage.

Lepidozamia peroffskyana occurs in upland rainforest in Qld, from the Blackall Range to the southern Border Ranges. Growing to about 6m high it is a spectacular plant with bright red fruit and fronds up to 2m long. All species in the Cycad group have separate male and female plants and are very slow-growing.

Wattle Blue *Theclinesthes miskini*

Size: Male 28mm, female 30mm.

Found throughout most of mainland Australia with the exception of the south-east corner. Three subspecies:
- ■ *T.m. miskini* is very widespread, being found in all states except Tas.
- ■ *T.m. eucalypti* in Qld from Cape York to about Townsville.
- ■ *T.m. arnoldi* in Torres Strait, Qld, and beyond into Papua New Guinea and islands.

Being so widespread it has a wide range of habitats from savannah and eucalypt woodland to the edge of gallery rainforest.

Attendant Ants: Occasionally *Dolichoderus, Froggattella, Iridomyrmex, Camponotus, Paratrechina, Opisthopsis.*

Host Plants: Usually *Acacia* (more then 20 species recorded); also *Cajanus reticulatus, Cathormion umbellatum, Sesbania cannabina, S. javanica, Paraserianthes lophantha, Corymbia bella, C. disjuncta, C. ferruginea, C. polycarpa, C. torelliana, Eucalyptus drepanophylla, Alectryon diversifolius, Atalaya hemiglauca, A. variifolia, Santalum lanceolatum, Xylomelum scottiana.*

Best Garden Host Plant: Juvenile plants or small suckers are preferred, especially *Acacia* plants with phyllodes rather than true leaves.

T.m. miskini.

T.m. eucalypti.

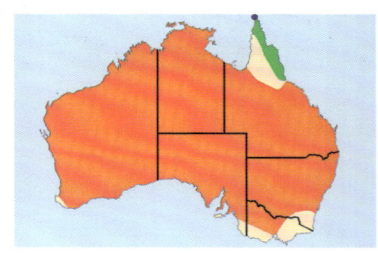

Wattle Blue *Theclinesthes miskini*

Cajanus reticulatus is a very widespread herb or small shrub with bright yellow flowers. It ranges from the Kimberley in WA to south-east Qld and is found in various types of eucalypt and open forest. The seed pods are densely covered with hairs which may cause irritation to some people.

Cathormion umbellatum can form a beautiful spreading tree if grown in the open, and in the influence of the summer monsoon rains. It has *Albizia*-like flowers and glossy green foliage. Often found in waterlogged plains in the top end of WA, it also occurs along streams and not far from mangroves along the northern coast. It ranges from the Kimberley in WA, across the top end of NT and the Gulf, to Cape York Peninsula, Qld. The Wattle Blue larvae are found on the soft new growth.

Growth rates are very poor in southern areas as it is best suited to the tropics.

Bitter-bush Blue *Theclinesthes albocinctus*

■ Coastal form.

■ Inland form.

Size: Male 24mm, female 28mm.

Has scattered populations from near Broome, WA, to central NSW. Inhabits low open shrubland on sand-dune areas in both coastal and inland areas, preferring disturbed open areas where the larval food plants grow.

Attendant Ants: Occasionally *Dolichoderus, Iridomyrmex, Ochetellus, Camponotus, Melophorus, Notoncus, Polyrhachis, Myrmecia, Crematogaster, Monomorium, Rhytidoponera*.

Host Plants: *Adriana tomentosa* in most localities and *A. quadripartita* in coastal SA and south-west Vic.

Best Garden Host Plant: *Adriana tomentosa*.

 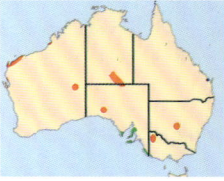

   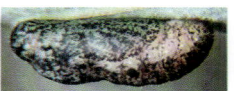

Western Bitter-bush Blue *Theclinesthes hesperia*

T.h. hesperia.

Size: Male 28mm, female 30mm.

Confined to the south-west corner of WA where two subspecies are recognised:
- ■ *T.h. hesperia* around Bunbury.
- ■ *T.h. littoralis* east of Albany.

Both inhabit coastal sand dunes where the larval host plant grows.

Attendant Ants: Occasionally *Iridomyrmex, Camponotus, Crematogaster*.

Host Plant: *Adriana quadripartita*.

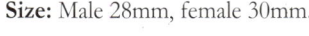

T.h. littoralis.

Saltbush Blue *Theclinesthes serpentatus*

T.s. serpentatus.

T.s. lavara.

Size: Male 20mm, female 21mm.

Found over a wide area of Australia, south of about a line through Townsville, Qld. Inhabits coastal and inland areas where saltbush plants (in the Chenopodiaceae family) grow. Two subspecies:
- ■ *T.s. serpentatus* across much of mainland Australia and in north-east Tas.
- ■ *T.s. lavara* in a small area of south-east Tas.

Attendant Ants: Occasionally *Iridomyrmex*, *Camponotus*, *Notoncus*, *Myrmecia*, *Monomorium*.

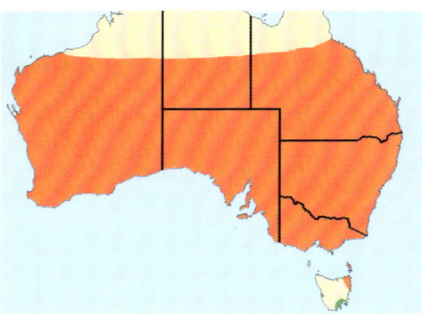

Host Plants: At least 30 species of Saltbush recorded, including *Atriplex*, *Einadia*, *Rhagodia*, *Chenopodium*, *Chenopodium* and one completely unrelated plant, *Atalaya hemiglauca*.

Best Garden Host Plant: *Atriplex* species.

Atriplex velutinella is a prostrate saltbush that occurs over a wide area of central Australia including southern NT, south-west Qld, western NSW and most of SA. The grey foliage is typical of many of these plants and they usually have succulent leaves.

FAMILY LYCAENIDAE – SUBFAMILY POLYOMMATINAE — BLUES AND COPPERS

Atriplex spongiosa is found in most of inland Australia from a line south of about Bowen, Qld, and west of the Great Dividing Range, with the exception of Vic.

Atriplex holocarpa has an almost identical range as the above species, reaching the coast in WA.

Samphire Blue *Theclinesthes sulpitius*

Size: Male 19mm, female 20mm.

Restricted to coastal areas where the Samphire host plants grow in saltmarshes and on mudflats along the tidal sections of creeks and rivers, usually behind mangroves. It is found from about Broome, WA, across the top and down the east coast to southern Vic.

Attendant Ant: Occasionally *Iridomyrmex* sp.

Host Plants: *Tecticornia indica, T. australasica, T. halocnemoides, T. pergranulata, Sarcocornia quinqueflora, Suaeda australis, S. arbusculoides, Enchylaena tomentosa*.

Best Garden Host Plant: It is probably not practical to grow any of these salt plants in a garden.

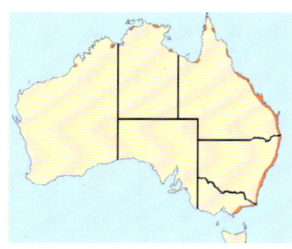

Suaeda arbusculoides.   *Suaeda australis.*

All the images show various types of Samphire plants. These are succulent plants that grow on saltflats along the coast or in the inland of Australia. They are becoming popular in the bushtucker trade and go under the names of Sea Asparagus, Swamp Grass, Salicorne, Glasswort, Pickleweed and Sea Beans.

These are mostly plants in the Amaranthaceae family and belong to the following genera: *Tecticornia, Sarcocornia, Suaeda*. Also *Enchylaena* species (Salt Bush) in the Camphorosmeae family.

They often have green foliage at some stage of growth which turns red or orange when stressed.

Zebra Blue *Leptotes plinius*

Size: 28mm.

Occurs from Cape York, Qld, to southern NSW and range extends into NT and SA. The native *Plumbago* host plant occurs in vine thickets, boulder clumps and sandstone breakaways, and wherever the plant grows the butterfly seems to be. The widespread growing of cultivated *Plumbago* has greatly increased the numbers of this species.

Attendant Ants: Mostly none, very occasionally *Iridomyrmex*, *Paratrechina*.

Host Plants: *Plumbago zeylanica* (flowers can be blue or white), **P. auriculata* in gardens, has bright blue flowers.

Best Garden Host Plant: **Plumbago auriculata*.

Plumbago zeylanica is a very widespread scrambling shrub that is found over most of the northern half of Australia, extending well into NSW on the eastern side of its range. It is a dry rainforest plant that occurs in vine thickets, softwood rainforests, sandstone gorges and breakaways and boulder piles. The flowers are mostly white but some populations are blue. The larvae of the Zebra Blue breed on the flower heads and are well camouflaged to match the buds and seed pods of the plant.

Bright Cerulean *Jamides aleuas*

Size: 34mm.

A truly spectacular little butterfly – if it were larger it would rival the Morphos of South America. The male is bright shimmering blue on the upperside. Even when flying in the shade it is very noticeable. Found mostly in lowland areas. Two subspecies:
- ■ *J.a. coelestis* from Cape Flattery to south of Townsville, Qld.
- ■ *J.a. pholes* in Torres Strait and the top of Cape York Peninsula, Qld.

Attendant Ants: Occasionally *Crematogaster*, *Rhytidoponera*, *Tetramorium*.

Host Plants: *Arytera pauciflora*, *Arytera bifoliolata*.

Best Garden Host Plant: *Arytera pauciflora*.

J.a. coelestis.   J.a. pholes.

Arytera pauciflora is a small tree that is confined to the wet tropics of north Qld where it occurs in wet to very wet rainforest. The new growth is bright red, fading gradually almost to white then green as the leaves mature.

Pale Cerulean *Jamides cyta*

♂

♀

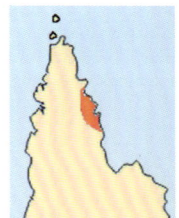

Size: Male 34mm, female 36mm.

Confined to Cape York Peninsula, Qld, where it occurs from about the Olive River to the Rocky River in well-developed rainforest.

Attendant Ants: Occasionally *Philidris cordatus*, *Camponotus*.

Host Plants: *Syzygium puberulum*, *S. tierneyanum*.

Best Garden Host Plant: *Syzygium puberulum*, although very few people live within the range of this butterfly.

Syzygium puberulum is an understorey rainforest tree that grows along streams on Cape York Peninsula from about the Pascoe River to the Rocky River. It has a weeping habit and produces flushes of large bright pink foliage. The very showy large flowers last for less than a day. These are followed by clusters of bright red fruit.

Syzygium tierneyanum is a large rainforest tree that grows along streams. It occurs from Torres Strait to about Townsville, also beyond Australia in Papua New Guinea and the Solomon Islands. The fruit can be either red or white; flowers occur along the branches.

Dark Cerulean *Jamides phaseli*

Size: Male 28mm, female 30mm.

Found from about Broome, WA, across the top end of NT then from Torres Strait, Qld, to northern NSW. Can occur in open eucalypt forest and savannah woodland where most of its pea-flowering host plants grow.

Attendant Ants: Occasionally small ants.

Host Plants: Flower buds and flowers of *Bossiaea bossiaeoides*, *Cajanus aromaticus*, *C. reticulatus*, *Canavalia rosea*, *Indigofera pratensis*, *Millettia*

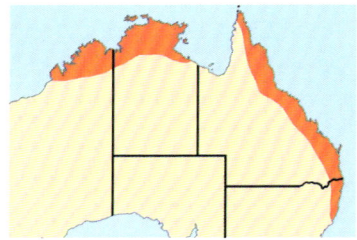

pinnata, *Sesbania simpliciuscula*, *Tephrosia rufula*, *T. spechtii*, **Phaseolus vulgaris*, **Vigna caracalla*.

Best Garden Host Plant: Any of the above that will grow in a particular location. *Millettia pinnata* is a large tree so if you have a small garden this is not suitable.

Bossiaea bossiaeoides is a very attractive shrub that is found from the Kimberley region of WA, across the top end of NT to the southern Gulf of Carpentaria. It is a plant of the open eucalypt forest and does best in full sun. It is an unusual plant insomuch as it does not have leaves, rather the stems are flattened out and provide the same functions as leaves.

Shining Cerulean *Jamides amarauge*

Size: Male 30mm, female 32mm.

Does not occur on the Australian mainland, being restricted to the Torres Strait islands and beyond to Papua New Guinea and the Solomon Islands. The males have deep blue on the top of their wings with a brown border.

Attendant Ants: Not recorded.

Host Plants: Not recorded.

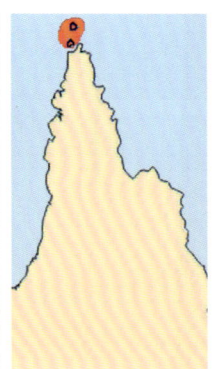

Orange-tipped Pea Blue *Everes lacturnus*

Size: 26mm.

Quite widespread, with a range extending from the Kimberley region in WA to central NSW. Usually found in open riparian forest and on the edges of monsoon forest along streams.

Attendant Ants: Occasionally a few ants.

Host Plant: Flowers and seed pods of *Desmodium heterocarpon*.

Best Garden Host Plant: *Desmodium heterocarpon*.

Desmodium heterocarpon is a small shrub or herb that is found from the Kimberley region of WA to northern NSW and matches almost exactly the range of this butterfly. It has bright pink flowers. The seed pods are divided into distinctive sections for each seed.

Pale Pea Blue *Catochrysops panormus*

C.p. platissa.

Size: 30mm.

Found from the Kimberley area, WA, across the top end of NT and then from Torres Strait, Qld, to northern NSW. The larvae feed on various pea-flowered herbs and shrubs that grow in open eucalypt forest and savannah woodland. There are two subspecies:

■ *C.p. platissa* from WA to NSW.

■ *C.p. papuanus* only within the Australian limits in Torres Strait.

Attendant Ants: Occasionally small black ants.

Host Plants: Flower buds and flowers of *Cajanus acutifolius, C. aromaticus, C. confertiflorus, C. pubescens, C. reticulatus, Crotalaria alata, Dendrolobium umbellatum, Flemingia lineata, Galactia tenuiflora, Sesbania simpliciuscula, S. cannabina*.

Best Garden Host Plant: Any of the above species that are local to your area or will grow satisfactorily.

C.p. papuanus.

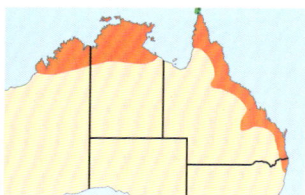

Flemingia lineata is a small shrub that grows to about 1.5m high in the wild or 2m in cultivation. The pink and white flowers are quite attractive but are small and do not make much of a display on the plant. The range of this *Flemingia* species matches almost perfectly with that of the **Pale Pea Blue** except that it extends only to south-east Qld and does not occur in northern NSW. All pea-flowered herbs and shrubs are easy to grow from seed and this is the best way to get them established.

Long-tailed Pea Blue *Lampides boeticus*

Size: Male 32mm, female 35mm.

One of only a few butterflies that is found in Tas as well as all over mainland Australia. Basically it occurs wherever there are pea-flowered plants growing.

Attendant Ants: Occasionally *Dolichoderus*, *Froggattella*, *Iridomyrmex*, *Camponotus*.

Host Plants: *Crotalaria*, *Cajanus*, *Cullen*, *Gompholobium*, *Indigofera*, *Kennedia*, *Lotus*, *Pultenaea*, *Sesbania*, *Swainsona*, *Templetonia*, *Chamaecytisus, *Dipogon, *Dolichos, *Lathyrus, *Lupinus, *Macroptilium, *Medicago, *Pisum, *Phaseolus, *Vicia, *Vigna, *Virgilia, *Wisteria.

Best Garden Host Plant: While there are numerous genera of Fabaceae (Pea-flowering plants) listed the author has found this butterfly using a much wider range, from the giant flowers of *Sesbania formosa* to the smallest introduced herb. If there was a favourite it would probably be *Crotalaria*.

Crotalaria spectabilis is an introduced plant that has become naturalised over most of northern and eastern Australia. It puts on a spectacular display of large yellow flowers and is often grown in gardens, although like most *Crotalaria* species it is basically an annual. Usually there is enough seed to keep it going year after year. One advantage of this species is that in addition to the Long-tailed Pea Blue it will also attract all male Danaid (Crow and Tiger) butterflies. They often gather in large numbers on this plant to extract alkaloids from the flowers and old seed pods.

Spotted Pea Blue *Euchrysops cnejus*

Size: Male 30mm, female 32mm.

Has a similar range to that of the Pale Pea Blue, extending from south of Broome, WA, across the top and down to northern NSW. It is found in savannah woodland, paperbark woodland and on rock screes were the larval host plants grow.

Attendant Ants: Occasionally *Iridomyrmex*, *Camponotus*, *Opisthopsis*, *Polyrhachis*, *Pheidole*.

Host Plants: Flower buds, flowers and seed pods of *Cajanus reticulatus*, *Sesbania cannabina*, *Vigna lanceolata*, *V. luteola*, *V. radiata*, *V. vexillata*, *Cajanus cajan*, *Macroptilium atropurpureum*, *M. lathyroides*, *Phaseolus vulgaris*, *Vigna caracalla*, *V. unguiculata*.

Best Garden Host Plant: *Sesbania cannabina*.

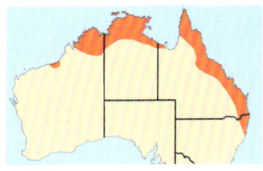

Vigna vexillata is a small twining vine that is found in northern and eastern Australia from the Kimberley area, WA, to about Sydney, NSW, in open forest. It usually twines over grass or small shrubs. For a small vine the flower is quite large and very showy.

Small Pied Blue *Megisba strongyle*

Size: Male 22mm, female 26mm.

Found in Qld from Torres Strait to about Townsville, usually inhabiting the edge of rainforest in both lowlands and uplands where the larval host plants grow.

Attendant Ants: None.

Host Plants: Flower buds of *Macaranga inamoena*, *Mallotus paniculatus*, *M. philippensis*, *Allophylus cobbe*.

Best Garden Host Plant: *Allophylus cobbe*.

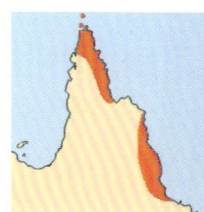

There are possibly three species combined into *Allophylus cobbe*. This one is a small tree to about 10m high which grows in monsoon rainforest in Qld from Cape York to just south of Cooktown and possibly also in NT. The leaves are soft and furry to touch.

Allophyllus sp. Cape York is a small shrub about 1–2m high that grows in coastal rainforest (usually on old sand dunes) on Cape York Peninsula, Qld.

This form of *Allophylus cobbe* was previously called *Allophylus crenulatus*. It grows behind mangroves and along the edge of rainforest fronting the beach. It is a scrambling shrub with glossy leaves that are crenulated (wavy) along the edge.

Black-spotted Grass Blue *Famegana alsulus*

Size: Male 20mm, female 22mm.

Confined to the northern half of Australia, occurring more often within a few hundred kilometres of the coast but also in scattered populations in the inland. This butterfly uses small pea-flowering herbs and shrubs as host plants so it will be found in open eucalypt and savannah woodland where these plants grow.

Attendant Ants: Occasionally *Iridomyrmex, Camponotus, Rhytidoponera*.

Host Plants: Flower buds and flowers of *Cajanus acutifolius, C. pubescens, Galactia tenuiflora, Indigofera pratensis, Vigna lanceolata, V. radiata, V. vexillata*.

Best Garden Host Plant: Any of the above plants.

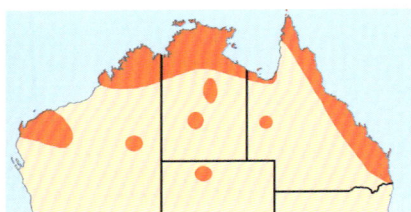

Indigofera pratensis is found from the Kimberley region of WA to northern NSW in open forest, extending a considerable distance inland from the coast. It is a small shrub that grows to about 1m high with bright pink flowers and many leaflets to each leaf.

Spotted Grass Blue *Zizeeria karsandra*

Size: Male 24mm, female 25mm.

Found from the Kimberley district, WA, across the top of NT and from Torres Strait, Qld, to southern NSW. Occurs in coastal areas where *Tribulus* grows in saline conditions and along roadsides as well as inland where *Glinus* plants grow.

Attendant Ants: Occasionally black ants.

Host Plants: Usually *Tribulus cistoides*, *T. terrestris*, also *Tribulopis bicolor*, *Glinus lotoides*, *G. oppositifolia* in the inland.

Best Garden Host Plant: Any *Tribulus* in your area. Be warned, their fruit are quite nasty burrs.

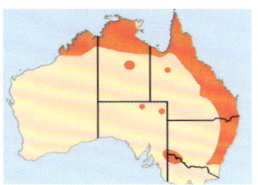

The image on the right shows a typical *Tribulus* plant. They have yellow flowers and grow flat on the ground with small soft leaflets and usually burr fruit.

Grass Jewel *Freyeria putli*

Size: Male 18mm, female 19mm.

A very small butterfly that has a range extending from the Kimberley region in WA, across the top end of NT, and then from about the Pascoe River on Cape York Peninsula to south-east Qld. Usually found in open eucalypt forest and savannah woodland where the small pea-flowering shrubs/herbs that are used as host plants grow.

Attendant Ants: Occasionally *Iridomyrmex*, *Ochetellus*, *Polyrhachis*, *Opisthopsis*, *Tetramorium*.

Host Plants: Leaves and flowers of *Indigofera linifolia*, *L. hirsuta*, *L. colutea*, *Flemingia lineata*.

Best Garden Host Plant: Any of the above.

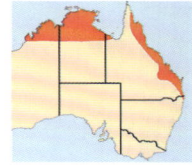

Common Grass Blue *Zizina otis*

■ *Z.o. labradus.*

■ *Z.o. labdalon.*

Size: Male 28mm, female 29mm.

Occurs Australia-wide and breeds wherever a supply of pea-flowering plants occur. They prefer to fly and lay in the full sun so plants in this situation will give the best results.

Attendant Ants: Occasionally *Iridomyrmex, Tapinoma, Paratrechina, Prolasius, Rhytidoponera.*

Host Plants: Numerous host plants have been listed but many more species are utilised. Small pea flowers are preferred, the larvae feeding on young leaves, flower buds, flowers and seedpods if they are soft enough. Recorded plants are *Cullen, Crotalaria, Desmodium, Glycine, Hardenbergia, Indigofera, Lotus, Neptunia, Pultenaea, Swainsona, Trigonella,* **Desmodium,* **Glycine,* **Lupinus,* **Macroptilium,* **Medicago,* **Phaseolus,* **Pisum,* **Trifolium,* **Vicia,* **Vigna,* **Virgilia.*

Best Garden Host Plant: Any small native pea-flowering plant – *Cullen tenax* gets very good results.

Hardenbergia comptoniana in WA. Hardenbergia species are small twining vines that scramble over shrubs. They usually have mauve or purple flowers.

Pultenaea millarii in north Qld. *Pultenaea* species are widespread in eastern and southern Australia, including Tas. They are small shrubs with yellow or orange flowers, sometimes with red markings.

Tiny Grass Blue *Zizula hylax*

Male Tiny Grass Blues gathering around moisture in a gully near Winton, Qld.

Size: Male 20mm, female 22mm.

The **Tiny Grass Blue** is one of Australia's smallest butterflies and often goes unnoticed unless there are large numbers of them on the wing. This often happens when they are breeding in remote inland areas where the main host plant *Dipteracanthus australasicus* grows in sheltered gorges and gullies where there is moisture.

Attendant Ants: Occasionally small black ants.

Host Plants: Flower buds, flowers and soft new growth of *Hygrophila angustifolia*, *Dipteracanthus australasicus*, *Dipteracanthus prostratus*, *Hemigraphis*, *Hygrophila costata*.

Best Garden Host Plant: *Dipteracanthus australasicus*.

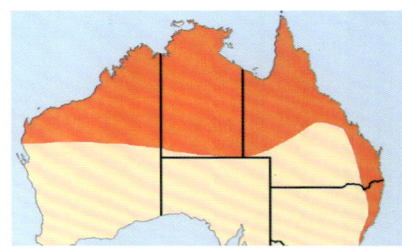

Dipteracanthus australasicus subsp. *corynothecus* is the inland variety that grows in the Winton area in breakaways on escarpments where moisture is retained and shelter provided from the harsh sun. Huge numbers of the **Tiny Grass Blue** breed in these areas. *Dipteracanthus australasicus* is found in all states except Victoria and Tasmania. Four subspecies have been named.

Harlequin Metalmark *Praetaxila segecia*

Size: Male 40mm, female 43mm.

Found in well developed rainforest from Cape York to the Rocky River on Cape York Peninsula..

Attendant Ants: None.

Host Plants: Myrsine *(Rapanea) porosa*.

Usually not very common and somewhat localised.

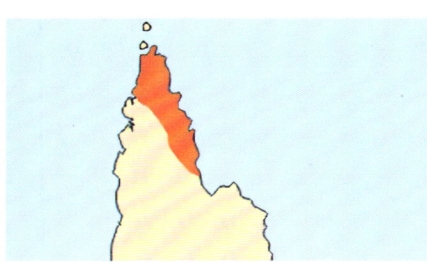

Moth Butterfly *Liphyra brassolis*

Size: Male 68mm, female 74mm.

Occurs in the top end of Australia in the Kimberley, northern Territory and from Torres Strait to south of Rockhamption in Queensland. Found in many habitats, wherever the Green Tree Ant lives. The larvae of the Moth Butterfly actually eat the larvae of the Green Tree Ant.

The adult butterflies are rarely seen.

Larval Food: Larvae of the Green Tree Ant (*Oecophylla smaragdina*).

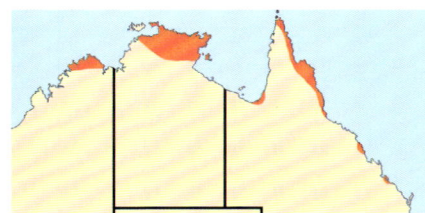

Cultivating Mistletoes

Mistletoes are a very important part of any eco-system and about twenty five butterflies and a number of other insects rely on them. As well as these insects most small honeyeaters utilise the nectar and fruit together with the Mistletoebird, Silvereyes, and many other birds as well as possums and gliders. There are about 90 species of mistletoe in Australia and they exist in most forest types. Over the years mistletoes have received bad press, probably because of the parasitic way they attach to other plants. Mistletoes do however photosynthesise and actually become part of the plant, rather than just suck the goodness out of it. Mistletoes continue to flower during very dry times and contribute a very important supply of nectar when other plants are not doing so. Certainly in heavily cleared areas individual trees in the open can get an abnormal number of mistletoe plants on them; many of the species that use eucalypts have a short life span of less than ten years. When most of the foliage on the tree is mistletoe, the tree is likely to die with the mistletoe. Species of mistletoe that parasatise rainforest trees do not seem to have a short life and live for as long as the host tree does. Usually in a balanced system like a rainforest no tree is heavily infested.

Because so many butterflies must have mistletoe for their larvae to live on you may want to grow some on your trees in the garden. It is not easy, but if you go about it in the correct way you will get a result.

The above two mistletoe seed have been deposited on branches by a bird. The one on the left is most likely too far below the branch for the shoot that comes out of the seed to reach it, so it will die. The one on the right has already shot and the shoot/root is attaching to the branch. Mistletoe seed have a very effective glue on them that in a short while sets hard and attaches them firmly to where they land.

When fixing the seed to a branch yourself you carefully squeeze the sticky seed out of the fruit and wipe in *under* a branch. Seeds positioned under a branch have a much better chance of survival because they will not be knocked off by birds and animals walking on the branch and very often at night a drop of dew will form on the seed thus giving it moisture. The fruit is usually red, yellow or orange when ripe. It should be picked carefully so as not to squash it, and be placed in a small plastic container, again to avoid squashing. Only when planting on a tree should the fruit be carefully squashed as it is pressed against a branch, using its own glue to fix it firmly.

The image on the left shows a seed that has just been attached under a branch. The one on the right shows the germinating seed attaching itself to the host plant. This usually takes only a couple of weeks but it may take a year or so before it looks like a plant.

It has taken a tiny seed of the Golden Mistletoe (*Notothixos leiophyllus*), the host plant of the Yellow-banded Jezebel, a whole year to get to the stage illustrated in the image on the left. One year later it will look like the one in the image on the right; after that growth will be quite rapid.

It is not just a simple matter of collecting a few mistletoe seed, attaching them to branches and sitting back to watch them grow. The majority of seed is rejected and killed by the host tree after they attach. The attached seed can remain on a branch for a year or more without advancing any further, then it dies. This is much like our immune system preventing infections from invading our bodies. It is best to place ten or more seed on a branch to improve the chance of getting a mistletoe plant to grow. There is one exception, mistletoe plants themselves cannot reject the seeds so the ideal tree to use is a Sandalwood, *Santalum*. This is a mistletoe tree and the commercial Sandalwood is ideal and quite easy to grow. They grow readily from cuttings under a mist system and will grow very well in a pot in normal potting mix with controlled release fertiliser till large enough to plant out.

Young mistletoe plants becoming established.

Once you have mistletoe established you can enjoy the beautiful Jezebel butterflies in your garden. There are some for anywhere in Australia except Tasmania.

Apart from the butterflies many mistletoes have beautiful flowers like the following.

INDEX

Acacia decurrens 318
Acacia flavescens 321
Acacia holosericea 320
Acacia humifusa 319
Acacia melanoxylon 317, 327
Acacia podalyriifolia 322
Acacia victoriae 323
Acraea andromacha 131
Acraea terpsicore 131, 132
Acrodipsas arcana 275
Acrodipsas aurata 275
Acrodipsas brisbanensis 274
Acrodipsas cuprea 274
Acrodipsas myrmecophila 275
Acronychia peninsularis 29
Adenia heterophylla subsp. *australis* 128
Adenia heterophylla subsp. *heterophylla* 126
Aegiceras corniculatum 286
Albizia procera 139
Albizia retusa 139
Alexfloydia repens 177
Alexfloydia repens 257
Allophylus cobbe 364, 385
Allophylus crenulatus 385
Allophylus sp. Cape York 385
Allora doleschallii 198, 199
Allora major 199
Alphitonia excelsa 295, 333, 354
Alphitonia incana 334, 355
Alphitonia oblata 355
Alphitonia petriei 355
Alphitonia pomaderroides 293
Alphitonia sp. Selwyn Ranges 355

Alpine Sedge Skipper 229
Alpinia caerulea 249
Alternanthera angustifolia 146
Alternanthera nana 146
Alternanthera nodiflora 146
Ambrax Swallowtail 37, 38
Amethyst Imperial Blue 325
Amyema bifurcata 101
Amyema biniflora 341
Amyema congener subsp. *congener* 312
Amyema miquelii 310
Amyema preissii 89
Amyema quandang 309
Amyema quandang var. *bancroftii* 309
Amyema quandang var. *quandang* 309, 308
Amyema queenslandica 101
Amyema sanguinea 98
Amylotheca dictyophleba 99
Anderson's Grass Skipper 226
Anisynta cynone 221
Anisynta dominula 222
Anisynta monticolae 222
Anisynta tillyardi 221
Annona muricata 59
Anthene lycaenoides 338
Anthene seltuttus 339
Antipodia atralba 241
Antipodia chaostola 239
Antipodia dactyliota 241
Apollo Jewel 282, 283
Apophyllum anomalum 84
Appias melania 86, 87
Appias paulina 85

Archidendron grandiflorum 363
Archontophoenix alexandrae 267
Archontophoenix maxima 267
Archontophoenix tuckeri 266
Argynnina cyrila 186
Argynnina hobartia 186
Argynnis hyperbius 137
Arhopala eupolis 302, 303
Arhopala madytus 304
Arhopala micale 305
Arhopala wildei 306
Arid Bronze Azure 316
Aristolochia acuminata 12
Aristolochia chalmersii 20
Aristolochia esperanzae 15
Aristolochia grandiflora 15
Aristolochia holtzei 19
Aristolochia indica 24
Aristolochia macroura 14
Aristolochia meridionalis subsp. *centralis* 23
Aristolochia meridionalis subsp. *meridionalis* 23
Aristolochia nauseifolia 20
Aristolochia pubera var. *aromatica* 22
Aristolochia pubera var. *pubera* 22
Aristolochia thozetii 21
Arrhenes dschilus 260
Arrhenes marnas 260
Artemis Owl 172
Arytera bifoliolata 360
Arytera divaricata 359
Arytera pauciflora 378
Asclepias curassavica 115
Asystasia australasica 151

Asystasia gangetica 152
Atkins's Ochre 215
Atriplex holocarpa 375
Atriplex spongiosa 375
Atriplex velutinella 374
Australian Admiral 164, 165
Australian Fritillary 137
Australian Gull 83
Australian Hairstreak 326, 327
Australian Lurcher 153, 154
Australian Painted Lady 163
Australian Rustic 134, 135
Australian Vagrant 133
Avicennia marina 292
Badamia exclamationis 200
Banded Demon 249
Banded Red-eye 206
Banks's Brown 190
Barnard's Azure 308
Barred Skipper 221
Bathurst Copper 279
Beach Tamarind 339
Belenois java 84
Big Greasy 11, 19–24
Bindahara phocides 328
Bitter-bush Blue 373
Black-and-white Aeroplane 169
Black-and-white Swift 270
Black-and-white Tiger 119, 120
Black-and-white Tit 335
Black Bean 342
Black Wattle 317
Black-ringed Ochre 218
Black-spotted Grass Blue 386

INDEX

Black-veined Ant-blue 275
Blady Grass 174
Blotched Dusky Blue 347
Blue Argus 161, 162
Blue-banded Eggfly 141, 149
Blue Flash 329
Blue-flash Skipper 248
Blue Iris Skipper 247
Blue Jewel 295
Blue Moonbeam 300
Blue Tiger 102, 122, 123
Blue Triangle 53, 54
Blush Macaranga 300
Borbo cinnara 250
Borbo impar 251
Boronia glabra 350
Boronia rosmarinifolia 351
Bossiaea bossiaeoides 380
Breynia cernua 76
Breynia sp. Iron Range 76
Breynia stipitata 75
Bright Cerulean 378
Bright Copper 279
Bright Cornelian 332
Bright Forest Blue 281
Bright Oak Blue 304
Bright Purple Jewel 293
Bright Shield Skipper 228
Bright-eyed Brown 191
Bright-orange Darter 264
Broad-banded Awl 193, 194
Broad-margined Azure 308
Bronze Ant-blue 274
Bronze Lineblue 364
Brown Awl 200
Brown Ochre 219
Brown Soldier 157, 158
Brunoniella acaulis 162
Brunoniella australis 162
Buchanania arborescens 303
Buchanania obovata 302
Bursaria incana 277
Bursaria spinosa 278
Capparis spinosa var. *nummularia* 82
Cabbage White 88
Cairns Birdwing 11–5
Cairns Hamadryad 103, 104
Cajanus reticulatus 372
Calamus caryotoides 171
Calamus moti 272
Callerya australis 196
Callerya megasperma 196
Callicoma serratifolia 207
Calotropis gigantea 117
Calotropis procera 117
Candalides albosericea 350, 351
Candalides caesia 351
Candalides caesia urumelia 352
Candalides delospila 347
Candalides erinus 346
Candalides heathi 349
Candalides medicea 352
Candalides noelkeri 344

Candalides xanthospilos 348
Canopus Swallowtail 42
Capaneus Swallowtail 39–41
Cape Coogara 360
Cape York Hamadryad 105
Caper White 63, 84
Capparis arborea 80
Capparis canescens 78
Capparis lasiantha 77
Capparis lucida 83
Capparis nummularia 82
Capparis laxiflora 81
Capparis sp. aff. *ornans* 80
Capparis spinosa var. *nummularia* 82
Carissa laxiflora 112
Carissa ovata 112
Carissa spinarum 112
Cassia brewsteri 67
Cassia queenslandica 67
Cassia sp. Kalpowar 68
Cassia sp. Paluma Range 67
Cassia tomentella 68
Cassytha pubescens 345
Castanospermum australe 342
Cathormion umbellatum 372
Catochrysops panormus 382
Catopsilia gorgophone 70, 71
Catopsilia pomona 66–8
Catopsilia pyranthe 64, 65
Catopsilia scylla 69
Catopyrops ancyra 364
Catopyrops florinda 365
Cedar Bush-brown 175
Cephrenes augiades 266, 267
Cephrenes trichopepla 268
Cepora perimale 83
Ceriops tagal 284
Ceropegia cumingiana 120
Cethosia cydippe 125, 126
Cethosia penthesilea 127, 128
Chaetocneme beata 205
Chaetocneme critomedia 206
Chaetocneme denitza 204
Chaetocneme porphyropis 203
Chalky Pearl White 87
Chamaecrista maritima 72
Charaxes latona 140
Charaxes sempronius 138, 139
Charaxinae 138-140
Chequered Grass Skipper 221
Chequered Sedge Skipper 233
Chequered Swallowtail 11, 44, 45
Cinderella Weed 147
Cinnamomum baileyanum 54
Citrus australasica 32
Citrus australis 31
Citrus garrawayi 32
Citrus glauca 32
Citrus inodora 38
Clausena brevistyla 33
Clausena smyrelliana 35

Clerodendrum floribundum 336
Clerodendrum grayi 337
Clerodendrum longiflorum 337
Clerodendrum tomentosum var. *lanceolatum* 337
Cocky Apple 204, 285
Commersonia bartramia 290
Common Aeroplane 166
Common Albatross 85
Common Banded Awl 195
Common Brown 188
Common Crow 102, 109–112
Common Dusky Blue 345
Common Eggfly 141, 145–7
Common Grass Blue 388
Common Grass Dart 255
Common Grass Yellow 75, 76
Common Imperial Blue 317
Common Jezebel 100, 101
Common Lineblue 359, 360
Common Migrant 63–5
Common Moonbeam 299
Common Oak Blue 273
Common Oak Blue 305
Common Pencilled Blue 342
Common Rayed Blue 349
Common Red-eye 205
Common Ringlet 177
Common Tit 336
Connarus conchocarpus 331, 353
Cooktown Azure 311
Copper Ant-blue 274
Copper Jewel 273, 284
Copper Pencilled Blue 344
Cordyline manners-suttoniae 271
Cressida cressida 19–24
Croitana aestiva 243
Croitana arenaria 242
Croitana croites 242
Crotalaria 122
Crotalaria cunninghamii 384
Crotalaria novae-hollandiae 384
Crotalaria spectabilis 383
Crotalaria verrucosa 384
Cruiser 124, 129, 130
Cryptocarya cunninghamii 205
Cryptocarya triplinervis 140
Cryptocarya vulgaris 54
Cullen australasicum 45
Cullen balsamicum 44
Cullen cinereum 45
Cullen pustulatum 44
Cullen tenax 43
Cupaniopsis anacardioides 339
Cupha prosope 134, 135
Curry Tree 40
Cyathostemma micranthum 56
Cycad Blue 369
Cycas media 370
Cynanchum carnosum 119
Cynanchum floribundum 117
Cynanchum ovalifolium 120
Cynanchum pedunculatum 118

Cyprotides cyprotus 344
Daemel's Imperial Blue 322
Dalbergia candenatensis 167
Dalbergia densa 167
Danaid Eggfly 148
Danaus affinis 119, 120
Danaus genutia 118
Danaus petilia 115–7
Danaus plexippus 121
Danis danis 353
Daphnandra repandula 52
Dark Cerulean 380
Dark Ciliate Blue 339
Dark Forest Blue 280
Dark Grass Dart 259
Dark Grass Skipper 227
Dark Opal 352
Dark-orange Grass Dart 257
Dark Pencilled Blue 343
Dark Purple Azure 312
Darwin Blue Flash 330
Daviesia divaricata 296
Decaisnina angustata 98
Decaisnina brittenii subsp. *brittenii* 98
Delias aestiva 95
Delias aganippe 90, 91
Delias argenthona 97, 98
Delias aruna 96
Delias ennia 94, 95
Delias harpalyce 89
Delias mysis 99
Delias nigrina 100, 101
Delias Nysa 92, 93
Delicate Pearl White 82
Dendrocnide cordifolia 143
Dendrocnide moroides 143
Dendrocnide photinophylla 143
Dendrophthoe curvata 99, 100
Dendrophthoe glabrescens 96
Dendrophthoe vitellina 286
Derris sp. Claudie River 194
Derris sp. Tolga 194
Derris trifoliata 193
Desert Sand Skipper 243
Desmodium heterocarpon 381
Desmos polycarpus 48
Deudorix democles 329
Deudorix diovis 332
Deudorix epijarbas 331
Deudorix smilis 330
Diamond Sand Skipper 241
Diggles' Jewel 292
Dingy Bush-brown 176
Dingy Grass Skipper 226
Dingy Ring 170, 173
Dingy Ringlet 177
Dingy Swallowtail 31, 32
Dingy Swift 251
Dioscorea transversa 208
Diospyros fasciculosa 281
Diplatia furcata 314
Dipteracanthus australasicus 154

Dipteracanthus australasicus
 subsp. *corynothecus* 389
Dipteracanthus bracteatus 154
Dipteracanthus prostratus 154
Dipteracanthus
 sp. Kalpowar 154
Dispar compacta 221
Dodder-laurel 345
Doleschallia bisaltide 150–2
Doryphora aromatica 52
Drynaria quercifolia 289
Drypetes acuminata 87
Drypetes deplanchei 85
Drypetes sp. aff. *deplanchei* 87
Dull Copper 277, 278
Dull Cornelian 331
Dull Heath Blue 368
Dull Jewel 292
Dull Oak Blue 302, 303
Dull Shield Skipper 228
Dusky Grass Skipper 225
Eastern Brown Crow 113
Eastern Flat 207
Eastern Iris Skipper 245
Eichhorn's Crow 108
Eirmocides absimilis 342
Eirmocides consimilis 343
Eirmocides helenita 340
Eirmocides margarita 341
Elattostachys microcarpa 366
Elgner's Jewel 285
Elodina angulipennis 78
Elodina padusa 77
Elodina parthia 82
Elodina perdita 82
Elodina queenslandica 79, 80
Elodina walkeri 81
Elymnias agondas 171
Enchylaena 376
Entada rheedii 356
Erina acasta 347
Erina erina 346
Erina hyacinthinus 345
Erycibe coccinea 169
Erysichton lineatus 366
Euchrysops cnejus 384
Euploea eichhorni 108
Euploea corinna 109–112
Euploea darchia 114
Euploea sylvester 106, 107, 110
Euploea tulliolus 113
Eurema alitha 74
Eurema brigitta 72
Eurema hecabe 75, 76
Eurema herla 73
Eurema laeta 72
Eurema smilax 73
Euschemon rafflesia 201, 202
Evening Brown 173, 174
Everes lacturnus 381
Exocarpos cupressiformis 91
Exometoeca nycteris 209
Famegana alsulus 386
Ficus opposita 299

Fiery Jewel 294
Fitzalania bidwillii 57
Fitzalania heteropetala 56
Fitzalania
 sp. Groote Island 57
Five-bar Swordtail 48–50
Flacourtia
 sp. Shipton's Flat 134
Flacourtia territorialis 136
Flagellaria indica 248, 264
Flame Sedge Skipper 234
Flemingia lineata 382
Forest Brown 186
Four-bar Swordtail 46–7
Freyeria putli 387
Fringed Heath Blue 367
Gahnia aspera 179
Gahnia clarkei 180
Gahnia grandis 180
Gahnia melanocarpa 180
Gahnia sieberiana 179
Galactia tenuiflora 74
Geijera salicifolia
 var. *latifolia* 36
Geijera salicifolia
 var. *salicifolia* 36
Geitoneura acantha 184
Geitoneura klugii 184
Geitoneura minyas 185
Glasswing 124, 131
Glasswort 376
Glinus lotoides 389
Glistening Lineblue 367
Glistening Pearl White
 79, 80
Glycosmis trifoliata 40
Golden Ant-blue 275
Golden Canola 88
Golden Mistletoe 95
Golden Sedge Skipper 232
Golden-haired Sedge
 Skipper 233
Golden-rayed Blue 344
Gomphocarpus physocarpus 121
Graphium agamemnon 60–2
Graphium aristeus 48–50
Graphium choredon 53, 54
Graphium eurypylus 55–7
Graphium macfarlanei 58, 59
Graphium macleayanum 51, 52
Grass Jewel 387
Greater Peacock Awl 199
Green Awl 197
Green Triangle 58, 59
Green-banded Jewel 289
Green-spotted Triangle 11,
 60–2
Greenish Darter 263
Grey Albatross 63, 86, 87
Grey Sedge Skipper 237
Grey Swift 250
Guioa acutifolia 280, 362
Gymnanthera oblonga 108
Hairy Lineblue 366

Halfordia kendack 34
Halfordia scleroxyla 34
Halfordia sp. Temple Bay 35
Hardenbergia comptoniana 388
Harlequin Metalmark 390
Harpullia ramiflora 332
Hasora chromus 195
Hasora discolora 197
Hasora hurama 193, 194
Hasora khoda 196
Heath Ochre 210
Heath Sand Skipper 239
Helena Brown 179
Heliotropium muelleri 115, 122
Hemigraphis alternata 156
Hemigraphis ciliata 156
Hemigraphis colorata 156
Hemigraphis repanda 156
Hemigraphis reptans 156
Herimosa albovenata 243
Hesperilla chrysotricha 233
Hesperilla crypsargyra 232
Hesperilla crypsigramma 238
Hesperilla donnysa 235
Hesperilla flavescens 236
Hesperilla furva 237
Hesperilla hopsoni 232
Hesperilla idothea 234
Hesperilla malindeva 236
Hesperilla mastersi 233

Hesperilla ornata 231
Hesperilla picta 230
Hesperilla sarnia 238
Heteronympha banksii 190
Heteronympha cordace 191
Heteronympha merope 188
Heteronympha mirifica 187
Heteronympha paradelpha 190
Heteronympha penelope 189
Heteronympha solandri 172, 191
Heterostemma acuminatum 123
Heterostemma magnifica 123
Heterostemma
 sp. Bellenden Ker 123
Heterostemma sp. Mt Edith 123
Hobart Brown 186
Homalium circumpinnatum 133
Huberantha nitidissima
 (*Polyalthia*) 49, 56, 58
Hyaline Swift 250
Hybanthus enneaspermus 131
Hybanthus monopetalus 131
Hybanthus stellarioides 131
Hygrophila angustifolia 157
Hygrophila costata 158
Hygrophila sp. Rocky River
 158
Hypochrysops apelles 284
Hypochrysops apollo 282, 283
Hypochrysops byzos 291

INDEX

Hypochrysops cyane 293
Hypochrysops delicia 295
Hypochrysops digglesii 292
Hypochrysops elgneri 285
Hypochrysops epicurus 292
Hypochrysops halyaetus 296
Hypochrysops hippuris 287
Hypochrysops ignitus 294
Hypochrysops miskini 287
Hypochrysops narcissus 286
Hypochrysops polycletus 288
Hypochrysops pythias 290
Hypochrysops theon 289
Hypocysta adiante 178
Hypocysta euphemia 178
Hypocysta irius 176
Hypocysta metirius 177
Hypocysta pseudirius 177
Hypolimnas alimena 149
Hypolimnas bolina 145–7
Hypolimnas misippus 148
Hypolycaena danis 335
Hypolycaena phorbas 336
Imperata cylindrica 174
Imperial Jezebel 89
Indigo Flash 333
Indigofera pratensis 386
Inland Sand Skipper 242
Ionolyce helicon 364
Iron Range Lurcher 155–6
Isoglossa eranthemoides 151
Jalmenus clementi 324
Jalmenus daemeli 322
Jalmenus eichhorni 320, 321
Jalmenus evagoras 317
Jalmenus icilius 325
Jalmenus ictinus 318
Jalmenus inous 324
Jalmenus lithochroa 323
Jalmenus pseudictinus 319
Jamides aleuas 378
Jamides amarauge 381
Jamides cyta 379
Jamides phaseli 380
Junonia hedonia 157, 158
Junonia orithya 161, 162
Junonia villida 159, 160
Kimberley Spotted Opal 351
Klug's Xenica 184
Knight's Grass Dart 257
Korthalsella japonica 93
Korthalsella rubra subsp. *geijericola* 93
Korthalsella taenioides 93
Lampides boeticus 383, 384
Laportea interrupta 154
Large Bronze Azure 316
Large Brown Skipper 240
Large Green-banded Blue 353
Large Moonbeam 297
Large Yellow Grass Dart 252
Leafwing 150–2
Leichhardt Tree 285

Lemon Migrant 66–8
Leopard 136
Lepidozamia peroffskyana 370
Leprea Brown 185
Leptaspis banksii 265
Leptomeria preissiana 315
Leptotes plinius 377
Lesser Wanderer 115–7
Lilac Grass Skipper 225
Lined Grass Yellow 72
Liphyra brassolis 390
Litsea breviumbellata 206, 297
Litsea leefeana 298
Livistona humilis 269
Livistona muelleri 268
Lomandra filiformis 210, 212
Lomandra longifolia 211
Lomandra multiflora 218
Lomandra obliqua 213
Lomandra spicata 214
Long-tailed Lineblue 362
Long-tailed Pea Blue 383, 384
Lophostemon confertus 204
Lucia limbaria 276
Lurcher 155, 156
Luvunga monophylla 36
Lyell's Swift 252
Lysiana exocarpi 311
Macaranga involucrata 301
Macaranga tanarius 300
Macleay's Grass Yellow 73
Macleay's Swallowtail 51, 52
Macqueen's Imperial Blue 319
Macqueen's Ochre 217
Mallee Ochre 215
Mangrove Jezebel 95
Maranthes corymbosa 303
Marsdenia geminata 107
Marsdenia hemiptera 111
Marsdenia pleiadenia 106
Marsdenia straminea 107
Marsdenia tricholepis 107
Marsdenia velutina 123
Meadow Argus 159, 160
Megisba strongyle 385
Meiogyne cylindrocarpa 62
Melanitis leda 173, 174
Melicope affinis 30
Melicope bonwickii 29
Melicope elleryana 27
Melicope peninsularis 28
Melicope rubra 30
Melodorum leichhardtii 47
Melodorum rupestre 48
Mesodina aeluropis 244
Mesodina cyanophracta 247
Mesodina gracillima 246
Mesodina halyzia 245
Mesodina hayi 246
Metal Plant 158
Micromelum minutum 41
Miliusa brahei 50
Miliusa horsfieldii 50

Miliusa traceyi 49
Millettia pinnata 195
Miskin's Jewel 287
Monoon australe (Polyalthia australis) 61
Monoon patinatum 61
Montane Ochre 210
Motasingha dirphia 239
Motasingha trimaculata 240
Moth Butterfly 390
Mottled Grass Skipper 221
Mountain Grass Skipper 222
Mountain Heath Blue 368
Mountain Iris Skipper 244
Mountain Sedge Skipper 230
Mucuna gigantea 197
Muellerina eucalyptoides 313
Murraya koenigii 40
Musa banksii 172
Mycalesis perseus 176
Mycalesis sirius 175
Mycalesis terminus 175
Mynes geoffroyi 142–4
Myrmecodia beccarii 283
Myrsine variabilis 358
Nacaduba berenice 359, 360
Nacaduba biocellata 361
Nacaduba cyanea 356
Nacaduba kurava 358
Narcissus Jewel 286
Narrow-banded Awl 196
Narrow-brand Darter 265
Narrow-brand Grass Skipper 224
Narrow-winged Pearl White 77
Native Broom 84
Nauclea orientalis 285
Neohesperilla crocea 224
Neohesperilla senta 223
Neohesperilla xanthomera 224
Neohesperilla xiphiphora 223
Neolitsea dealbata 203
Neolucia agricola 367
Neolucia hobartensis 368
Neolucia mathewi 368
Neptis praslini 169
Neptunia gracilis 73
Nesoxenica leprea 185
Netrocoryne repanda 207
No-brand Grass Dart 253
No-brand Grass Yellow 72
Northern Grass Dart 254
Northern Imperial Blue 320, 321
Northern Iris Skipper 246
Northern Jezebel 63, 97, 98
Northern Large Azure 314
Northern Large Darter 262
Northern Lineblue 357
Northern Pearl White 81
Northern Ringlet 176
Northern Sassafras 52
Northern Sedge Darter 261

Northern Silver Ochre 212
Nothocnide repanda 142
Notocrypta waigensis 249
Notothixos leiophyllus 95
Nysa Jezebel 92, 93
Ocybadistes ardea 257
Ocybadistes flavovittatus 255
Ocybadistes hypomeloma 255
Ocybadistes knightorum 257
Ocybadistes walkeri 256
Ogyris abrota 312
Ogyris aenone 311
Ogyris amaryllis 307
Ogyris barnardi 308
Ogyris genoveva 313
Ogyris ianthis 309
Ogyris idmo 316
Ogyris iphis 310
Ogyris olane 308
Ogyris oroetes 307
Ogyris otanes 315
Ogyris subterrestris 316
Ogyris zosine 314
Oncoba spinosa 135
Oplismenus aemulus 175
Oplismenus compositus 187
Orange Aeroplane 167, 168
Orange Alpine Xenica 183
Orange Bush-brown 175
Orange Emperor 140
Orange Grass Dart 258
Orange Jezebel 96
Orange Lacewing 127, 128
Orange Migrant 69
Orange Ochre 219
Orange Palm Dart 266, 267
Orange Ringlet 178
Orange Swift 271
Orange Tiger 118
Orange-tipped Azure 310
Orange-tipped Pea Blue 381
Orchard Swallowtail 33–6
Orchid Butterfly 273
Oreisplanus munionga 229
Oreisplanus perornatus 230
Oreixenica correae 183
Oreixenica kershawi 183
Oreixenica lathoniella 182
Oreixenica latialis 181
Oreixenica orichora 181
Oreixenica ptunarra 182
Ornate Ochre 214
Ornithoptera euphorion 12, 14
Ornithoptera richmondia 16, 17, 18
Oxalis 276
Oxalis perennans 276
Oxystelma (Sarcostemma) esculentum 115, 118
Pachliopta polydorus 25, 26
Paddy's Lucerne 147
Painted Sedge Skipper 230
Pale Blue Triangle 55–7
Pale Cerulean 379

Pale Ciliate-blue 338
Pale Pea Blue 382
Pale-orange Darter 262
Palmfly 171
Palmijuncus caryotoides 141
Pandanus conicus 172
Pantoporia consimilis 167, 168
Paper daisy 165
Papilio aegeus 33–6
Papilio ambrax 37, 38
Papilio anactus 31, 32
Papilio demoleus 43–5
Papilio fuscus 40
Papilio fuscus canopus 42
Papilio fuscus capaneus 39, 41
Papilio ulysses 27–30
Papuan Lineblue 364
Paradise Jewel 287
Paralucia aurifera 279
Paralucia pyrodiscus 277, 278
Paralucia spinifera 279
Pararistolochia australopithecurus 13
Pararistolochia deltantha 26
Pararistolochia laheyana 18
Pararistolochia linearifolia 26
Pararistolochia peninsulensis 26
Pararistolochia praevenosa 18
Pararistolochia sp. Gilles Crater 14
Pararistolochia sparusifolia 13
Parnara amalia 250
Parnara bada 250
Parsonsia ferruginea 105
Parsonsia latifolia 104
Parsonsia lenticellata 104
Parsonsia straminea 111
Parsonsia velutina 103
Pasma tasmanica 223
Passiflora (Hollrungia) aurantioides 126
Passiflora (Hollrungia) kuranda 126
Passiflora aurantia 129
Passiflora caerulea 130
Passiflora foetida 130, 132
Passiflora herbertiana 130
Patersonia fragilis 245
Patersonia occidentalis 247
Patersonia sericea 244
Peacock Awl 198, 199
Peacock Jewel 290
Pelopidas agna 251
Pelopidas lyelli 252
Persian Shield 154
Petrelaea tombugensis 357
Phaedyma shepherdi 166
Phalanta phalantha 136
Philiris fulgens 298
Philiris innotata 299
Philiris nitens 300
Philiris papuana 297
Philiris sappheira 301
Pickleweed 376

Pied Flat 208
Pieris rapae 88
Pimelea latifolia subsp. *latifolia* 348
Pimelea linifolia 348
Pipturus argenteus 144, 364
Pipturus sp. Archer Creek 144
Planchonia careya 204
Planchonia careya 285
Plantago debilis 160
Plantago major 160
Platycerium hillii 289
Plumbago zeylanica 377
Polyalthia patinata 61
Polyalthia xanthocarpa 61
Polyscias elegans 343
Pomaderris lanigera 291
Pongamia pinnata 166, 195, 200
Pongamia pinnata var. *minor* 166, 195
Portulaca australis 148
Portulaca oleracea 148
Praetaxila segecia 390
Proeidosa polysema 243
Prosotas dubiosa 363
Prosotas felderi 361
Prosotas nora 362
Protographium leosthenes 46–7
Pseudalmenus chlorinda 326, 327
Pseuderanthemum variabile 149
Pseudodipsas cephenes 281
Pseudodipsas eone 280
Pseuduvaria froggattii 60
Psychonotis caelius 354
Ptychosperma elegans 267
Ptychosperma macarthurii 269
Pultenaea millarii 388
Purple Dusk Flat 203
Purple Moonbeam 298
Purple Swift 270
Purple Waffle Plant 158
Pyrrosia lanceolata 287
Rachelia extrusa 248
Rapala varuna 333
Rare Red-eye 204
Red Lacewing 124–6
Red Wattle 321
Red-bodied Swallowtail 25, 26
Regent Skipper 192, 201, 202
Rhyssopterys timorensis 199
Rice Swift 250
Richmond Birdwing 16–8
Ringed Xenica 184
River Cherry 305
Rock Ringlet 178
Rostellularia adscendens 162
Rostellularia adscendens subsp. *glaucoviolacea* 162
Rostellularia adscendens var. *latifolia* 161
Rourea brachyandra 353
Royal Jewel 288

Rusty Parsonsia 105
Sabera caesina 270
Sabera dobboe 271
Sabera fuliginosa 272
Sabulana scintillata 367
Salacia chinensis 328
Salicorne 376
Salt Bush 376
Saltbush Blue 374, 375
Samphire Blue 376
Sandpaper Fig 299
Sandstone Ochre 213
Santalum lanceolatum 91
Santalum spicatum 90
Sapphire Moonbeam 301
Sarcocornia 376
Suaeda 376
Satin Azure 307
Satin Blue 350, 351
Scalloped Grass Yellow 74
Scolopia braunii 134
Scrub Darter 260
Sea Almond 357
Sea Asparagus 376
Sea Beans 376
Secamone elliptica 123
Senna acclinis 71
Senna artemisioides 325
Senna artemisioides subsp. *helmsii* 325
Senna auriculata 71
Senna barclayana 64
Senna gaudichaudii 69
Senna magnifolia 68
Senna notabilis 66
Senna sophera 65
Senna surattensis 70
Sesbania cannabina 385
Shining Cerulean 381
Shining Pencilled Blue 340
Short-tailed Lineblue 361
Shouldered Brown 189
Sida Retusa 149
Sida rhombifolia 147
Signeta flammeata 228
Signeta tymbophora 228
Silky Azure 307
Silver Sedge Skipper 232
Silver Xenica 182
Silver-spotted Ochre 216
Silver-studded Ochre 211
Small Alpine Xenica 181
Small Ant-blue 275
Small Bronze Azure 315
Small Copper 276
Small Darter 265
Small Dingy Grass Dart 253
Small Dusky Blue 346
Small Grass Skipper 224
Small Grass Yellow 73
Small Green-banded Blue 354
Small Iris Skipper 246
Small Oak Blue 306

Small Orange Ochre 216
Small Pied Blue 385
Smilax australis 280
Solander's Brown 170, 191
Soursop 59
Southern Large Azure 313
Southern Large Darter 263
Southern Pearl White 78
Southern Sedge Darter 261
Southern Silver Ochre 213
Spathoglottis paulinae 335
Spathoglottis plicata 335
Speckled Lineblue 365
Spinifex Sand Skipper 243
Splendid Ochre 220
Spotless Grass Skipper 226
Spotted Alpine Xenica 181
Spotted Brown 190
Spotted Dusky Blue 347
Spotted Grass Blue 387
Spotted Grass Skipper 223
Spotted Jezebel 90, 91
Spotted Opal 352
Spotted Pea Blue 384
Spotted Sedge Skipper 231
Stencilled Imperial Blue 318
Stigmaphyllon australiense 199, 288
Stinging Nettle 165
Striped Xenica 183
Strobilanthes dyerianus 152
Strychnos lucida 330
Strychnos minor 329
Strychnos psilosperma 122
Suniana lascivia 259
Suniana sunias 258
Swamp Darter 260
Swamp Grass 376
Swift Sedge Skipper 238
Sword-brand Grass Skipper 223
Swordgrass Brown 180
Sword-tailed Flash 328
Sydney Azure 309
Synedrella nodiflora 147
Syzygium puberulum 379
Syzygium tierneyanum 305, 379
Taenaris artemis 172
Tagiades japetus 208
Tailed Emperor 138, 139
Tailed Green-banded Blue 356
Tailless Lineblue 363
Taractrocera anisomorpha 252
Taractrocera dolon 253
Taractrocera ilia 254
Taractrocera ina 253
Taractrocera papyria 254
Tasmanian Alpine Xenica 182
Tawny Coster 131, 132
Tecticornia 376
Telicota ancilla 263
Telicota anisodesma 263
Telicota augias 264

INDEX

Telicota brachydesma 265
Telicota colon 262
Telicota eurotas 261
Telicota eurychlora 261
Telicota mesoptis 265
Telicota ohara 262
Tellervo zoilus gelo 105
Tellervo zoilus zoilus 103, 104
Terminalia catappa 200
Terminalia catappa 357
Terminalia sericocarpa 304
Terminalia subacroptera 306
Tetratheca hirsuta 209
Theclinesthes albocinctus 373
Theclinesthes hesperia 373
Theclinesthes miskini 371, 372
Theclinesthes onycha 369
Theclinesthes serpentatus 374, 375
Theclinesthes sulpitius 376
Tiny Grass Blue 389
Tirumala hamata 122, 123
Tisiphone abeona 180
Tisiphone helena 179
Toxidia andersoni 226
Toxidia doubledayi 225
Toxidia inornata 226
Toxidia melania 227
Toxidia parvula 224
Toxidia peron 226
Toxidia rietmanni 227
Toxidia thyrrhus 225
Trapezites argenteoornatus 216
Trapezites atkinsi 215
Trapezites eliena 219
Trapezites genevievae 214
Trapezites heteromacula 216
Trapezites iacchoides 211
Trapezites iacchus 219
Trapezites luteus 217
Trapezites macqueeni 217
Trapezites maheta 212
Trapezites petalia 218
Trapezites phigalia 210
Trapezites phigalioides 210
Trapezites praxedes 213
Trapezites sciron 215
Trapezites symmomus 220
Trapezites taori 213
Trapezites waterhousei 216
Trema tomentosa 365
Tribulus 387
Trichospermum pleiostigma 290
Trident Pencilled Blue 341
Trophis scandens 113, 114
Turquoise Imperial Blue 324
Twin Dusky Blue 346
Twin-spotted Lineblue 361
Two-brand Crow 102, 106–7
Two-brand Grass Skipper 222, 223
Two-spotted Sedge Skipper 236
Tylophora erecta 116
Tylophora flexuosa 116
Tylophora sp. aff. *flexuosa* 116
Ulysses Swallowtail 27–30
Union Jack 99
Urtica incisa 165
Uvaria rufa 48
Vagrans egista 133
Vanessa itea 164, 165
Vanessa kershawi 163
Varied Imperial Blue 324
Varied Sedge Skipper 235
Ventilago pubiflora 340
Verbena bonariensis 159
Verbena rigida 160
Vigna vexillata 384
Vindula arsinoe 129, 130
Viola betonicifolia 137
Walker's Grass Dart 256
Wanderer 121
Waterhouse's Imperial Blue 323
Waterhouse's Ochre 216
Wattle Blue 371, 372
Western Bitter-bush Blue 373
Western Brown Skipper 239
Western Flat 209
Western Jewel 296
Western Sand Skipper 241
Western Xenica 185
Westringia fruticosa 349
White-margined Crow 114
White Nymph 142–144
White-banded Grass Dart 254
White-banded Lineblue 358
White-brand Grass Skipper 227
White-fringed Swift 272
White-margined Grass Dart 255
White-veined Sand Skipper 243
Wide-brand Sedge Skipper 238
Wilkiea angustifolia 201
Wilkiea huegeliana 202
Wilkiea macrophylla 202
wintering colonies 110
Wire-leaf Mistletoe 89
Wonder Brown 187
Woolly Pomaderris 291
Xerochrysum bracteatum 163
Xylopia maccreae 62
Xylosma sp. Hunter Creek 133
Xylosma sp. Mt Lewis 135
Xylosma sp. Temple Bay 133
Xylosma terrae-reginae 135
Yellow Grass Skipper 224
Yellow Migrant 70, 71
Yellow Ochre 217
Yellow Palm Dart 268
Yellow Sand Skipper 242
Yellow Sedge Skipper 236
Yellow Swift 251
Yellow-banded Jezebel 94, 95
Yellow-spot Blue 348
Yellow-spot Jewel 291
Yoma algina 155, 156
Yoma sabina 153, 154
Ypthima arctous 173
Zanthoxylum brachyacanthum 34
Zanthoxylum ovalifolium 38
Zanthoxylum parviflorum 42
Zanthoxylum veneficum 41
Zebra Blue 377
Zizeeria karsandra 387
Zizina otis 388
Zizula hylax 389
Zygocactus Mistletoe 93

References

Braby, M.F. 2000. *Butterflies of Australia. Their Identification, Biology and Distribution.* CSIRO Publishing.

Braby, M.F. 2016. *The Complete Field Guide to Butterflies of Australia.* Second edition. CSIRO Publishing.

Common, I.E.B, and Waterhouse, D.E. 1981. *Butterflies of Australia.* Angus and Robertson.

Hoskins, A. 2015. *Butterflies of the World.* Reed New Holland.

Hoskins, A. 2017. *1,000 Butterflies.* Reed New Holland.

Orr, A., and Kitching, R. 2011. *The Butterflies of Australia.* Jacana Books.

Sankowsky, G. 2015. *All About Butterflies of Australia.* Reed New Holland.

Systematic revision of the *Ogyris idmo* (Hewiston, 1862) group (Lepidoptera: Lycaenidae); implications for the conservation management of Australia's most threatened butterflies.
Ethan P. Beaver, Michael F. Braby, Richard V. Glatz, and D. Andy Young.
Invertebrate Systematics 11/10/2023

Zborowski, P. 2019. *Insects of the World.* Reed New Holland.

Further Information

Australian Entomological Society – austentsoc.org.au
PO Box 546, East Melbourne, Vic 3002.

Entomological Society of Queensland – esq.org.au
P.O. Box 537 Indooroopilly, Qld 4048.

Key to Mistletoes of Australia –
keys.lucidcentral.org/keys/v4/australian-mistletoe/

The Entomological Society of NSW –
entsocnsw.org.au
c/– Australian Museum, 6 College St, Sydney, NSW 2000.

The Entomological Society of Victoria –
entsocvic.org.au

Australian Butterfly Conservation on Facebook –
facebook.com/australianbutterflyconservation

Western Australian Insect Study Society –
museum.wa.gov.au/waiss

Butterfly Conservation South Australia –
butterflyconservationsa.net.au

For help in identifying larval host plants

AusGrass2 – ausgrass2.myspecies.info
A very valuable tool for idenitfying grasses which are host plants for many Skipper butterflies.

Australian National Herbarium –
anbg.gov.au/plantinfo
There are numerous links on this site to information on plants that may be of use in identifying larval host plants.

eFlora –
eflora.library.sydney.edu.au/taxon/lomandra-obliqua
Vascular Plants of the Sydney Region.

Key Base –
keybase.rbg.vic.gov.au
Links to numerous online keys for identification of plants.